Lecture Notes
in Economics and
Mathematical Systems

Managing Editors: M. Beckmann and W. Krelle

251

Input-Output Modeling

Proceedings of the Fifth IIASA (International Institute
for Applied Systems Analysis) Task Force Meeting
on Input-Output Modeling
Held at Laxenburg, Austria, October 4–6, 1984

Edited by A. Sm

Springer-Verlag
Berlin Heidelberg New York Tokyo

ISBN 3-540-15698-4 Springer-Verlag Berlin Heidelberg New York Tokyo
ISBN 0-387-15698-4 Springer-Verlag New York Heidelberg Berlin Tokyo

Printing and binding: Beltz Offsetdruck, Hemsbach/Bergstr.
2142/3140-543210

PREFACE

Input—output modeling has, through the years, provided a consistent and unifying focus for IIASA's economic research. Scientists working in the Institute, first in the economic modeling task of the System and Decision Sciences area and later within the Economic Structural Change project, have cooperated extensively with colleagues throughout the world in advancing and contributing to input—output work.

Perhaps the most notable aspect of these efforts has been the joint work with the INFORUM Project to develop linked systems of national models. Experience gained from the INFORUM—IIASA studies has been of great benefit to other members of the I/O community, but this is by no means the end of the story. Contributors not connected with INFORUM have also brought their own very valuable insights and knowledge to bear on the subject, and input—output modeling has moved progressively away from being a purely academic specialization. A number of the methods developed have direct application to economic analysis and policy formulation, and I/O techniques have achieved widespread use in both governmental and commercial environments.

This volume presents the results of the fifth in a series of meetings organized by IIASA to promote methodological advances in the subject and to draw on a pool of I/O expertise so as to further the aims of the Institute's in-house economic research.

ANATOLI SMYSHLYAEV
Project Leader
Comparative Analysis of
Economic Structure and Growth

CONTENTS

Introduction   1
Anatoli Smyshlyaev

A Multi-Country, Multi-Industry Historical View
Of International Trade Competitiveness   7
Douglas Nyhus

Austrian—Italian Interdependence: Some Linking
Experiments   19
Maurizio Grassini and Josef Richter

Proposals for the Linkage of CMEA-Country Models   29
B. Czyzewski, Andrzej Tomaszewicz, and Lucja Tomaszewicz

The INFORUM—IIASA Family of Input—Output Models: A Brief
Historical Review, Progress in 1984, and Future Prospects
for Growth   43
Dwight A. Porter

The Potential Contributions of Mutually Consistent,
Sectorally Disaggregated National Economic Models
to Analyses of National Environmental Policies and
Global Environmental Interdependence   51
Stephen P. Dresch

Changes in the Structure of the Finnish Economy, 1970—1980   61
Osmo Forssell

Patterns of Industrial Change in the Federal Republic
of Germany. Part I: Flows of Manufacturing Output and
Energy Input   73
Claire P. Doblin

On Modeling Structural Changes in Sectoral Wage Distribution
in a Modern Input-Output Model   79
Cristina Raffaelli

On Modeling Foreign Trade in an Input—Output
Model of an Open Economy   95
Marco Barnabani and Maurizio Grassini

Changes in Factor Input Coefficients
and the Leontief Paradox   105
Arvid Stentoft Jakobsen

Some Experience in the Planning of Input Coefficients   119
Rolf Pieplow

Stability of Import Input Coefficients   129
Joachim Schintke and Reiner Stäglin

Changes in Input Coefficients in the Germany Economy   141
Rudi Rettig

Estimation of Input—Output Coefficients
Using Neoclassical Production Theory   151
Christian Lager and Wolfgang Schöpp

On The Endogenous Determination of Import Coefficients
in an Input—Output Model: Theoretical and Practical
Problems   163
Laura Grassini

Input—Output Techniques in the Japanese Econometric
Model   173
Ryoichi Nishimiya

Endogenising Input—Output Coefficients by Means of
Industrial Submodels   183
Swami Amrit Terry (T.S. Barker)

Structural Change in the Belgian Economy   193
Hilda Tahon and Dirk Vanwynsberghe

An Econometric Model of the Soviet Iron and
Steel Industry   197
Anatoli Smyshlyaev

The Effects of Structural Changes on
Danish Energy Consumption   211
Ellen Pløger

The Role of Energy Intensity in Economic
Development   221
Pal Erdösi

Transformation Matrices in Input—Output
Compilation   225
Carsten Stahmer

Seton's Eigenprices: Comparisons Between
Post-War Holland and Hungary   237
Erik Dietzenbacher and Albert E. Steenge

An Attempt to Evaluate the Impact of Changes in
Interindustry Interactions   249
Maurizio Ciaschini

INTRODUCTION

Anatoli Smyshlyaev

International Institute for Applied Systems Analysis,
Laxenburg, Austria

The Fifth IIASA Task Force Meeting on Input—Output Modeling took place in Laxenburg from 4th to 6th October 1984 and this volume is the proceedings of the meeting.

Input-output modeling is a lively area of research; despite many years of accumulated experience there still remain significant problems with the statistics used in the models as well as their application for international comparisons. Efforts to link various national models were reviewed during the meeting and general agreement was reached on proposals to expand and develop a basic linked system involving seven countries.

Participants were also asked to devote some attention to the question of input structures and to report on their experience in analyzing and forecasting interindustry interactions. This was intended, in part, to complement the great success achieved in recent years in developing the final demand side, involving models of personal consumption, investment, exports, and imports. Changes in industrial structure brought about by technological progress in resource utilization, as well as the effects of improving energy efficiency, were discussed at some length.

Programming issues had been extensively examined during an IIASA workshop in May 1984 and therefore did not figure explicitly on this meeting's agenda. Nevertheless, the flexibility of the software now being used by INFORUM partners on a number of different computers has been clearly demonstrated, for example in the demand-side developments mentioned above.

All of these topics have also been encountered in the research work of IIASA's Economic Structural Change project during 1984 and the experience and "collective wisdom" of the INFORUM family has been of great benefit to IIASA's in-house efforts. Twenty-five external specialists in input—output work and five IIASA staff members participated in the meeting, and twenty-four papers (reproduced here) were presented. For the purposes of this volume, the papers are grouped into five main areas, and each of these will now be briefly reviewed.

I. LINKAGE OF INPUT—OUTPUT MODELS AND RELATED PROBLEMS

The first section opens with a paper by *Douglas Nyhus* examining international trade data for the last twenty years in order to assess the trade performance of various countries, with special emphasis on the United States, Japan, and Western Europe. Import penetration is also considered; this required a great deal of work in making international and national data sets compatible, although previous INFORUM studies helped significantly here. Nyhus rejects assessments that characterize the US economy as uncompetitive; he asserts that Japan is highly competitive in certain areas rather than across the board and compares the relative trading strength of the United States and of Japan to that of the EEC.

The joint efforts during 1984 of *Maurizio Grassini* and *Josef Richter* in linking a 45-sector model of Italy with a 48-sector model of Austria demonstrate the usefulness of such an exercise, both for improving the quality and reliability of forecasts for individual countries and for analyzing the likely impacts of external changes on the domestic economy. A common 19-sector classification of tradable goods was developed to enable foreign trade data to be married with the national accounting systems, and *vice versa*. Only a few months were needed to derive results of value to both partners once the models were ready for linkage, as is frequently the case with linked input—output models. Methodological problems solved here are also of benefit to other prospective partners in multicountry linking efforts, for example our colleagues in Poland who have been working for the past two years to develop their model to a level where linkage can be easily implemented. *B. Czyzewski, Andrzej Tomaszewicz*, and *Lucja Tomaszewicz* review classification difficulties arising from the different systems used by the CMEA and the OECD, and they present bridge matrices and estimated trade-share matrices for countries within the CMEA as possible solutions.

Dwight Porter gives an extended overview of the INFORUM—IIASA work on input—output modeling since 1978; after this "historical" introduction he discusses at some length the organizational changes that may be advisable to increase the policy relevance of these activities and match them more closely with IIASA's current research directions. *Stephen Dresch*, who has had considerable experience with input—output modeling together with Wassily Leontief and in developing multiregional models for the United States, made a plea for economists associated with INFORUM to explore new applications for the work. He notes that a tendency to "export" pollution-intensive activities may itself play a role in global structural economic change, and suggests that a linked system of input—output models with a significant contribution from environmental research could help bridge the gap between economists and environmentalists, as well as revitalizing IIASA research in general.

II. SECULAR CHANGES IN INTERINDUSTRY RELATIONS

Osmo Forssell opens the second section with a paper on recent changes in the industrial structure of the Finnish economy, which is analyzed from a macro economic perspective with the help of static input—output models for 1970 and 1980. The reasons for the differing growth of various industries during the seventies are studied via an examination of demand-side effects and the technological changes that have occurred since 1975. Forssell concludes that many of the major structural changes in the Finnish economy that followed the 1973 oil price hike were essentially complete by 1980; and he notes that at the 30-sector level of aggregation, 62 input coefficients showed significant changes between 1970 and 1980, although some were so marked that they were probably due to changes in classification procedure.

In the next paper, *Claire Doblin* reviews changes in the structure of industry in the FRG between 1950 and 1980. Using a 20-group disaggregation of the industrial sector, she divides it into "no-growth" industries such as the primary metals, which have seen a steep decline in their share of total output, "fast-growth" industries like electrical and electronic equipment for which the opposite is true, and industries whose growth behavior has changed markedly during the course of the study period. Doblin also traces out trends in investment, output, and the use of energy over the same period; she identifies a drying-up of investment in the late sixties and early seventies as postwar reconstruction was completed, and feels that the oil price rises probably only accelerated rather than caused the switch to more energy-efficient technologies.

Sectoral wage distribution is discussed by *Cristina Raffaelli* who is one of the team working on the Italian interindustry model INTIMO. She considers the patterns of wage changes produced by the *scala mobile* indexation system as well as the impacts on wages of changes in output and employment. Also included are some observations on the temporal development of the ratios for each sector between wages and value added and between wages and production costs.

The issue of sectoral effective exchange rates is raised by *Marco Barnabani* and *Maurizio Grassini*, who voice the widespread concern that serious bias can be introduced into the input—output analysis of foreign trade if one unique exchange rate is used instead of separate effective rates for exports and imports. They find specifically that the use of a unique rate in a national model is unsatisfactory in studies or forecasts of the impact on the domestic economy of the devaluation (or revaluation) of a foreign currency. In their opinion, the actual effective exchange rates experienced by individual sectors may differ by 15—45% from the averaged, unique rate — thus explaining much otherwise anomalous export/import behavior. These results indicate the importance of further work on purchasing power parities (such as the UN's ICP project) and the need to account for this phenomenon in future input—output work.

Arvid Jakobsen returns to the well-known Leontief paradox, first enunciated in 1954, which represented the United States as a net exporter of labor services and a net importer of capital services. Jakobsen finds the origin of the paradox in the over-rigidity associated with straightforwardly applying input—output techniques to such topics as the factor content of foreign trade. His regression analysis, relating changes in the composition of industrial output to changes in the corresponding factor coefficients (using Danish data for 46 sectors between 1966 and 1972), indicates that the weight of the empirical evidence has shifted in favor of the Hecksher—Ohlin theorem rather than the traditional industry technology assumption. This study deals with the product-mix effect, that is, the fact that changes over time in the composition of goods in total output will lead to corresponding changes in input requirements.

III. CHANGES IN INPUT STRUCTURES

Section III begins with a paper by *Rolf Pieplow*, which reports on work in the GDR on the analysis and forecasting of input coefficients. Using input—output techniques within a strongly planning-oriented environment, Pieplow notes that typically only 10—20% of the input coefficients in the GDR input—output table are of major importance; he illustrates this with examples concerning the use of electricity in the chemicals industry, and demonstrates the usefulness of detailed information on product demands within an input—output framework.

Joachim Schintke and *Reiner Stäglin* examine the stability over time of input coefficients, in a paper that complements Doblin's overview of the economy of the FRG; in addition they compare various sources of these data. The intertemporal analysis covers the years 1967, 1972, and 1976 at a 56-sector level of disaggregation, and about 150 out of 3000 coefficients are found to be important, covering approximately two-thirds of intermediate transactions. Despite what appears at first sight to be an enormous task in data compilation, Schintke and Stäglin stress that most of the empirical work is in fact concentrated on relatively few significant parameters, which may increase the applicability of such input—output models. *Rudi Rettig* studies much the same problem for the FRG input—output data covering the period 1960—1981. In addition to presenting a general overview he deals at some length with the topic of energy utilization, where substitution between energy carriers and other factors has contributed to relatively rapid changes in coefficients.

A joint paper by *Christian Lager* and *Wolfgang Schöpp* deals with the estimation of input—output coefficients using neoclassical production theory. They draw upon and combine well-known theoretical approaches and apply them to a data base constructed within the framework of modern input—output statistics. The technique is illustrated by examining changes in the coefficients of the Canadian basic metal industry and attributing these to changes in microtechnologies brought about shifts in relative prices and in the output structure of the industry.

Laura Grassini turns her attention to the endogenous determination of import coefficients in input—output models. Within the framework of the Italian INTIMO model she describes theoretical and practical approaches to analyzing imports sector by sector, so that the effects of foreign prices on domestic prices and demand can be determined. Time series of Italian imports by sector for the period 1975—1983 are given by way of illustration, and the analytical and numerical techniques are discussed in some detail.

The final paper in the section, by *Ryoichi Nishimiya*, describes the use of input—output techniques in an econometric model of Japan. This model has been developed primarily to analyze the major energy-supply problems facing the country; in common with many other non oil-producing countries, Japan has experienced a sharp cutback in GNP growth and a significant rise in inflation compared to their pre-1973 levels. Nishimiya describes the major characteristics of the model — the method of disaggregating final demand, the application of input—output techniques to the price equations, and the two-level CES-type neoclassical production function representing the supply side of the economy — and reports the results of various model simulations.

IV. CHANGES IN INDUSTRIAL STRUCTURES

Swami Amrit Terry (T.S. Barker) approaches the problem of endogenizing input—output coefficients via the development of submodels for groups of closely-related industries. He identifies the main advantages of the method as being three-fold: first, the size of the main model can be held constant whilst allowing for more detailed treatment of particular industrial groups; second, the use of submodels makes it easier to allow for product-mix and technological-change effects; and third, submodels can be constructed for groups of industries whose coefficients are particularly important. He then illustrates the technique with estimates and projections using the Cambridge multisectoral dynamic model of the British economy.

The paper by *Hilda Tahon* and *Dirk Vanwynsberghe* presents a method of quickly updating input—output tables so that recent data can be brought to bear on the modeling of industrial development. The example described concerns a 50-sector analysis of structural change in the Belgian economy, and concentrates on those changes in input structure that can be discerned using constant or current prices. My own paper then describes an econometric model of the Soviet iron and steel industry, drawing on numerous studies of the industry's development over the past twenty years. Step-by-step analysis of each technological process involved produces useful comparisons of energy-input requirements and makes it possible to study the importance of product-mix effects and energy-saving processes at each stage of production.

Ellen Pløger examines how changes in output mix have influenced the energy consumption of Danish manufacturing industries. Her preliminary conclusions are that output-mix effects have important explanatory power in tracing the development of energy coefficients and that changes in production shares can adequately represent changes in output mix. Pløger's argument is illustrated by model results based on a time series of Danish input—output tables for the years 1966—1980. *Pal Erdösi*'s paper on the role of energy intensity in the development of an economy brings Section IV to a close. Erdösi reports on some of the responses of the Hungarian economy to the oil price rises of the seventies, and describes the use of an input—output model in developing planned structural shifts away from energy-intensive processes.

V. THEORETICAL DEVELOPMENTS

The final section of the volume contains three papers on theoretical areas of input—output analysis. *Carsten Stahmer* reviews the role of transformation matrices in compiling input—output tables. Using special matrices for certain rows and columns of input tables, he presents improved procedures for transforming the input data; these methods build upon the UN System of National Accounts proposals and have already been adopted by the Federal Statistical Office of the FRG.

Erik Dietzenbacher and *Albert Steenge* compare economic developments over the past forty years in two open economies, those of the Netherlands and Hungary. They propose a method involving "eigenprices" recently developed by Francis Seton, which combines within one framework "cost-side" arguments imputing all value to primary factors and "use-side" arguments that derive the prices of input factors from those of the final products.

In the last paper in the volume, *Maurizio Grassini* sets out to evaluate the impact of changes in interindustry interactions. Input—output models are used for various simulation work and also to study the dynamic behavior of an economic system under a given set of econometric equations. Analysis of these models from a system-dynamic perspective can be used to learn more about the structure of the parameters involved.

CONCLUSION

The latest in our series of annual meetings once again proved valuable in bringing together members of the input—output community to share their experience and to discuss problems and challenges arising in the course of their work. A significant proportion of the participants have had links with the INFORUM—IIASA group for some years, and the interested reader can trace the development of many of the results presented here through previous proceedings volumes.

I was particularly impressed this year by the results reported by our Italian colleagues working on the INTIMO project: this work appears to be of considerable relevance for input—output modelers elsewhere. Many participants stressed the importance of concentrating on a relatively limited number of input coefficients (perhaps between 50 and 200) when attempting to analyze or forecast structural change at either the national or the international level. Staff of IIASA's Economic Structural Change group also contributed results that may be of interest to other input—output researchers. All in all, the meeting proved to be a worthwhile and stimulating experience and I hope this volume will succeed in conveying its results to a wider audience.

A MULTI-COUNTRY, MULTI-INDUSTRY HISTORICAL VIEW OF INTERNATIONAL TRADE COMPETITIVENESS

Douglas Nyhus

Department of Economics, University of Maryland, College Park, Maryland, USA

1. INTRODUCTION

The task of assessing a country's true trade performance is, at best, difficult. There has, however, been no lack of assessors. Several assessments have been highly critical of the US economy's ability to meet the threat of foreign economic competition domestically and in its ability to compete in foreign markets. Others have studied the question and come to the opposite conclusion. This study tends to agree with the later. The data shown in the following report do not support the negative assessment of US industrial competitiveness. They do show that some industries such as Ferrous Metals do face significant problems. On the other hand, many traditional industries such as those in the machinery area appear to be in a relatively strong position and in some fast growing industries such as Computers the US has increased its already strong position. Further, the study shows that the contention that the Japanese economy is highly competetive in all areas is false. The strong Japanese position is only apparent in the durable manufacturing area. The third result of the study is that a comparison of major trading blocks, North America, the European Economic Community (EEC), and Japan, shows the EEC as the weakest competetor and Japan the strongest with North America holding its own.

The general approach here will be to examine a country's share of world exports of a particular commodity or group of commodities over time. We will then compare both the levels of the shares and the movements in those levels for different countries or aggregations of them. A second method of comparison will be to look at import penetration into domestic markets.

The next section will explain the data sources and methods. Some of the results of the study will be shown in the third part. The last section will briefly discuss some directions for future research.

2. DATA - SOURCES AND METHODS

The data used in this study may be divided into two broad categories: data from international sources for which international comparisons may be done and data from national sources for which comparison within a country can be examined. The reasons for such a division are clear to everyone who has ever had to deal on a practical level with data purportedly measuring the same thing put derived from different sources. The data do not agree. Making comparisons based on such data could lead to erronous conclusions due solely to the fact that the basic methods of derivation and classification of the data were different.

Such is the case for exports. For each individual country an estimate of exports at an industry level has been obtained. These estimates have been so derived that there are consistent with industry production levels and with the import levels of that industry. The methods however differ between countries; the definitions of certain industries also differs; and, the levels of detail for the industries also differs. At the international level we have exports as reported to the United Nations by each country in the Standard International Trade Classification (SITC). These data are comparable across countries but are not comparable to the nationally derived output and import data. In this report all ratios and comparisions shown are only shown for data which are strictly comparable. Hence an export to output ratio would be built by using the national source data for both exports and outputs.

2.1 Internationally based data

Exports by individual country by three digit (and a few four digit) Standard International Trade Classification (STIC) commodites were obtained from the United Nations and the Organization for Economic Cooperation and Development.

World trade by commodity was derived from United Nations data on world market economy trade by three digit SITC found in the UN's Yearbook of International Trade Statistics.

Both sets of data were aggregated to 119 commodity level.

2.2 National data

Data for output, imports, and exports by industry were obtained through national sources. In most cases the data were only indirectly obtained from official government sources. Indeed, only Canada and France have such series made in current and constant prices. For each set of national data, the national data was first converted into constant prices (national currency) of the year 1977. Then the trade conversion ratio of national currency to the United States dollar for 1977 was used to convert the entire series to volumes evaluated in 1977 dollars. The conversion to dollars did not disturb any ratios of exports to output or imports to output since the same scaler was applied to both series. Nor were any trends in those ratios altered since the scaler was the same for all years. The following is a brief description of the principal sources of the national data used.

United States: the INFORUM model "LIFT" data bank.

Canada: Statistics Canada's time series on the input-output structure of the Canadian economy for 1961-79. Additional price data (for 1980-82) came from the same source derived from Industry Selling Price indicies found in the Canadian Statistical Review.

Japan: From a data bank developed by Prof. Sukuramoto of the Keio Economic Observatory of Keio University in Tokoyo. This data base is the basis for the INFORUM system's model of Japan. The time period of this data base is 1955-1978. The 1979-82 period was derived from various sources mainly the Japan Statistical Yearbook and a monthly publication Monthly Economic Indicators.

Federal Republic of Germany: From a data base derived by Dr. Rudi Rettig of the Rheinish-Westfaelish Institut fuer Wirtschaftsforschung (RWI) in Essen. The period covered is 1960-1981. Additional data for 1981 came principally from the Statistisches Jahrbuch for 1983.

France: INSEE provided a time series of input-output tables for 1970-1982 in current and constant prices. The data for 1959 to 1969 were derived from an eariler series of INSEE input-output tables.

Italy: The INTIMO model of Italy supplied the data base for the period 1959-1982.

Belgium: The Belgium model of the INFORUM family was the source of the data source for the period 1955-1981. 1982 data was derived from the

Statisical Office's monthly publication <u>Statistisch Tijdschrift</u>.

Netherlands: Our Dutch collaborators from Erasmus University generously supplied the data base for Holland.

United Kingdom: Various issues of <u>The Annual Abstract of Statistics</u> supplied the data for time series on imports and outputs and prices. The OECD and UN supplied export series were used to make time series on exports. The 1974 input-output table was used to calibrate the time series to offical British data series.

Rest of the World: The <u>International Financial Statistics</u> published by the International Monetary Fund provided price indices for principal commodities (such as oil, wheat, various ores, rubber, etc.) traded in international markets. The <u>IFS</u> was also the source for the trade conversion ratios used to convert from the UN and OECD data series which are in dollars to national currency.

2.3 Combinations of the two data sources

The principal area where both sets of data were used was in the deflation of the international trade data from current dollars to constant dollars of the year 1977. From each national source price deflators for each of the 119 commodities were derived. This was done for the most part with bridging. For a given commodity of the 119 estimates were made of the proportion contained in each of the nationally defined industrial sectors. In most cases only one national sector was involved because in all of the models the number of goods producing sectors is smaller than 119. There were, of course, many cases were the international classification was broader than the national. In these cases the bridge matrix was derived through a combination of mechanical RAS procedures and judgment. The RAS procedure began with the a matrix of 119 columns and as many rows as goods producing sectors in the model. The international data was converted to national currency using the trade conversion ratios of the <u>IFS</u>. The sums of the international and national data were then compared. The sums differed for every country but by greatly differing amounts. Upon reflection these differences were mostly the result of differing methods in evaluating the national data. The obvious area is the use of evaluating exports in producer prices. This means taking the port price and stripping away the costs of transporting the goods to the port. Hence the national valuation was lower. When the transportation and trade margins were considered the differences in the totals for the data almost disappeared. Even with the sums of the two data sources agreeing the balancing procedure was difficult and left many question marks. Judgment was used in many instances to allow for more reasonable results when the mechanical RAS method did not or could not work. The goal was <u>not</u> a perfect balance but the most reasonable relationship between the two data sets. Thus certain questions of inconsistency were left unresolved when the alternative of consistency would involve absurd results such as linking textile products to machinery.

Such a procedure as outlined above was followed for each of the nine countries named above. The rest of the world's price was determined in either of two ways. The first was the direct method as given in the above section. The second was to define it as the trade-weighted, exchange rate adjusted average price of the prices of the nine. Manufactures were the main area where the second method was used.

2.4 Construction of deflated international trade

Time series by 119 commodity classification of exports in constant prices for each of the nine and for the rest of the world were made. The five major steps in the construction are given below.

(1) Produce estimates of world trade for each of our 119 commodities in current dollars.

> Let o = the exports (in U.S. dollars) of all the OECD countries; and
> w = the exports of¤the world's market economies.

Now let

$$r_t = o_t/w_t \qquad \text{for } t = 1970\text{-}1981$$

Perform the regression

$$r = a + bt$$

and calculate w (for t = 1962-1969, and 1982) by

$$w_t = o_t/r_t \quad .$$

Finally, we adjust w by the factor, f, necessary to make our estimates of world trade agree with the broad estimates of the UN. Hence for trade sector k which is wholly or principally part of the one digit SITC, m, we have

$$W_{k,t} = w_{k,t}f_{m,t}$$

(2) Dervive by subtraction exports for the rest of the world in current dollars. If we let S be the sum of the exports for nine countries treated individually in this study then the exports of the rest of the world may be calculated as W - S.

(3) Take each national price series, d, and adjust it for each rate changes with 1977 as the base year of the index.
That is, for each country k and product i, and year t

$$p_{k,i,t} = d_{k,i,t} \, e_{k,t}$$

> where d is the domestic price index
> e is the index of country k's exchange rate vis-a-vis the dollar in year t

(4) Deflate the current price series by the price series derived in (3) country by country. The price of the rest of the world was calculated, where necessary, by the formula

$$p_{10,i,t} = \sum_{k=1}^{9} s_{k,i,t} \, p_{k,i,t}$$

where

$$s_{k,i,t} = \frac{X_{k,i,t} / p_{k,i,t}}{\sum_{l=1}^{9} X_{l,i,t} / p_{l,i,t}}$$

where
$X_{k,i,t}$ are the exports of country k of product k in year t.

(5) Sum the resulting individual country series to obtain a series of constant priced world trade by industry.

The individual series derived in step (4) are the basis of the tables on shares of world trade in the report. No constraints on the aggregate sums beyond that applied in step (1) were used. The resulting series on volumes of world trade by industry may very well be unique. The sums across industries do not necessarily agree with other estimates of the volume of world trade because of fundmentally different methods used. The method described above is the only one using such detailed methods.

3. The View Itself

The task of assessing a country's true trade performance is at best difficult. Several measures are suggested here. The measures used divide into two parts. The first is a direct country by country, industry by industry comparions of shares of world exports. We shall call this comparison an assessment viewed from an international perspective. We shall find that there exits no country for shich shares of world exports have either increased or decareased for all industries. Therefore a label such as "uncompetetive" ascribed to a particular country can be misleading. The data used for this view are those described in section 2.1.

A second group of measures shall be called the assessment as viewed from a national perspective. In this view we will look primarily at the relationships between domestic production, exports and imports by industry. The data used are all taken from national sources as described in section 2.2. A cautionary note is in order in using these data for cross-country comparisions. Since each data set is based primarily on a single country's classification scheme, there will necessarily exist cases where data may appear to be comparable but in fact are not. Therefore, such international comparisions using this data should be done with great care.

3.1 An Assessment from the International View

The general approach here will be to examine a country's share of world exports of a particular commodity or group of commodities over time. We will then compare both the levels of the shares and the movements in those levels for different countries or aggregations of them.

The use of the actual export levels may, however, lead to some wrong conclusion about a country's trade performance. The error may occur because during the period 1962-1982 there have been numerous efforts to reduce trade barriers between countries or larger trading blocks. The success in reducing those barriers has not been uniform. The formation of the Common Market (EEC) eliminated barriers, for the most part, between member countries but did not alter trade relations with non-members. Another example is the United States-Canadian auto aggrement of 1965. The response of the Canadian auto industry was dramatic. The Canadian share of world exports of auto's climbed from 1% in 1962 to 11% ten years later. If Canada's exports to the US are not counted then the Canadian share remains at 1% for 1972. An attempt to eliminate this "trade creation" effect was tried. The "internal" exports of the six Common Market countries were removed from their total exports and all "internal" US-Canadian trade was stricken. World trade totals were correspondingly reduced by the amount taken out when the exports shares were computed. One final note is that this procedure probably over-estimates the "trade creation" effect because, in the theory of customs unions, there exists a "trade diversion" effect as well. This last effect works in the opposite direction of the first one.

Table 1: Share (%) of World Exports

Country	Actual Total			Total − "internal"		
	1962	1972	1982	1962	1972	1982
North America	16	14	16	14	12	15
USA	12	10	12	12	10	13
Canada	4	4	4	2	2	2
Japan	4	6	9	5	8	12
EEC −six	31	34	35	22	22	23
Germany	10	11	12	7	8	8
France	5	6	6	3	3	4
Un. Kingdom	6	5	5	6	5	4
Italy	3	4	5	2	3	3
Netherlands	4	5	4	2	2	2
Belgium	3	4	4	2	1	2
Rest of World	49	48	40	59	58	50

Table 2: Share (%) of World Manufacturing Exports

Country	Actual Total			Total − "internal"		
	1962	1972	1982	1962	1972	1982
North America	19	17	16	17	14	15
USA	15	12	12	15	12	14
Canada	4	5	4	2	2	1
Japan	6	10	12	7	13	16
EEC −six	45	46	41	36	34	28
Germany	15	16	14	12	13	11
France	6	7	7	5	5	5
Un. Kingdom	10	7	5	10	8	4
Italy	4	5	6	4	4	4
Netherlands	4	5	4	3	3	2
Belgium	5	5	5	3	2	2
Rest of World	30	27	31	40	39	41

For example, the "trade diversion" effect occurs if a German chemical exporter merely shifts his exports sales from Sweden to France after the creation of the Common Market containing both Germany and France but not Sweden.

The figures in Table 1 show each country's share (as a percentage) of world exports for the three selected years 1962, 1972 and 1982. The first three columns show the shares of actual world exports; the next three, the shares after striking out the "internal" trade. The total for the six EEC countries illustrated the importance of the distinction between actual and the adjusted shares. The actual shares show substantial growth between 1962 and 1972 and a smaller growth later. The adjusted shares show no growth for the first period and again some increase for 1972-82. We can infer that the increase in the EEC share ovaer the first period was due primarily to the "trade creation" effect of the formation of the Common Market during the early period. Once in place no more effect is seen and both series move approximately in the same manner.

Since both raw agricultural products and mineral ores (including crude petroleum) are substantially resource dependent and subject to a myriad of supports, subsidies, etc, the results in Table 2 may make for a better comparision. In Table 2 the basis for the shares is world exports of manufactured products. Certain features stand out. The sharp rise in the Japanses shares: the steep decline of the British share. The US share fell in the first ten years but recovered later (even though 1982 was not a good export year for the US); the EEC showed a steady erosion on the adjusted basis and even a decline based on the actual unadjusted figures. Indeed, the direction of movement for the Common Market strongly suggests that its manufacturers are losing out to the those from Japan and elsewhere.

Table 3 shows a major subgrouping of manufactures: Durables. The growth of the Japanese share is quite dramatic. A close look at the detailed Japanese data (not reported here) shows that the increase is widespread including all of the machinery sectors. In fact, of the 27 sectors classified as Durables only two have falling shares - Lumber and Miscellaneous Manufactures. The US had generally slightly falling shares, but, once again, there are two industries who buck the trend. The two are Computers and Office Machinery. The EEC data show a very substantial drop in the overall share. The largest decreases are in the Motor Vehicle and in the machinery sectors. Increases were observed in the Lumber, Furniture and Copper sectors. Country differences are also apparent within the EEC. The largest decrease is for the United Kingdom with Germany second. Only France and Italy seem able to retain their overall shares.

With Table 4 which shows the data for the other major part of manufactures, Nondurables, we see the first major break with the trends we have seen in Tables 1-3. The first sharp difference can be seen in the Japanese case. Instead of rising, the shares are falling. The fall is widespread with Food, Apparel, Plastics and Shoes showing the most decrease. On the other hand, both Chemical and Rubber products have increases. The US share appears to have remained about constant over the period. Increases in Textiles and Agricultural Fertilizers were offset by decreases in Shoes and Chemicals. The rise in the EEC is nearly as dramatic as its fall for the Durable subgroup. All countries except for the United Kingdom experienced growth. Increases in Food, Textiles and Paper more than offset losses in Plastics and Shoes.

Tables 5 and 6 illustrate two industries where the US has been getting progressively weaker. For Ferrous Metals the US weakness do not, in fact, imply that the other two blocks are gaining strength. The EEC share has fallen tremendously. Japan's has increased, but that increase has almost ceased since 1972. Indeed, it appears that the Japanese strength in steel has already crested and that the major new competetors are now elsewhere. The case for Autos is in similar for the US and the EEC but for Japan the

Table 3: Share (%) of World Durable Manufacturing Exports

Country	Actual Total			Total – "internal"		
	1962	1972	1982	1962	1972	1982
North America	21	18	18	20	15	15
USA	17	13	14	18	13	14
Canada	4	5	4	2	2	1
Japan	5	12	16	7	16	21
EEC – six	53	47	40	45	37	29
Germany	21	18	16	18	15	12
France	6	7	7	5	5	5
Un. Kingdom	13	8	5	13	9	4
Italy	4	5	5	3	4	4
Netherlands	3	3	2	2	2	2
Belgium	6	6	5	4	2	2
Rest of World	21	23	26	27	32	35

Table 4: Share (%) of World Non-Durable Manufacturing Exports

Country	Actual Total			Total – "internal"		
	1962	1972	1982	1962	1972	1982
North America	15	14	14	13	13	13
USA	11	10	10	12	11	12
Canada	4	4	4	1	2	1
Japan	6	6	4	8	8	7
EEC – six	34	45	43	25	30	27
Germany	8	12	11	6	9	8
France	7	8	8	5	5	5
Un. Kingdom	7	6	5	7	6	4
Italy	5	7	7	4	4	5
Netherlands	5	8	7	3	4	3
Belgium	3	5	6	1	2	2
Rest of World	45	35	39	54	49	53

Table 5: Share (%) of World Ferrous Metals Exports

Country	Actual Total			Total - "internal"		
	1962	1972	1982	1962	1972	1982
North America	9	6	6	9	5	4
USA	7	4	3	8	4	3
Canada	2	2	3	1	1	1
Japan	9	21	24	13	31	31
EEC - six	66	55	47	56	40	35
Germany	12	11	13	16	13	14
France	12	10	9	10	8	7
Un. Kingdom	10	6	3	13	7	3
Italy	4	4	6	5	4	5
Netherlands	2	4	4	1	2	2
Belgium	18	14	9	12	6	4
Rest of World	16	18	23	22	24	30

Table 6: Share (%) of World Motor Vehicle Exports

Country	Actual Total			Total - "internal"		
	1962	1972	1982	1962	1972	1982
North America	17	23	17	15	8	7
USA	16	12	8	14	7	6
Canada	1	11	9	1	1	1
Japan	3	14	26	4	24	41
EEC - six	73	52	45	70	49	34
Germany	32	23	24	33	26	21
France	10	10	7	8	7	6
Un. Kingdom	21	7	3	24	10	3
Italy	6	5	3	4	5	3
Netherlands	1	1	1	0	0	1
Belgium	3	6	6	1	2	1
Rest of World	7	11	12	11	19	18

increase in world market share is tremendous.

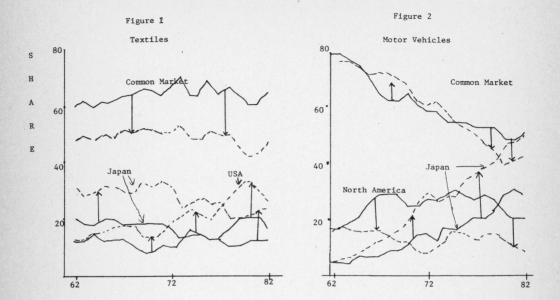

Figure 1
Textiles

Figure 2
Motor Vehicles

The snapshots of time shown in the tables do not illustrate   the momentum of the events described above. Figures 1 and 2 show the data for Textiles and Motor Vehicles in graph form. The solid lines show the movements of the shares of total trade of the major blocks. The dashed lines show the movements of the shares after adjustment for "internal" trade. The arrows indicate the shifts in the lines caused by the adjustment. The first figure shows the gradual decline of the Japanese share. After adjustment the Japanese share is higher but the basic trend is the same. The figure for Motor Vehicles shows the importance of the adjustment made to correct for "internal" trade. The North American and, to a lessor extent, the EEC shares move quite differently depending upon when we consider the total or the total less the "internal" trade.

3.2 An Assessment from a National View

The national view from the USA is given here. The most interesting from the standpoint of competitiveness is the import penetration into the domestic market. Increased import penetration of the domestic market by itself should not be a cause for alarm. Since world trade has historically grown faster than world production, import penetration world-wide must be increasing. The converse is more popular. The ratio of exports to output is also increasing. Table 7 shows the ratio of imports to domestic production over the historical period. It is interesting to note that between 1972 and 1982 import penetrationa actually fell in 12 of the 40 manufacturing industries. In 27 there was either a decrease or the increase was under three percentage points. In only six industries did the import penetration account for more than twenty percent of output. These were for consumer electronics , Shoes, Office Equipment, Motor Vehicles, Special Industry Machinery and Miscellaneous Manufacturing.

Table 7 Ratio of Imports to Domestic Production

MANUFACTURING		0.030	0.066	0.093
	NON-DURABLES	0.037	0.052	0.062
9	FOOD & TOBACCO	0.037	0.041	0.043
10	TEXTILES, EXC. KNITS	0.089	0.075	0.057
11	KNITTING	0.010	0.028	0.014
12	APPAREL, HOUSEHOLD TEXTILES	0.043	0.113	0.182
13	PAPER	0.095	0.072	0.082
14	PRINTING & PUBLISHING	0.004	0.010	0.009
15	AGRICULTURAL FERTILIZERS	0.034	0.037	0.035
16	OTHER CHEMICALS	0.021	0.036	0.039
17	PETROLEUM REFINING	0.023	0.039	0.021
18	FUEL OIL			
19	RUBBER PRODUCTS	0.022	0.101	0.086
20	PLASTIC PRODUCTS	0.017	0.030	0.037
21	SHOES AND LEATHER	0.055	0.246	0.678
	DURABLES	0.026	0.076	0.115
22	LUMBER	0.063	0.081	0.091
23	FURNITURE	0.008	0.038	0.059
24	STONE, CLAY, GLASS	0.030	0.049	0.053
25	FERROUS METALS	0.024	0.083	0.185
26	COPPER	0.058	0.052	0.103
27	OTHER NONFERROUS METALS	0.080	0.101	0.086
28	METAL PRODUCTS	0.012	0.029	0.037
	NON-ELEC MACHINERY	0.022	0.058	0.098
29	ENGINES AND TURBINES	0.011	0.049	0.157
30	AGRICULTURAL MACHINERY	0.101	0.101	0.129
31	CONSTR, MINING, OILFIELD EQ			
32	METALWORKING MACHINERY	0.017	0.044	0.148
33	SPECIAL INDUSTRY MACHINERY	0.034	0.140	0.243
34	MISC NON-ELECTRICAL MACH.	0.005	0.034	0.061
35	COMPUTERS	0.070	0.063	0.035
36	OTHER OFFICE EQUIPMENT	0.134	0.318	0.457
37	SERVICE INDUSTRY MACHINERY			
	ELECTRICAL MACHINERY	0.020	0.076	0.127
38	COMMUNIC EQ, ELECTRONIC COMP	0.013	0.049	0.126
39	ELEC INDL APP & DISTRIB EQ	0.013	0.045	0.053
40	HOUSEHOLD APPLIANCES	0.034	0.091	0.101
41	ELEC LIGHTING & WIRING EQ	0.008	0.040	0.099
42	TV SETS, RADIOS, PHONOGRAPHS	0.224	0.789	0.775
	TRANSPORTATION EQ	0.015	0.112	0.161
43	MOTOR VEHICLES	0.019	0.150	0.276
44	AEROSPACE	0.009	0.031	0.059
45	SHIPS, BOATS	0.009	0.024	0.016
46	OTHER TRANSP. EQUIP.	0.042	0.254	0.166
47	INSTRUMENTS	0.060	0.105	0.195
48	MISC. MANUFACTURING	0.087	0.180	0.206

4. Future Directions and Conclusions

It is clear that the above report only begins to touch the wealth of analysis that is contained in the data base. Clearly the historical data base can be improved in several ways. The most apparent concern the data on domestic prices. Since prices are the connecting link between the national and international data great care must be exercised in the collection and use of such prices. There may exist cases where, because of increasing domestic subsidies, the ratios of domestic to export prices may change substantially over time. Greater input from national sources would help in this area. The data on prices needs to be extended to cover more countries. A base that included more of the smaller European countries would help with the assumptions about prices of manufactured products especially in such areas as pulp, paper and ferrous metals. Extension of the data base to include some of the larger developing countries, such as Argentina, Brazil, Korea, Malaysia, Mexico and Singapore, would also be extremely helpful. Future study areas going beyond that of data expansion by country could involve such topics as the effects on developed countries of an increased penetration by developing countries into the domestic markets of the developed countries.

AUSTRIAN—ITALIAN INTERDEPENDENCE: SOME LINKING EXPERIMENTS

Maurizio Grassini[1] *and Josef Richter*[2]

[1] Faculty of Political Science, University of Florence, Florence, Italy; [2] Federal Economic Chamber, Vienna, Austria

1. INTRODUCTION

Linking of IO models has two different though closely related aspects. First, to achieve more consistency among the results of IO models and thus to increase the quality and reliability of forecasts. Second, to analyse the impacts of changes or exogenous shocks in one country on the various branches and variables in the other country; this includes the attempt to quantify all the involved feedback effects on the economy of the first country, a repercussion which is usually neglected.

This paper describes the results of a number of exercises in which the Italian (INTIMO) and the Austrian (AUSTRIA III) member of the INFORUM family of IO models were linked together in a rather pragmatic way.

The experiments concentrated on the real side of the economies, on the impacts due to changes in trade flows. The exercises carried out were also limited to the bilateral effects, impacts on third markets with all their implications on the Austrian and the Italian economy were not included in these analyses.

2. BASIC RELATIONSHIPS

The basic relationship between Italian imports and Austrian exports can be written as

$$\widehat{SMI} \cdot MI = \widehat{SXA} \cdot XA \tag{1}$$

Italian total imports (MI) weighted with the Austrian market share in these imports (SMI) equal Austria's total exports (XA) weighted with the share of exports going to Italy in Austria's total exports.

The relationship between Austrian imports and Italian exports is given by

$$\widehat{SMA} \cdot MA = \widehat{SXI} \cdot XI \tag{2}$$

where
MI is a vector of Italy's total imports
MA is a vector of Austria's total imports
XI is a vector of Italy's total exports
XA is a vector of Austria's total exports
SMI is a vector of shares of Austrian commodities in total Italian imports MI
SMA is a vector of shares of Italian commodities in total Austrian imports MA
SXI is a vector of shares of exports with the destination Austria in total Italian exports XI

* This research has been partially supported by a C.N.R. grant, contratto n. 83.236.53.

SXA is a vector of shares of exports with the destination Italy in total
  Austrian exports XA

Since the Austrian model makes a distinction regarding the destination
of exports and exports to Italy are a category by their own, these exports
can directly be calculated by

$$XA_I = \widehat{SMI} \cdot MI \tag{3}$$

XA_I is a vector of Austrian exports with the destination Italy.

3. EMPIRICAL BACKGROUND OF THE ANALYSES

3.1. IO models

AUSTRIA III is a 48 sector model with a fairly detailed real side, the
price/income side is still in an experimental stage. Special characteristics
with some implications for the linking exercises are the regional breakdown
of commodity exports and the use of import matrices in determining import
demand. The model is primarily used for medium-term simulations up to 1990
and 1995, so little attention is paid to model business cycle fluctuations
accurately (Richter 1981).
The standard scenario as of May 1984 was taken as starting point and is
called BASE CASE in the following pages. This scenario makes use of final demand data coming from national accounts up to the year 1982.

INTIMO has 45 sectors; following a large grouping classification, agriculture is represented by one sector, industry by 26 sectors and the services
are described by the other 18 sectors. Among them, 4 sectors produce government goods and services (Grassini 1982). The real side of the model built two
years ago is continuosly updated; at present, the national account data usable
for defining the final demand components are included up to the year 1983. The
model has already been used for simulating medium term horizons; the BASE CASE
considered in this paper refers to the scenario which has guided the forecasts
published in CER (1983).

3.2. Classification

A common classification was found at a level of 19 sectors (see Appendix).
Bridge matrices were applied to transform foreign trade results in the national classifications to the common classification and back.

3.3. Shares

An adequate estimation of the various shares for the forecasting period
is of crucial importance for any linking exercise. Expecially, because the
little empirical evidence which is available indicates, that the shares are
rather unstable and changing over time quite rapidly.
Table 1 shows the changes in SXA in the period 1976 - 1981 in constant
prices. Although these shares are not used in the simulation, they illustrate
the rate of change and give an idea about the relative importance of exports
to Italy for some of the Austrian sectors. Table 1 concentrates on those branches for which exports to Italy really matter. The selected 10 of 19 sectors

account for more than 93 % of total Austrian exports to Italy. The figures
are presented in the common classification although the relative importance
of Italy as a market for its export products is, of course, more pronounced in
the more disaggregated national classification for many of the sectors.

TABLE 1 Italy as a market for Austrian exports (selected sectors)

Common classification	Italian market shares in constant prices		Share of total exports in total output 1976	Share of exports in total exports to Italy 1976
	SXA76	SXA81		
Agriculture & Forestry	0,47	0,33	0,05	0,091
Electricity, gas, water	0,25	0,25	0,06	0,032
Chemical products	0,05	0,08	0,36	0,067
Basic metals & products	0,10	0,10	0,35	0,178
Machinery	0,04	0,03	0,49	0,064
Electrical goods	0,02	0,03	0,41	0,040
Dairy products	0,32	0,26	0,11	0,034
Textiles & clothing	0,02	0,04	0,36	0,023
Wood & furniture	0,42	0,37	0,32	0,345
Paper & printing	0,08	0,10	0,33	0,058

SXA76 for agricultural products means that 47 % of all Austrian agricultural exports are delivered to Italy.

Both in 1976 and in 1981 about 10 % of Austria´s exports were delivered
to Italy but - as may be seen from Table 1 - the relative importance of Italy
as a market for Austrian products differs from sector to sector significantly.
The highest degree of dependence can be observed for "Wood & furniture". More
than 12 % (32 % of output is exported and 42 % of these exports are delivered
to Italy) of the output of this sector is going to Italy. The relatively high
concentration of Austrian exports to Italy on a limited number of products
- as shown in column 4 - should be kept in mind when some of the results given
in chapter 4 are analysed.
On the other side deliveries from Austria only account for 1,89 % of
Italy´s total imports in 1976 and show a slight positive trend (2,05 % in 1981
and 2,14 % in 1984).

TABLE 2 Austrian market shares in Italian sectoral total imports
         (selected sectors)

Common classification	1971	1976
Agriculture & Forestry	0,022	0,016
Non metal products	0,031	0,036
Iron, steel and metal products	0,019	0,028
Dairy products	0,023	0,028
Wood & furniture	0,357	0,344
Paper & printing products	0,052	0,057

As may be seen from Table 1 and Table 2 the trade flow of wood and furniture (primarily sawmill products) is of high relevance for both partners.

Austria is not a very big market for Italian exports. Total Italian exports going to Austria represent 2,83 % (1976),3,04 %(1981) and 3,22 % (1984) of total Italian exports. These exports are higher than those delivered to Japan or Canada and are in the order of magnitude of exports to Belgium or the UK.[1])

TABLE 3 Austrian market shares in Italian sectoral total exports (selected sectors)

Common classification	1971 SXI	1976 SXI
Agriculture & Forestry	0,049	0,048
Mining	0,024	0,029
Crude oil refinery	0,022	0,036
Iron, steel and metal products	0,073	0,037
Vehicles	0,037	0,039
Leather & shoes	0,012	0,038
Wood & Furnitures	0,022	0,031
Chemical products	0,032	0,037
Non metal products	0,034	0,039
Optical precision instruments	0,032	0,039

The Austrian market shares for the selected sectors recording the higher shares show that Austria does not represent an important market for any Italian product. Since year 1971, Italian exports to Austria have increased, following the general trend in the growth and the opening of the Italian economy; the market shares of Italian exports to Austria did show remarkable changes but the market shares are always under 5 %.

Imports from Italy account for about 8,2 % of total Austrian imports both in 1976 and 1981.

TABLE 4 Austria as a market for Italian imports (selected sectors)

Common classification	Italian market shares in current prices		Share of imports of this commodity group in total Austrian imports
	SMA76	SMA81	
Agriculture & Forestry	0,142	0,106	0,050
Oil & refinery products	0,082	0,036	0,097
Chemical products	0,052	0,065	0,131
Basic metals & products	0,065	0,096	0,107
Machinery	0,068	0,068	0,135
Electrical goods	0,055	0,052	0,088
Vehicles	0,076	0,060	0,115
Other food	0,052	0,051	0,031
Textiles & clothing	0,123	0,165	0,097
Paper & printing	0,024	0,016	0,037

1) See also Barnabani, Grassini (1984)

The two commodity groups for which Italy holds the highest market share in the Austrian import market namely "Non-metallic mineral products" (1976: 22 %) and "Leather & leather products" (1976: 42 %) do not show up among the ten most important commodity groups of Austrian imports.

3.4. Computing the basic relationship and forecasting market shares

As may be seen from all the tables, market shares hardly can be assumed to remain stable for the entire forecasting period.

From the Italian dataset in foreign trade, market shares of imports from Austria and exports to Austria have been computed. These shares refer to flows in current values. The available data allowed the construction of time series of market shares from 1964 to 1977. Filtering the time series of (sectoral) Italian imports and exports with the market shares, time series of Italian imports ed exports exchanged with Austria were calculated.

The comparison between the data from the Italian side with the data on the Austrian side has been rather unsatisfactory.

Since data from the UN Trade Statistics showed a high degree of consistency between the Austrian and the Italian foreign trade statistics at the two digit SITC level[2] the dismatch on the aggregate level is probably due to aggregation problems. When we like to proceed in linking experiments we feel that more work has to be devoted to classification problems, in order to achieve more homogenity among sectors belonging to different models.

In order to "solve" the problem of inconsistency, we decided to live with each set of national data and to limit the exchange of information on the rate of change of sectoral imports and exports implied by the modifications introduced into each national scenarios.

The changes in imports of one country had to be transformed into the change in exports of the partner country. This has been accomplished by extrapolating the market shares. On the Italian side, the market shares, SXI and SMI, have been projected by simple trends; when the decreases or increases recorded in the past led to values unexpectedly high or too low (as the case in which strong contractions in the past would produce a negative value for the future,if a simple trend would have been applied) a moving average covering a period of four years has been adopted.

On the Austrian side it was not necessary to estimate SXA since exports to Italy are a category by the own, as already has been mentioned. Since no time series for SMA were available (only data for 1976 and 1981) SMA was assumed to remain constant.

This simple model has been used to estimate the Italian imports from Austria to be transformed into exports from Austria to Italy and viceversa.

This procedure has made possible the following exercises.

4. SELECTED POLICY SIMULATIONS

Given the BASE scenarios for both countries we planned to simulate the effect of home policies influencing final demand components. We decided to concentrate on private consumption and to analyse the impacts on both countries in a stepwise procedure.

In the first step (reported in 4.1.) private consumption in Italy was increased and the impacts on the Austrian economy were analysed.

In the second step (4.2.) private consumption in Austria was also increased;

---

[2] The authors are indebted to Jan Stankovsky (Austrian Institute for Economic Research) who provided this information

Private consumption was choosen because of the magnitude of this final demand component and because national income policy can in fact influence disposable income and thus consumer expenditures in a significant way.

4.1. Increasing private consumption in Italy

For the years 1985 to 1987 an increase of 2 % per year was superimposed on the private consumer expenditures of the BASE forecasts. On the basis of this modified scenario INTIMO was rerun and provided higher import estimates. These increased import estimates were filtered through SMI. In addition it was assumed that the increase of Italian imports does not change the market shares as compared to the BASE scenario. Therefore it was possible to apply the rates of change between the BASE scenario and the modified scenario directly to the estimate of the Austrian exports to Italy. A run of AUSTRIA III (BASE CASE + higher exports to Italy) led to a higher level of economic activities in Austria.

TABLE 5 First step: The increase of 2 % in the disposable income in Italy; growth rates

	BASE CASE 84 - 87	+ 2 % Cons. 84 - 87
GDP	2,67	4,44
Private Consumption	1,92	3,90
Public Consumption	1,76	1,76
Exports	5,40	5,40
Imports	4,74	6,97
Total investment	4,18	7,85

As may be seen from Table 6 the impact of higher personal consumption in Italy on the overall level of economic activities in Austria is not very high. More exports to Italy (an average annual growth rate of 4,76 % instead of 4,15 %) lead to higher outputs and via the income effect also to higher domestic consumption and investment. Imports also go up from an annual rate of 4,70 % to 4,74 %. The resulting growth rate of GDP is 2,47 % compared to 2,44 % in the BASE CASE.

TABLE 6 Overall impacts of step 1 on the Austrian economy; growth rates

	BASE CASE 84 - 87	STEP 1 84 - 87
GDP	2,44	2,47
Private Consumption	2,25	2,28
Public Consumption	2,40	2,44
Exports	5,24	5,29
Italy	4,15	4,76
Imports	4,70	4,74
Total investment	2,44	2,47
Total output (selected sectors in national classification)		
Agriculture	1,48	1,53
Glass	2,99	3,06
Leather	2,12	2,18
Radio & TV	4,92	4,98
Sawmills	3,08	3,42
Plywood	3,77	3,88
Paper	2,84	2,90

Some of the sectors in the Austrian economy are affected more significantly. The largest increase can be observed for the total output of sawmills. Higher consumption in Italy would mean an increase in the growth rate
of this sector of more than 10 %. Austrian agriculture would gain directly
and indirectly from higher consumption in Italy. Directly via better export
opportunities, indirectly via higher domestic demand for agricultural inputs
primarily coming from sawmills and paper industry. The higher level of
Austrian consumption also would stimulate demand for agricultural products.
Other branches like those of the sheltered sector are only affected indirectly. But even for sectors like trade, insurances, real estate, services the
impacts are at least visible.

4.2. Increasing private consumption in Austria also

In analogy to the procedure described in 4.1. an alternative scenario
was calculated for Austria which assumes a higher private consumption than
in the BASE CASE. Total private consumer expenditures were increased by 2 %
compared to the BASE CASE for the years 1985, 1986 and 1987. This approach
implies that the rates of increase differ significantly from consumer expenditure to consumer expenditure catagory according to different income elasticities.
On the basis of increased consumer expenditures AUSTRIA III was re-
calculated which led to a new set of import estimates which became input
into INTIMO.
The main results of this exercise are shown in Table 7.

TABLE 7 Overall impacts of increased consumption in both countries;
         Linked run; growth rates 84 - 87

	ITALY		AUSTRIA	
	BASE	STEP 2	BASE	STEP 2
GDF	2,67	4,46	2,44	3,36
Private consumption	1,92	3,90	2,25	4,26
Public consumption	1,76	1,76	2,40	3,21
Exports	5,40	5,45	5,24	5,29
Imports	4,74	6,99	4,70	5,63
Total investment	4,18	7,88	2,44	2,65

To a certain extent the results reported in Table 7 are due to differences in the structure of the two models.

Public consumption is exogeneous in INTIMO and has been assumed to be
constant over time. This hypothesis was adopted in the BASE CASE and in the
other scenarios because we thought to stick to the official declaration of
Italian governments to fight for decreasing public deficits; this should
imply an unchanged rate of growth of public consumption even if private consumption is expected to increase. In AUSTRIA III public consumption is
endogeneous.

The most striking difference in the final reaction to an increased consumption and increased export opportunities may be observed for investment.
Since investment in INTIMO is dependent on change in output, an increase in
output is immediately detected especially when such an increase is prolonged
over time. In AUSTRIA III investment is treated semi-exogeneously and the
increase in total outputs has no direct impact on investment.

The effect of the linking for Italy can be isolated by comparing the
results of Table 7 with those of Table 5. The additional demand for Italian
exports caused by an increase in consumption in Austria accounts only for
an annual increase of about 0,02 % in GDP. This low effect hides a peculia-
rity of the multiplier effect of the Austrian contribution to the Italian
total output. The multiplier of output/increased exports is about 3. At
sectoral level the multiplier is greater than 1 for many branches like coke,
oil, mining, ferrous and non ferrous ores, metal products, dairy products,
paper, rubber and, of course, all the service sectors. Many other sectors
have an elasticity close to 1.

The isolated effects of an increased consumption in Italy on the
Austrian economy were already reported in 4.1..

The additional imports induced by exports (due to higher consumption in
the other country) are small both in Italy and in Austria. Given the size
of market shares it was therefore decided not to perform further iterations.

5. CONCLUDING REMARKS

The experiences gained from the attempt to link the Austrian and the
Italian model were quite encouraging.

First, the experiments with the two models showed that linking is even
possible under circumstances which can by no means considered as ideal. Only
three month (including the traditional vacation time) were available to
collect the necessary data, to estimate market shares and to run scenarios.
As usual most of the time was absorbed by computer problems. Both models were

operated on their home computers and no computer- or tele-network was available for fast communication. The transfer of ideas, data and results of simulations had to be based on old fashioned surface mail.

The second conclusion is that linking is even meaningful in the case of two countries with moderate trade relationships. Although exports to Austria only account for about 3 % of total Italian exports and exports to Italy for about 10 % of total Austrian exports, changes in one country´s scenario have significant inpacts on the other country. Changes in the overall aggregates are not very pronounced but the outputs of some of the sectors differ quite remarkablywhether the models are linked or not.

The exercises carried out also indicate that linking should start from a firm basis as regards data and classifications. The problems of forecasting market shares on a detailed level also deserve further attention. If the involved difficulties with data can be solved in a satisfactory way, bilateral or trilateral linking seems to be a second best solution to achieve more consistency among scenarios. Needless to say,that such a pragmatic solution will never offer an alternative to a multilateral link within a family of IO models.

REFERENCES

Barnabani, M., Grassini, M. (1984). On modeling the foreign trade of an input-output model of an open economy. Paper presented to 5 th IIASA Task Force Meeting on IO Modeling.
CER (1983). Effetti Strutturali Delle PoliticheMacroeconomiche: Previsioni Settorali 1984-'86. Rapporto 6, Rome.
Grassini, M. (1982). A national scenario for a regional model. WP-82-131 IIASA, Laxenburg, Austria.
Richter, J. (1981). Szenarien der österreichischen Wirtschaft bis 1990; Modellbeschreibung, Vienna.

APPENDIX

INTIMO-AUSTRIA III Key for tradeable commodities

Common classification	INTIMO classification	AUSTRIA III classification
1	1 Agriculture	1 Agriculture
2	2 Coal 7 Ferrous & non ferrous	2 Mining (incl.magnesite + magnesit products)
3	4 Petroleum, gas	3 Crude oil, refinery
4	5 Electricity, gas, water 6 Nuclear	40 Electricity 41 Gas, water
5	8 Non metal min.products	4 Non metal mineral products 5 Cement 6 Glass
6	9 Chemical products 25 Rubber & plastic prod.	18 Chemical products
7	10 Metal products 3 Coke	19 Iron & steel 22 Foundries 23 Non ferrous metals 24 Metal products
8	11 Agric.&ind.machinery 12 Office, preci.ind.	20 Machinery 25 Precision machinery
9	13 Electrical goods	26 El. motors etc. 27 El. wires & cables 28 Other El. goods 29 Radio & TV
10	14 Motor vehicles 15 Other transp.equip.	30 Vehicles 21 Ships, locomotives
11	16 Meat	7 Meat
12	17 Milk	11 Dairy products
13	18 Other food	8 Mills 9 Bakery 10 Sugar 12 Other food
14	19 Beverages	13 Beverages
15	20 Tabacco	14 Tabacco
16	21 Textiles & clothing	15 Textiles 16 Clothing
17	22 Leather & shoes	17 Leather & shoes
18	23 Wood & furniture	32 Sawmills 33 Plywood 34 Furniture etc.
19	24 Paper & print.prod.	35 Paper 36 Paper products 37 Printing& publishing

PROPOSALS FOR THE LINKAGE OF CMEA-COUNTRY MODELS

B. Czyżewski, Andrzej Tomaszewicz, and Lucija Tomaszewicz

Department of Statistics and Econometrics,
University of Łódź, Łódź, Poland

1.   FOREIGN TRADE STATISTICAL DATA FOR POLAND

The INFORUM-type model for the Polish economy covers 31 branches (see the Annex) of material production. This level of disaggregation was chosen mainly because of the comparability of the sectoral classification of balances for the 1970s. However, when considering the basic matrix of input—output coefficients and of conversion coefficients for a given year, a higher sectoral disaggregation can be assumed (according to Systematic Specification of Products, SSP).

In the input—output balances (the comparable period of 1971–82, excluding 1976, 1978 and 1981) the data dealing with exports and imports at current domestic prices are reported in a branch system that neglected commodity SITC or CTN cross-classification and a division into geographical regions. These data were the only source of information about exports and imports at current domestic prices up to 1980. Other available data in this area were reported either in devisa zloty or at current foreign currency prices. This situation has changed significantly since 1981, when foreign trade statistics reporting in current domestic prices was introduced.

For the purposes of construction of bridge matrices between domestic classification of branches (SSP) and CTN or SITC classification, two sources of data can be used — on the one hand, the data on the main exports/imports commodities and main country partners in a branch division, and on the other hand, the data on exports/imports in a geographical subdivision (socialist and non-socialist countries) and in an international commodity classification (CTN or SITC).

Input—output data include information about exports and imports not only of commodities but of services as well. The above mentioned sets of branch data concern main commodity groups and main country partners only, so the bridge matrices can only be obtained as estimates. In this paper we present an attempt of such an estimation for 1982.[1]

---

[1]Our earlier estimates were based on a larger number of assumptions than given in this paper (caused by the additional problem of conversion between devisa zlotys and current domestic prices) and were concerned with 1977 and 1980.

The additional problem consists of the constraint possibility of disaggregation of CTN or SITC items. The data published in Statistical Yearbooks have a very general character and consist of four groups according to CTN and of six groups according to SITC, both divided into two geographical regions (see the Annex). So, only these disaggregations could be used in INFORUM. The example presented below of bridge matrices for CTN is based on a four-group classification, extended by the inclusion of services as a fifth group.

2. ON THE POSSIBILITY OF CONSTRUCTING A BRIDGE MATRIX FROM SSP CLASSIFICATION TO CTN CLASSIFICATION

The exports and imports data from input—output balances are global data (with services) 'not divided into commodity groups and countries, the data of which, in turn, concern only main countries and main commodities (without services). Thus, the construction of bridge matrices of CTN or SITC into SSP requires a solution of, at least, two problems:

1. The construction of the bridge matrix between CTN classification and branch classification for commodities (with the subdivision into socialist and non-socialist countries).

2. The construction of the matrix of connections between services and branches offering services — divided into two groups of countries.

Because we have no better suggestions about the distribution of commodities originating from a given branch according to CTN groups we assume that the distribution is proportional to the incomplete distribution we were able to obtain for the main commodities on the basis of foreign trade statistics. It is worth adding that in different branches the differences between incompletely distributed commodities according to CTN and global exports/imports by branches were different — from a 100% distribution in the fuel and energy industry to 70–80% in electromachinery.

Let us introducte the symbol U_{shg} for exports/imports values.

The s, h, and g subscripts denote:

s: $s = 1$ for socialist, $s = 2$ for non-socialist countries,

h: number of the branch, $h = 1, 2, \cdots, 31$,

g: GTN trade group index, $g = 1, 2, 3, 4$ for commodities and $g = 5$ for services.

When, instead of any subscript, a point is written the symbol represents the sum of values, for instance,

$$U_{.h.} = \sum_s \sum_g U_{shg} .$$

Moreover, the asterisk denotes that summing concerns the commodity group ($g = 1, 2, 3, 4$) only. For instance,

$$U_{s.*} = \sum_{g=1}^{4} U_{s.g} ,$$

Analogical symbols are used for denoting the values obtained on the basis of a preliminary incomplete distribution, replacing the letter U for F.

The following assumptions were introduced:

1. The global exports/imports services were divided into socialist and non-socialist countries and are proportional to the global exports/imports of commodities divided into these areas

$$U_{1.s} / U_{2.s} = U_{1.*} / U_{2.*}$$

e.g.,

$$U_{s.5} = U_{..5} \frac{U_{s.*}}{U_{..*}} \quad , \quad s = 1,2 \quad .$$

2. The differences between the levels of exports/imports commodities and services and their preliminary distribution are biproportional to a certain binary matrix (with elements B_{shg}) characterizing the distribution and the possibility of the appearance of commodities and of services in the particular branches, e.g., there exist such coefficients ρ_{sh} and σ_{sg} that

$$U_{shg} = F_{shg} + \rho_{sh} B_{shg} \sigma_{sg} \quad .$$

Bridge matrices for 1982, whose elements were defined as $U_{shg}/U_{s.g}$, are presented in the Annex.

3. ON THE POSSIBILITY OF APPLICATION OF THE TRADE SHARE MATRICES AND BRIDGE MATRICES

The trade share matrix method is an important analytical tool for modeling the transmission of economic activity between various countries of the world. The well-known project Link model [1] and many subsequent models of similar design make use of the trade share matrix method in linking national econometric models.

In forecasting with "Link-Type" models, it is necessary to take into account changes in the trade share matrices. The methods that attempt to capture changes in trade share matrices can be classified into two groups: (1) direct methods and (2) indirect methods. Direct methods attempt to forecast each coefficient of the trade share matrix explicitly. A theoretical framework for the direct approach was developed by Armington [2] and a linearized version of this method was used by Hickman and Lau [3]. Indirect methods make adjustments to export forecasts obtained from a base year trade share matrix without explicitly predicting each element of the trade share matrix. The Linear Expenditure System method of Klein and Van Peeterssen [4] can be classified as an indirect method.

Application of a trade share matrix method for modeling the transmission of economic activity between CMEA countries requires solving two problems:

empirical and methodological. Empirical difficulties result from constraints in publishing adopted in foreign trade statistics in CMEA countries.[2] For example, there is no official information about intra-CMEA trade flows in CTN categories. There is also no information about foreign trade price movement for CMEA countries, except for some global quantities. The lack of data has limited linkage methods for models of CMEA countries to a "pool" approach developed by Vanous [5]. A similar approach has been used in IE&S model of CMEA countries [6]. The pool approach is based on the assumption that all commodities traded on the intra-CMEA market are homogenous from the buyers point of view. However, taking into account the predominance of a bilateral form of foreign exchange on the intra-CMEA market and the dominating share of the trade with the Soviet Union, a trade share matrix approach seems to be superior to the "pool" approach. However, a prerequisite for an application of the trade share matrix method is to have the matrix of trade flows between linked countries.

Having no statistical information about intra-CMEA trade flows we have attempted to derive estimates of intra-CMEA trade flows matrices for four CTN groups of commodities from a set of *a priori* assumptions about the allocation of exports of particular countries. The calculation was carried out for seven European CMEA countries: Bulgaria, Czechoslovakia, GDR, Poland, Romania, Hungary, and the Soviet Union, using 1980 data about global intra-CMEA exports and imports of these countries in four CTN groups of commodities: CTN 1, CTN 2+3+4+5, CTN 6+7+8, and CTN 9, evaluated in 1980 US dollars. Obtained trade share matrices are given in the Annex.

Moreover, we have derived from the published data[3] for Poland, exports flows to and imports flows from six CMEA countries in the same CTN division. These data are evaluated in 1982 Polish zlotys. The initial information about the Polish trade with each of the six CMEA countries disaggregated into 450 SSP products, covering from 86% (exports to Hungary) to 97% (exports to Romania) of the total trade with these countries. Final exports and imports flows are given in the Annex.

Overcoming the data problems enables us to use trade flow matrix, but does not solve the problem of how to use it in modeling the transmission of economic activity between CMEA countries.

The solution to this problem is the next methodological difficulty. A straightforward translation of "Link-Type" procedures[4] does not appear reasonable. The reasoning based on Armington's assumption, which justifies theoretically an application of "Link-Type" methodology to the case of market economies,

---

[2]A brief description of the Polish data was given in the first section of the paper, and it is worth mentioning that Polish and Hungarian statistics are more comprehensive than those in the other CMEA countries.

[3]Rocznik statystyczny handlu zagranicznego 1983, GUS, Warszawa 1983. The same data were used to construct the bridge matrix SSP–CTN.

[4]Transformation of import demands into exports.

cannot be valid for CMEA countries. Armington's hypothesis assumes the existence of price-competitive equilibrium on international markets. It implies that, given foreign trade prices, there is enough capacity in each country to meet foreign demand for each country's products. This is not the case where CMEA countries are concerned.

Historical conditions, namely:

— unconvertible currency,
— central planning based on material balances accounts,
— protection of domestic and intra-CMEA price system against world price movement,
— necessity of trading with market economies,

have contributed to the permanent lack of supply of primary products, such as fuels, raw materials, and food on the intra-CMEA markets. On the other hand machinery and equipment are in excess supply on the intra-CMEA market.

Supply restrictions and the weak sensitivity of CMEA countries' economies to changes in foreign demand and foreign trade prices make up the necessity of evolving distinct solutions.

If the assumption about an excess demand of "hard" goods is accepted[5] the quantity of traded goods on the CMEA market will be determined by the supply of exports of "hard" goods into the CMEA market. The quantity of exports to CMEA countries depends on the trade conditions on non-CMEA markets faced by each CMEA country. Higher demand for non-CMEA products usually has to be covered by higher exports to non-CMEA countries. Therefore, for a given CMEA country, the quantity of imports from CMEA should depend on the quantity of exports supply directed by other CMEA countries on the intra-CMEA market. In that case the trade share matrix should transfer the supply of exports into the quantity of imports, and its entries λ_{ij} should be defined as a ratio of trade flow from the i-th to the j-th country, U_{ij}, and the total exports of the i-th country, U_i.

$$\lambda_{ij} = U_{ij} / U_i \ .$$

There are several important consequences of the above assumption for the specification of models for individual countries. Because imports of hard goods from CMEA markets are supply-restricted they cannot depend on changes in import demands. Any increase of total demand for imports resulting from the solution of a country model should be directed to non-CMEA markets. The possibility of meeting the increase of that demand depends on the significance of the balance of payments restrictions.

―――――――――

[5]For justification of the assumption see Vanous [5] and Tomczyk–Czyżewski [6], and also Plowiec [7], and Winiecki [8].

The bridge matrices between the domestic and international division of imports and exports, if they exist in any country model, should transform: exports of hard goods to CMEA countries from the domestic division to the international division and imports of these goods from the international to the domestic division.

The next implication of Armington's assumption is that trade shares change according to changes in foreign trade prices. Unfortunately, there is no operational theory to explain the rules of bilateral trade patterns on the intra-CMEA markets. As a result the factors that cause changes in trade shares on these markets are not identified. It can hardly be assumed that intra-CMEA prices adjust these trade shares, since these prices are not equilibrium prices.

Because the dominating part of intra-CMEA exports and imports is covered by long and medium-term bilateral agreements, the quantities of trade flows result from the accepted strategies of development of the trade partners.

Therefore, one should expect very smooth changes in the trade flows, which should be captured by the time variable. Because the planning of development strategies takes into account the expected conditions on world trade markets, which are subject to very rapid and dynamic changes, there is quite a high probability of error in this expectations. If an unexpected course of events on the non-socialist markets causes a meaningful distortion on one country economy, it will imply an action of other CMEA members (mostly of the Soviet Union) to relieve the effects of the distortion in the economy of this country and to protect against expansion of the distortion over the other CMEA countries. Therefore, one of the most important factors explaining deviations from long term tendency are conditions of trade with non-socialist countries, measured by changes in the trade balances with these countries. Any further suggestions in the trade flow matrix will have to be prerequisited by detailed empirical studies.

ANNEX

Groups of branches — by Systematic Specification of Products (SSP) used in the INFORUM-Type Model for the Polish Economy

1. Coal, briquettes
2. Fuels and fuel products, excluding coal and briquettes
3. Production of electricity and thermal energy
4. Ferrous metallurgy
5. Non-ferrous metallurgy
6. Metal products
7. Machines and applicances
8. Precision instruments
9. Means of transportation
10. Electrical and electronical appliances
11. Chemical industry
12. Building materials
13. Glass and fine ceramic industry
14. Wood industry
15. Paper industry
16. Textile industry
17. Clothing industry
18. Leather industry
19. Food processing industry
20. Other manufacturing industries
21. Common building construction
22. Productive and service building construction
23. Special construction services
24. Other construction services
25. Agriculture: plant production
26. Agriculture: animal production
27. Agricultural services
28. Forestry
29. Transportation and communication
30. Trade
31. Other material goods and services

CMEA Trade Nomenclature

CTN 1 — metallurgy and equipment

CTN 2+3+4+5 — fuels and non-food raw materials

CTN 6+7+8 — food and raw materials for food

CTN 9 — industrial consumers goods

TABLE 1

Import Bridge Matrix for the Socialist Countries.

	1	2	3	4	5
1	0.000	0.011	0.000	0.000	0.000
2	0.000	0.542	0.000	0.000	0.009
3	0.000	0.008	0.000	0.000	0.000
4	0.000	0.151	0.000	0.000	0.013
5	0.000	0.045	0.000	0.000	0.027
6	0.046	0.012	0.000	0.087	0.010
7	0.359	0.000	0.000	0.000	0.107
8	0.083	0.000	0.000	0.094	0.004
9	0.353	0.000	0.000	0.047	0.027
10	0.089	0.009	0.000	0.071	0.029
11	0.044	0.121	0.000	0.242	0.039
12	0.005	0.015	0.000	0.000	0.003
13	0.004	0.002	0.000	0.010	0.004
14	0.000	0.013	0.000	0.079	0.002
15	0.000	0.020	0.000	0.000	0.005
16	0.000	0.018	0.000	0.128	0.045
17	0.000	0.000	0.000	0.028	0.003
18	0.000	0.000	0.002	0.134	0.001
19	0.000	0.016	0.813	0.000	0.032
20	0.017	0.000	0.000	0.066	0.005
21	0.000	0.000	0.000	0.000	0.021
22	0.000	0.000	0.000	0.000	0.001
23	0.000	0.000	0.000	0.000	0.000
24	0.000	0.000	0.000	0.000	0.000
25	0.000	0.010	0.184	0.000	0.028
26	0.000	0.005	0.000	0.000	0.002
27	0.000	0.000	0.000	0.000	0.000
28	0.000	0.001	0.000	0.000	0.000
29	0.000	0.000	0.000	0.000	0.567
30	0.000	0.000	0.000	0.000	0.004
31	0.000	0.000	0.000	0.014	0.011

TABLE 2

Import Bridge Matrix for the Non-Socialist Countries.

	1	2	3	4	5
1	0.000	0.000	0.000	0.000	0.000
2	0.000	0.106	0.000	0.000	0.009
3	0.000	0.000	0.000	0.000	0.000
4	0.000	0.099	0.000	0.000	0.013
5	0.000	0.086	0.000	0.000	0.027
6	0.063	0.018	0.000	0.018	0.010
7	0.445	0.000	0.000	0.000	0.107
8	0.076	0.000	0.000	0.008	0.004
9	0.164	0.000	0.000	0.000	0.027
10	0.099	0.015	0.000	0.031	0.029
11	0.110	0.351	0.000	0.620	0.039
12	0.000	0.026	0.000	0.000	0.003
13	0.000	0.003	0.000	0.007	0.004
14	0.000	0.001	0.000	0.000	0.002
15	0.000	0.026	0.000	0.000	0.005
16	0.000	0.054	0.000	0.187	0.045
17	0.000	0.000	0.000	0.092	0.003
18	0.000	0.011	0.000	0.002	0.001
19	0.000	0.138	0.292	0.000	0.032
20	0.035	0.006	0.002	0.034	0.005
21	0.000	0.000	0.000	0.000	0.021
22	0.000	0.000	0.000	0.000	0.001
23	0.000	0.000	0.000	0.000	0.000
24	0.000	0.000	0.000	0.000	0.000
25	0.000	0.026	0.706	0.000	0.028
26	0.000	0.032	0.000	0.000	0.002
27	0.000	0.000	0.000	0.000	0.000
28	0.000	0.001	0.000	0.000	0.000
29	0.000	0.000	0.000	0.000	0.567
30	0.000	0.000	0.000	0.000	0.004
31	0.000	0.000	0.000	0.000	0.011

TABLE 3

Export Bridge Matrix for the Socialist Countries.

	1	2	3	4	5
1	0.000	0.351	0.000	0.000	0.000
2	0.000	0.129	0.000	0.000	0.000
3	0.000	0.051	0.000	0.000	0.000
4	0.000	0.165	0.000	0.000	0.000
5	0.000	0.044	0.000	0.000	0.000
6	0.056	0.045	0.000	0.053	0.000
7	0.407	0.000	0.000	0.000	0.000
8	0.096	0.000	0.000	0.012	0.000
9	0.296	0.000	0.000	0.079	0.000
10	0.118	0.003	0.000	0.117	0.000
11	0.020	0.177	0.028	0.258	0.002
12	0.000	0.008	0.000	0.000	0.000
13	0.003	0.002	0.000	0.010	0.000
14	0.000	0.007	0.000	0.097	0.000
15	0.000	0.007	0.000	0.000	0.000
16	0.000	0.004	0.000	0.187	0.000
17	0.000	0.000	0.000	0.000	0.116
18	0.000	0.000	0.023	0.121	0.000
19	0.000	0.000	0.576	0.028	0.000
20	0.004	0.000	0.000	0.018	0.000
21	0.000	0.000	0.000	0.000	0.045
22	0.000	0.000	0.000	0.000	0.118
23	0.000	0.000	0.000	0.000	0.140
24	0.000	0.000	0.000	0.000	0.002
25	0.000	0.006	0.370	0.000	0.000
26	0.000	0.000	0.003	0.000	0.000
27	0.000	0.000	0.000	0.000	0.000
28	0.000	0.000	0.000	0.000	0.014
29	0.000	0.000	0.000	0.000	0.562
30	0.000	0.000	0.000	0.000	0.001
31	0.000	0.000	0.000	0.020	0.000

TABLE 4

Export Bridge Matrix for the Non-Socialist Countries.

	1	2	3	4	5
1	0.000	0.367	0.000	0.000	0.000
2	0.000	0.042	0.000	0.000	0.000
3	0.000	0.004	0.000	0.000	0.000
4	0.000	0.099	0.000	0.000	0.000
5	0.000	0.187	0.000	0.000	0.000
6	0.072	0.022	0.000	0.077	0.000
7	0.388	0.000	0.000	0.000	0.000
8	0.029	0.000	0.000	0.010	0.000
9	0.355	0.000	0.000	0.087	0.000
10	0.113	0.010	0.000	0.081	0.000
11	0.032	0.171	0.013	0.072	0.002
12	0.000	0.012	0.000	0.000	0.000
13	0.004	0.003	0.000	0.055	0.000
14	0.000	0.021	0.000	0.151	0.000
15	0.000	0.004	0.000	0.000	0.000
16	0.000	0.008	0.000	0.279	0.000
17	0.000	0.000	0.000	0.000	0.116
18	0.000	0.004	0.016	0.114	0.000
19	0.000	0.019	0.759	0.029	0.000
20	0.007	0.000	0.000	0.025	0.000
21	0.000	0.000	0.000	0.000	0.045
22	0.000	0.000	0.000	0.000	0.118
23	0.000	0.000	0.000	0.000	0.140
24	0.000	0.000	0.000	0.000	0.002
25	0.000	0.011	0.021	0.000	0.000
26	0.000	0.014	0.176	0.000	0.000
27	0.000	0.000	0.000	0.000	0.000
28	0.000	0.000	0.015	0.000	0.014
29	0.000	0.000	0.000	0.000	0.562
30	0.000	0.000	0.000	0.000	0.001
31	0.000	0.000	0.000	0.022	0.000

Table 5: Intra-CMEA trade share matrices for CTN divisions, exports shares $\lambda_{ij} = U_{ij} / U_{i.}$, for 1980.

CTN 1	BG	CS	GDR	PL	R	H	SU	Σ
BG	0	10.9	11.4	10.9	9.6	9.9	47.3	100
CS	7.4	0	16.9	16.2	6.3	6.5	46.8	100
GDR	7.4	16.4	0	16.3	6.3	6.5	47.1	100
PL	7.4	16.2	16.9	0	6.3	6.5	46.7	100
R	11.1	10.8	11.2	10.7	0	9.8	46.5	100
H	11.2	10.8	11.2	10.7	9.4	0	46.6	100
SU	17.6	20.7	27.0	20.5	6.2	7.9	12.9	100
Σ	14.8	18.0	22.5	18.0	6.2	7.6	12.9	100

CTN 2–5	BG	CS	GDR	PL	R	H	SU	Σ
BG	0	8.0	9.2	7.8	7.0	6.8	61.2	100
CS	5.9	0	14.5	12.3	3.9	3.8	59.6	100
GDR	6.0	12.9	0	12.5	4.0	3.9	60.7	100
PL	5.9	12.6	14.5	0	3.9	3.8	59.4	100
R	10.2	7.7	8.9	7.5	0	6.6	59.2	100
H	10.1	7.7	8.8	7.5	6.8	0	59.0	100
SU	18.6	17.6	23.4	26.0	7.6	6.8	0	100
Σ	8.2	10.2	11.8	11.9	5.0	4.7	48.1	100

CTN 6–8	BG	CS	GDR	PL	R	H	SU	Σ
BG	0	5.9	5.8	7.4	2.3	3.7	74.8	100
CS	4.2	0	5.9	7.6	2.4	3.7	76.1	100
GDR	4.2	6.0	0	7.6	2.4	3.7	76.1	100
PL	4.3	6.1	6.0	0	2.4	3.8	77.4	100
R	4.1	5.7	5.7	7.3	0	3.6	73.5	100
H	4.1	5.8	5.8	7.4	2.3	0	74.5	100
SU	10.5	21.0	20.9	37.1	2.9	7.6	0	100
Σ	4.4	6.2	6.2	8.6	2.2	3.8	68.6	100

CTN 9	BG	CS	GDR	PL	R	H	SU	Σ
BG	0	6.6	11.2	7.5	2.6	3.6	68.4	100
CS	3.4	0	11.6	7.7	2.7	3.7	70.8	100
GDR	3.5	7.2	0	8.1	2.8	3.9	74.4	100
PL	3.4	6.9	11.7	0	2.7	3.8	71.4	100
R	3.2	6.6	11.2	7.4	0	3.6	68.0	100
H	3.3	6.7	11.3	7.5	2.6	0	68.7	100
SU	9.4	19.1	32.3	21.4	7.5	10.3	0	100
Σ	4.1	9.8	16.4	11.0	3.6	4.9	50.3	100

Table 6: Intra-CMEA trade share matrices for CTN divisions, imports shares $a_{ij} = U_{ij} / U_{.j}$, for 1980.

CTN 1	BG	CS	GDR	PL	R	H	SU	Σ
BG	0	1.3	1.1	1.3	3.3	2.8	7.9	2.2
CS	3.3	0	5.0	6.0	6.8	5.8	24.3	6.7
GDR	3.8	6.9	0	6.9	7.7	6.6	27.8	7.6
PL	3.0	5.4	4.5	0	6.1	5.2	21.8	6.0
R	2.2	1.8	1.5	1.7	0	3.8	10.6	2.9
H	1.6	1.3	1.0	1.3	3.2	0	7.6	2.1
SU	86.1	83.4	86.9	82.8	72.9	75.9	0	72.5
Σ	100	100	100	100	100	100	100	100

CTN 2–5	BG	CS	GDR	PL	R	H	SU	Σ
BG	0	9.3	9.2	7.7	16.5	17.2	15.0	11.8
CS	13.2	0	22.6	19.0	14.4	15.0	22.8	18.4
GDR	15.9	27.4	0	22.8	17.3	18.1	27.4	21.8
PL	11.9	20.5	20.4	0	13.0	13.5	20.5	16.6
R	6.3	3.8	3.8	3.2	0	7.1	6.2	5.1
H	8.1	4.9	4.9	4.1	8.8	0	8.0	6.5
SU	44.7	34.1	39.1	43.2	30.0	29.0	0	11.8
Σ	100	100	100	100	100	100	100	100

CTN 6–8	BG	CS	GDR	PL	R	H	SU	Σ
BG	0	9.1	9.1	8.3	10.4	9.4	10.5	9.7
CS·	18.2	0	18.2	16.6	20.8	18.8	21.0	19.0
GDR	18.8	18.7	0	17.1	21.4	19.4	21.7	19.6
PL	21.9	21.7	21.9	0	25.0	22.6	25.3	22.4
R	10.0	9.9	10.0	9.1	0	10.4	11.6	10.8
H	8.5	8.4	8.5	7.7	9.7	0	9.8	9.0
SU	22.8	32.2	32.3	41.0	12.8	19.4	0	9.6
Σ	100	100	100	100	100	100	100	100

CTN 9	BG	CS	GDR	PL	R	H	SU	Σ
BG	0	18.1	18.4	18.2	19.4	19.7	36.4	26.7
CS	3.6	0	3.1	3.1	3.3	3.3	6.2	4.4
GDR	5.3	4.5	0	4.5	4.8	4.9	9.0	6.1
PL	3.9	3.3	3.4	0	3.6	3.6	6.7	4.7
R	11.6	9.9	10.0	9.9	0	10.7	19.8	14.6
H	12.9	11.0	11.1	11.0	11.8	0	22.0	16.1
SU	62.7	53.3	54.0	53.4	57.1	57.8	0	27.4
Σ	100	100	100	100	100	100	100	100

Estimates of intra-CMEA trade share matrices given in Tables 5 and 6 are derived from the following assumptions about cross-the-row structures:

- share of exports to the Soviet Union ($\lambda_{i\,7}$)
- shares of Czechoslovakia, GDR, and Poland in exports of these countries (λ_{ij} i,j = Czechoslovakia, GDR, Poland)
- the row structure of the Soviet Union exports (λ_{7j})
- equality of other shares in each row.

Particularly we set:

- for CTN 1: $\lambda_{i\,7}$ = 50% for each i; λ_{ij} = 15% for Czechoslovakia, GDR, Poland; λ_{7j} = global imports of j-th country divided by global imports in the CTN group less the Soviet Union imports; other shares equal.
- for CTN 2–5: $\lambda_{i\,7}$ = 60% for each i; λ_{ij} = 15% for Czechoslovakia, GDR, Poland; λ_{7j} as for CTN 1, other shares equal.
- for CTN 6–8: $\lambda_{i\,7}$ = 70%; λ_{7j} as for CTN 1, other shares equal.
- for CTN 9: trade flow from i to j is proportional to the product of country i exports and country j imports.

Then the R.A.S. method was used for biproportional adjustment of the preliminary matrices.

Used abbreviations mean: BG – Bulgaria, CS – Czechoslovakia, GDR – German Democratic Republic, PL – Poland, R – Romania, H – Hungary, SU – the Soviet Union.

Table 7: Trade flows from Poland to CMEA countries in CTN divisions, millions of zloty, 1982.

CTN	BG	CS	GDR	R	H	SU	Σ
1	21223	34248	27678	8621	16180	173026	280976
2+3+4+5	5029	13875	14482	16331	7801	45952	103470
6+7+8	585	836	862	725	980	5876	9864
9	2701	2050	2112	704	3984	61701	73252
Σ	29538	51009	45134	26381	28945	286555	467562

Table 8: Trade flows from CMEA countries to Poland in CTN divisions, millions of zloty, 1982.

	CTN				Σ
	1	2+3+4+5	6+7+8	9	
BG	9285	3938	2516	2553	18292
CS	30987	13938	388	5510	50823
GDR	34488	16628	321	7855	59292
R	5667	9478	2382	5748	23275
H	12804	5105	2802	5610	26321
SU	64974	245268	6600	11907	328749
Σ	158205	294355	15009	39183	506752

Computations based on *Statistical Yearbook of Foreign Trade 1983*
(*Rocznik Statystyczny Handlu Zagranicznego*).

BIBLIOGRAPHY

1. Ball, R.J., ed., *The International Linkage of National Economic Models*, North Holland Publishing Co., Amsterdam, 1973.

2. Armington, P.S., "A Theory of Demand for Products Distinguished by Place of Production", *International Monetary Fund Staff Papers*, Vol.XVI, No.1, March, 1969.

3. Hickman, B.G. and L.J. Lau, "Elasticities of Substitution and Export Demands in a World Trade Model", *European Economic Review*, Vol.4, 1973.

4. Sawyer, J.A., ed., *Modelling the International Transmission Mechanism*, North Holland Publishing Co., 1979.

5. Vanous, J., *An Econometric Model of World Trade of Member Countries of the Council for Mutual Economic Assistance*, Ph.D. Thesis, Yale University, 1979.

6. Czyżewski, A.B., and P. Tomczyk, Foreign Trade Flows Model of the CMEA Countries, paper presented at the conference *Models and Forecasts '82*, Budapest 1982.

7. Plowiec, V., *Centralne Sterowanie Handlem Zagranicznym* (Central Management of Foreign Trade), PWE, Warszawa, 1975.

8. Winiecki, J., Orientacja proeksportowa w gospodarce centralnie planowanej, kilka uwag teoretycznych (Pro-export orientation in centrally planned economy, some theoretical remarks) *Ekonomista* No.3—4, Warszawa, 1983.

THE INFORUM-IIASA FAMILY OF INPUT—OUTPUT MODELS: A BRIEF HISTORICAL REVIEW, PROGRESS IN 1984, AND FUTURE PROSPECTS FOR GROWTH

Dwight A. Porter

College of St. Thomas, St. Paul, Minnesota, USA

The initiative for the INFORUM-IIASA venture in cooperation and coordination in international economic model building began in 1978. Drs. Clopper Almon and Douglas Nyhus of the Interindustry Forecasting Project of the University of Maryland (INFORUM), spent 1978-79 at IIASA, as members of the Systems Decisions Sciences Project, laying the groundwork for and forging the beginnings of a project which has made steady progress in the intervening five years. Much of that progress has been reported elsewhere, but it is useful at present to briefly review the initial conception of the project and to remind ourselves of its original goals.[1]

The project at its start was based on several propositions:

1) Multisectoral (input–output) models offered a very powerful tool for national economic analysis and forecasting. In particular, they offered industry detail not usually found in macroeconomic type models.

2) While efforts to develop world economic models were afoot in 1978, none used the input-output approach as its basis.

3) To build all the country models in one place was seen as an overwhelming task. Good, detailed economic models of a country were also most likely to be built and maintained best by professionals within that country, therefore the need to find collaborating national partners in each country.
It was also understood that each collaborating partner would have complete autonomy regarding decisions about the techniques used in their model, subject to the needs of linking (see point 8 below).

4) A major economic factor in all of the country models is international trade. By linking country models together using trade flows a consistent system of models could evolve which would provide a disciplined treatment of trade flows among the participating countries.

5) Input–output models are fairly large scale enterprises which usually require a long-term commitment to become useful. For example, the U.S. model at Maryland and a U.K. model at the Cambridge Growth Project in England had been under development and in use for over ten years.

6) Somehow the self-interest and goals of the participants within the system would need to be met to ensure their continued interest and participation.

7) With the growing concern about problems of a "world economy" a tool capable of modeling the detailed interactions of the world's major economies (and many minor ones) seemed increasingly important.

---

[1]Nyhus, Douglas, "An International System of Input-Output Models: Status Report, December, 1980", Report to IIASA, 1980.

8) A common model building software package could assist new model builders and would ensure common computer conventions for file creation and handling which would in turn facilitate the task of model linking.

9) A venture of this type had the potential of attracting participants from both the East and West.

10) Such a venture would need a long-term perspective and long-term connections with a research center for coordination and as a meeting place for participants. IIASA could fulfill these functions.

So, in 1978 the goals were to forge a network of independent, model building partners in each IIASA country, plus in others wishing to participate; to quickly develop a common software basis; and as models were developed to begin linking them together. Obviously, success in meeting these goals depended in large measure on the energy and interest of the national partners. The progress and lessons of those next five years are worthy of a brief review.

Overall, the system evolved as planned, though somewhat more slowly than originally hoped. In retrospect, the slower than expected progress may have been partially due to the lack of staffing at IIASA from 1981 to 1983. Slow progress was clearly also due to the inherent nature of the project. Some national partners made rapid and splendid progress. Others began well, but were slowed by the loss of key individual participants. Yet others dropped out altogether and new collaborating partners had to be sought, which in turn delayed that country's potential contribution to the system. The problems of some national partners were related to the fact that fairly little IIASA funding was available for individual country model building support after 1979. IIASA funds were primarily used to support the annual Input-Output Task Force Meeting and to provide some technical support to individual countries. Most of the on-going technical support and assistance was provided directly by INFORUM which was somewhat inconveniently located and costly for many European partners to visit, especially those from the Eastern European countries.

Nevertheless, good progress was made. By Fall, 1982, over fifteen countries could be counted as active participants in the project. Fewer had operating models that were sufficiently completed to be useful for linking. But at the 1982 Task Force Meeting reports were made on the successful linking of seven country models.[2] Those country models were for the United States, Italy, Japan, Canada, Belgium, France, and West Germany.

Not all of these country models were built by national partners within those countries. For eample, the West German model was one built by INFORUM. In addition to these seven, a well developed Austrian model was also running at that time and models were substantially in progress for Finland and Hungary. A subgroup within the system, called Nordhand, began focusing on building a linked model system for Denmark, Norway, Sweden and Finland. Some progress was also reported by the group in Poland. Other countries showed interest in the project but had not as yet developed a national model.

---

[2]Nyhus, Douglas, "Linking Seven Input-Output Models of the INFORUM System," in Input-Output Modding, M. Grassini and A. Smyshlaev, editors, IIASA, 1983.

From October, 1983, to September, 1984, IIASA had a full-time member of the scientific staff working with the INFORUM-IIASA model family. In addition, half the time of an extremely competent research assistant was made available to the project. As a result, a number of new initiatives were begun that year and a working meeting of participants within the system was held (Slimforp User's Meeting, May 22-24, 1984).

The progress of this period spanned three main areas:

1) Methodology
2) Computer software and models available at IIASA
3) Organizational structure of the project

In each of the areas steps were taken to consolidate the gains and progress of the prior five years and to find new directions which encouraged further growth and development. Following is a list of some of the major activities or events of that year:

1) The most recent and advanced version of the INFORUM U.S. model, LIFT, was provided to IIASA. It was adapted for use on IIASA's VAX. LIFT was a "closed" input-output model in the sense that it had a real (product) side, a price and income side, and that forecast prices and incomes were used to drive the equations determining the next periods real side. LIFT represented a major methodological step forward and was made available as a prototype for study by other model builders. For example, a visiting scientist from VNIISI in Moscow, Andrei Zamkov, spent over a month in close collaboration with IIASA staff working on LIFT.

   The LIFT model and its supporting data base were also used to support other research efforts at IIASA in the Forestry Project under the direction of Dr. A. Anderson[3] and on a study of energy use in the U.S. under an IIASA contract with the Electrical Power Research Institute (EPRI) under the direction of Claire Doblin.

2) A careful compilation of all recent INFORUM publications was completed. Copies are on file with the Economic Structural Change Group (attention M. Weinreich) and a list of titles is also available. These documents were compiled to provide a clear supplement to the Slimforp manual in areas where that manual provided assistance for the programmer, but not the economist, engaged in building or extending an I/O model.

3) The basic Slimforp program was reprogrammed to adapt it to several microcomputers, including the Altos. Working Altos versions of the Polish and basic Czech Slimforp models were adapted for use at IIASA.

4) On-going model building assistance was provided at IIASA to groups from Hungary, Poland, Czechosloakia, Bulgaria, and as mentioned above, the USSR. At INFORUM, during the same period, collaborative work took place with visitors from Italy, Holland, Columbia and Taiwan. During the year substantial progress was made by the team of Drs. Andrzej and Lucja Tomaszewicz in

---

[3]INFORUM's database for Canada was also provided to the Forestry Project for its use.

Poland as they developed a working Slimforp model. The Hungarian group, led by Dr. Andras Simon, virtually "completed" their model and the preparatory steps to link their model into the system were taken. The Italian model, under the direction of Professor Grassini, continued its rapid progress with substantial advances in developing a full price and income side and to closing the model.

The Belgium model, the most mature one in the system other than the U.S. model, under the direction of Dirk Vanwynsberghe, engaged in a major reestimation of its demand equations. Vanwynsberghe also produced results from a linked run of the seven models for distribution at the May Users meeting.

5) The models of seven countries were adapted to the IIASA computers along with the linking software. In conjunction with this exercise, substantial progress was made by Wolfgang Schoepp of IIASA by developing largely automatic procedures for moving these very large programs from one computer to another. Overall, substantial progress was made during 1984 in identifying and solving many of the time consuming problems associated with transporting computer programs from one machine to another.

6) A computer communications network was set up for participating partners within the group. This network utilized IIASA's "Telectr" system and the PDP computer to act as a "post office." About eight modeling groups are currently on-line. Others can be added provided a local postal telephone and telegraph hookup to a European computer-net is available. Contact Wolfgang Schoepp for details about participation. In the future, this network may also facilitate linking with the model system (see point 7).

7) During the year it became clear that substantial progress for the system could be accomplished if existing input-output models, which had been developed independently of this initiative, could be incorporated into the system. The original goal of software compatability would have to be sacrificed but perhaps at not too high a cost. Based on this new idea, tentative agreements have been reached with Dr. Rudi Rettig of the Rheinisch-Westfaelisch Institute fur Wirtshaftsforschung, Essen, Germany; Dr. Terry Barker of the Cambridge Growth Project, Cambridge, England; and Dr. Frederich Muller of Erasmus Universiteit, Rotterdam, Holland, to have them participate in the system with their existing, extensive input-output models. The addition of these three new partners filled two large holes in the system for the UK and Holland, and replaced the INFORUM model of West Germany with a West German based one. Because these additions mean that all the models are unlikely to be running at once in a central location for linking, a new approach to linking had to be developed. The categories of "center" and "satellite" models were coined and a tentative procedure for linking with both types of models was proposed. Because of the importance of this new approach for attracting new participants and working out new arrangements with old partners who are, as yet, not linked, the original proposal along these lines is included in this paper as an Appendix.

8) In a continuing search to find new collaborating national partners, especially in the developing world, conversations were held with UNIDO regarding possible collaboration between INFORUM, IIASA and UNIDO. While these discussions are far too tentative at present to say anything definite about them, it is fair to say that the potential for such cooperation is very real and very exciting.

9) In May the Slimforp User's Meeting was held. Unlike the Input-Output Task Force Meetings, the agenda of this meeting was very specifically and narrowly focused on the interests and needs of the model builders within the system. Thirteen of the modeling groups were represented. The meeting was balanced between East and West and between groups with developed and developing models. A lively and frank exchange of views occurred out of which some new ideas and initiatives have arisen. The meeting also pointed out some problem areas and difficulties which may need to be taken into account in the future. These included the diversity of computer equipment used by the various groups and the attendant problems of software transportability; the differences between Eastern and Western uses for and approaches to these models, and some apparent tension about the allocation of responsibilities between the center coordinating groups, IIASA and INFORUM, and some of the national partners. Some groups also expressed a desire to see the Slimforp manual revised.

At the meeting all interested groups were given tape copies of one of the more advanced models within the system for use in their further work. The microcomputer versions of Slimforp were running and available for inspection and experimentation. One other positive feature of the meeting was that two previously tentative participants, Czechoslovakia and the German Democratic Republic sent strong delegates to the meetings. Subsequently a Slimforp demonstration was run via a computer link in the GDR and specific plans have been made for developing the Czech Slimforp model with assistance from IIASA.

10) In May, ÍNFORUM made a proposal to IIASA to begin a new stage of development and a new level of activity for the model system. Copies of this proposal and a subsequent revision of it are available from the Economic Structural Change Group (see M. Weinreich) This proposal includes a thrust to move rapidly in the model building and linking stages and to begin analysis using the powerful tool created by the linked system.

Unfortunately the proposal came at a time when IIASA was in transition, with budgetary problems and about to change directors. As a result no definite answer has been forthcoming yet from IIASA about the future of this work. But, since IIASA has on several occasions in the period since May affirmed its belief in the usefulness of this work I should like to conclude this paper with a brief commentary on some of the issues which I see as important to the future of the proposal.

There are now enough developed and running models within the system that an annual cycle of linked runs can begin now. The software is prepared at IIASA and at INFORUM. Several new satellite models have been added to the system but the "Telectr" machinery is also in place to accommodate them. I would hope that, in almost any circumstances, one cycle of linked runs, including at least the models for the U.S., Canada, Italy, Belgium, France, Austria, the U.K., Holland, West Germany, Hungary and Japan, would occur in 1985.[4] Other countries which are ready and which want to participate should speak out soon.

---

[4] In fact at the Task Force meeting, arrangements were made to conduct such a cycle of linked runs with a target completion date of May 1985.

Smaller experiments in examining bilateral (and multilateral) trade linkages should take place. Already Italy and Austria have done so, with the results presented in another paper at these meetings. Other possible groupings, such as adding West Germany and Hungary to the Italian and Austrian case study, offer much promise. At the User's Meeting in May much was made of the possibility of working on some separate linking of COMECON economics. This idea might be strengthened by the growth of a third center for research within this project. Such a center, located in an Eastern country, using its national currency as a form of IIASA dues, could readily provide the manpower and facilities to work on tailoring Slimforp for socialist economies, to provide a center to explore linking the COMECON countries and to act as a bridge between the linked Western and Eastern models. One possible candidate is the University of Lodz in Lodz, Poland, which is hosting two major modeling conferences shortly after the conclusion of this meeting.

As this international cooperative effort grows, as surely it must, it should search for a new name for itself. Both IIASA and INFORUM have done much for it, but as new countries and older established models enter, the system outgrows its old boundaries. The selection of a new name would symbolize that transition and offer new visions for the future.

One preoccupation for the future is to fund the system and its growth and to provide adequate incentives for the participants. Serious attention, as well as creativity and ingenuity, need to be brought to these problems. The status quo will clearly not work too much longer. While IIASA may act as a clearing house and as a convenient location for many years to come, it cannot be a perpetual source of funds, even for a project so successfully leveraged as this one. In his speech to the IIASA staff on 3 September, 1984, the new Director of IIASA, Professor Lee, said ". . . I reported the Council's decision to make IIASA's work more useful to policy makers and industrial leaders.· . . . One absolutely 'nonarguable' way to insure relevance and to guarantee direct client involvement is to have potential clients fund part of the project." This seems as clear a signal as one could ask for regarding IIASA's new directions. The challenge of how to follow Professor Lee's prescription is one which should be taken up immediately. In fact, much of a revised INFORUM proposal to IIASA is along those lines. Since the commitment envisioned in such a project of international cooperation in economic model building is a long-term one, long-term mechanisms for its support must also be developed.

In conjunction with several possible other new developments, some attention needs to be given to software and manual development. If a movement in the direction of developing countries·takes place, or if the models are to be adapted to even the more powerful microcomputers or if a new language such as C proves to be a logical next step for the programming, care will need to be taken to not leave some groups too far behind while striving for growth improvement or growth for others. All the above developments can, perhaps even should, happen with time. Patience and flexibility will be needed to deal with them in a way compatible with such a cooperative endeavor.

But, the future begins now, or at least tomorrow, depending on one's energy. I hope that the afternoon of October 7 can be spent planning the next immediate steps regarding use of the "Telectr" network and plans for linking. This network may provide an important step bridge into the future and should be taken despite the uncertainties of the moment. The potential for development of the system is very high in 1985. One of the purposes of this paper is to inform you of recent developments in order to retain the momentum of 1984. Please respond with your ideas, energy, new initiatives and, most of all, with your models.

Appendix

MODEL LINKING WITHIN THE INFORUM–IIASA SYSTEM OF MULTISECTORAL MODELS

PROPOSED RIGHTS AND DUTIES FOR EACH PARTY

May, 1984

1. The current linking procedure within the system is based on an ad hoc matching of the specific commodity classification scheme of each country model. For a new model to be linked into the system a description (in English) of the classification scheme of the country is necessary. From that the ad hoc comparison of that country to all the other countries within the system can be formulated.

2. If the country model is of an INFORUM (Slimforp) type then the easiest procedure for linking is for a current version of the model to be available at the central location where the linked runs will be performed (called "center" models).

3. If for any reason the country model is not to be run at the center location (called "satellite" models) the group running the satellite model would have the following responsibilities for each linked run.

   a) To provide to the center (via means discussed below) specific model output from the "best" prelinked run of the model. That output would consist of a time series by commodity (including some history and the model forecast) of the domestic production, import and export vectors of the model.

   b) That information would be used by the center to produce the first linked run. The outcome of that run would be provided to each satellite participant in the form of vectors of domestic production, imports and exports for every country within the system. In this first run, the data sent back from the satellite models in the system to all participants would be their first "best" forecast and from the central models their first forecast conditioned by the best forecasts of the satellites. Each satellite modelling group would then take the new information on the demand for their exports and use it to modify their forecasts. The new forecasts would again be provided to the center which would run a second iteration of the center models. This procedure would be continued until the convergence criteria were met.

4. At the end of this cycle all country participants would receive domestic output, imports and exports of the countries in the system as well as a summary report of the results. In addition, each country would have an "improved" forecast from its own model due to the better export forecasts arising from the system.

5. The linking cycle will take place once or twice per year on a regular cycle. Each participating satellite group would need to provide the help of a responsible individual for about two weeks to handle the local details of the linking.

6. The maintenance and updating of all country models, whether satellite or central, are the responsibility of each country group.

7. There are currently plans to manage the linking process through the IIASA computer network, "Telectr". Each participating group is encouraged to consider the possibility of such a procedure. Other arrangements are possible and are certainly subject to discussion.

THE POTENTIAL CONTRIBUTIONS OF MUTUALLY CONSISTENT, SECTORALLY DISAGGREGATED NATIONAL ECONOMIC MODELS TO ANALYSES OF NATIONAL ENVIRONMENTAL POLICIES AND GLOBAL ENVIRONMENTAL INTERDEPENDENCE

Stephen P. Dresch

International Institute for Applied Systems Analysis,
Laxenburg, Austria

1. Overview of the Issue

Much of the contemporary concern for "structural change" in advanced economies has its origins in the significant changes in patterns of international trade which have occurred over the last two decades. While these changes in trade patterns are the joint consequences of developments in a number of interrelated dimensions (e.g., differentials in rates of technological innovation and diffusion and differential changes in relative factor prices, in rates of savings and capital formation, in the vintage of the capital stock and in primary materials and energy prices and availabilities), a growing emphasis in a number of countries on the environmental consequences of productive activities has constituted an important contributing factor, serving to discourage apparently "environmentally-adverse" ("pollution-intensive") production in some countries and to encourage the transfer of that production to countries in which environmental concerns are less intense (or impinge less severely on productive activity).

If "open economies" enjoyed "closed (natural) environments," then international trade would represent an effective means by which to "purchase" environmental amenities. In those societies in which these amenities were valued more highly, higher "prices" would be placed on "environmental services" as factors of production (either *de jure* or, through regulation, *de facto*). Other economies, placing lesser value on environmental services and amenities, would enjoy a comparative advantage with reference to commodities the production of which was environmentally "intensive." In consequence, patterns of trade would evolve exhibiting relative specialization, either in environmentally-adverse or in environmentally-neutral production. Those countries more highly valuing environmental amenities would experience an apparent deterioration in terms of trade, compensated by simultaneous increases in the consumption of environmental amenities relative to the consumption of other commodities. In the absence of barriers to international migration, individuals would distribute themselves over countries (characterized, *inter alia*, by closed environmental systems and open economies) so as to maximize welfare.[1] On the assumption that environmental services were efficiently priced in each country, i.e., that any given level of environmental quality (consumption of environmental amenities) in any country could not be achieved at lesser cost (higher real income and output in that country), it would follow that the the global distributions of population, production and environmental quality would be Pareto optimal.[2]

In fact, of course, virtually all of the assumptions (explicit or implicit above), necessary for the conclusion that independently-taken national decisions concerning the explicit or implicit pricing of environmental services will lead to a globally Pareto-optimal solution, can be expected to be violated. Thus:

- Individual countries are not characterized by open economies and closed (natural) environments.

    - Because of less than "complete" environmental closure, the transfer of production from one country to another may be offset to a greater or lesser extent by trans-border environmental impacts of production, i.e., consequences of production in any one country on the environments of other countries.

    - Because of less than "complete" economic openness, the anticipated benefits of national actions designed to raise the effective prices of environmental services may not materialize or may be inefficiently achieved. For example, adverse changes in international competitiveness of industries engaged in environmentally intensive production may lead to the imposition of import tariffs and quotas and to other trade interventions which preclude to some extent the efficient global reallocation of productive activity, erode the intended improvement in environmental quality in the initiating country and raise the effective economic cost of such environmental improvement as is achieved in that country. Similarly, restrictions on international capital movements may well prevent full adaptation of the global economy.

---

[1]What is required here is freedom of movement of individuals both as consumers (of environmental amenities) and as factors of production (labor). The absence of barriers to international movements of capital as a factor of production is implicit in the assumption of a perfectly "open" economy, and corresponding stipulations concerning knowledge and technology are also implicit.

[2]The general system, as just described, would be in the class described by James Buchanan's "economic theory of clubs" and Charles Tiebout's "pure theory of local government" (analysis of local governmental expenditure and taxation).

- Constraints on international migration preclude the conclusion that the market-determined global allocation of productive activity would be Pareto optimal even if individual countries were characterized by open economies and closed environments and if national environmental policies were efficient. Even in the absence of perfect mobility, constrained optimality could be achieved if political decisions in each country fulfilled the compensation criterion that beneficiaries of the policy be able to fully compensate victims, although this is also unlikely.

- It is apparent that national environmental policies are not even internally efficient, i.e., that given levels of environmental quality and amenity could generally be achieved even if prices of environmental services confronted by producers were reduced (or, conversely, that given levels of nonenvironmental output and income could be achieved at lesser cost in terms of the sacrifice of environmental amenities).[3]

In short, the net benefits/costs (not to mention optimality/efficiency) of environmental policies are unclear, not only globally but even at the level of the national economy.

2. Toward an Analytical Framework for the Analysis of National Policies and Global Environmental-*cum*-Economic Interdependence, With Particular Reference to the IIASA Research Program

A complete portrayal of global economic and environmental interdependence would require a fully articulated specification of both the global economy and the global environment. It would be necessary that this system capture all significant interdependencies between economic activity and the environment in the spatial dimension, with economic activity at any point in space influencing the environment at all other points, and *vice versa*.[4] Attempted construction of such a fully articulated

---

[3]This problem would also be mitigated by free international migration, in that population (and capital) would leave jurisdictions pursuing inefficient environmental policies.

[4]In fact, it would also be necessary to incorporate the time dimension, in that current productive activity will have implications for the global environment at subsequent points in time, and *vice versa*. Differently stated, optimality must be considered not only with reference to persons currently alive but also with reference to those who will be alive in the future. If all environmental externalities could be internalized, then this would not require a qualification of the above suggestion that market outcomes would constitute a global optimum, as discussed in the related context of exhaustible resources in Stephen P. Dresch, "Myopia, Emmetropia of Hypermetropia? Competitive Markets and Intertemporal Efficiency in the Utilization of Exhaustible Resources" [IIASA Working Paper, WP-84-48, June 1984 (revised September 1984)], forthcoming (in Russian translation) in J. Gvishiani and A. Wierzbicki, eds., *Soviet Yearbook on Systems Research* (Moscow: USSR Academy of Sciences and The State Committee on Science and Technology, 1985).

portrayal of the economic-*cum*-environmental systems would, obviously, be a preposterous undertaking, given the current states of our understanding of both the economy and the environment. However, a selfconscious recognition of the environmental implications of economic activity and of the economic implications of environmental actions would clearly be beneficial to the substantive interpretation of the conclusions of economic *and* environmental analyses and might well contribute also to the further development of capabilities in each dimension.

Unfortunately, most current economic and (exhibiting an economist's bias, especially) environmental analyses are not notably selfconscious with reference to implications in the other domain. Overstating, perhaps, but not radically, environmental analyses pay lip service to economic implications but proceed as though environmental amenities were virtually "unlimited goods" (the value of which is invariant with respect to the amount "produced" and almost invariably greater than the value of the alternatives sacrificed for their attainment), while economic analyses, until quite recently, have virtually ignored the issues of the environmental implications of productive activity and of the evaluation of these implications.

Substantively, there appear to be several interdependent but separately identifiable issues warranting explicit economic and/or environmental analysis:

- *Representation of the environment as a factor of production (environmental services as productive inputs).* While characterization of environmental consequences of productive activity as simply *negative externalities* (negatively valued byproducts) is formally equivalent to the characterization of environmental services as factor inputs, comprehension of the issue may well be clarified by election of the latter representation. The issue is then one of the role of environmental services in production functions, substitution possibilities between environmental services and other inputs, etc. An important subsidiary issue here concerns the probable environmental *nonneutrality* of technological change, both as it affects production processes of existing products and as it eventuates in new products and thus alters the composition of output. Involving a major technological, engineering component, this subject is clearly within the purview of both economics and the environmental sciences.

- *Behavioral determinants of the choice of technology (and thus the relative utilization of environmental services in production).* This issue is obviously related to but is also distinct from the foregoing. The production function provides a menu of possibilities involving differential utilization of different factors of production. The issue here is the selection of one production technology over others, focusing on the implications of alternative mechanisms by which to allocate and ration environmental services (prices versus regulation), substitutions between direct consumption *versus* factor input utilization of environmental services, etc.

- *Environmental consequences of specific environmental service flows.* The significant but often ignored issue here concerns the nonabsolute nature of the environmental implications of productive activity, i.e., the dependence of environmental consequences on the specific characteristics of the environment (e.g., its absorbtive or regenerative capacities, capacities which are probably not invariant either spatially or over time). This issue is significant in the international context because it indicates that, even holding the global level and composition of output constant, redistributions of productive activity in space may well not constitute environmentally zero-sum games.

- *Spatial transmission of the environmental consequences of productive activity (international externalities).* Explicit recognition of the openness of national environments is necessary not only with reference to the issue of internalizing international environmental externalities (alternative *supranational* mechanisms of pricing or otherwise rationing foreign environmental inputs into any country's domestic production activities) but also for purposes of evaluating any individual country's own environmental policies, in that the environmental effects of a national policy (e.g., increased prices of environmental services) may be more or less offset by transnational externalities. Thus, a shift of certain production activities out of a country may not eliminate the environmental consequences of those production activities if there are significant externalities of foreign production (for export to the policy-initiating country).

Significant initiatives have, of course, been undertaken in these and related areas. With reference only to current IIASA activities, the acid rain project is explicitly concerned with transnational environmental externalities, as is the regional water policy project and the much more ambitious "biosphere" proposal currently under discussion. In each of these, however, it would appear that the economic dimension, although perhaps recognized, is considered secondary (implicitly if not explicitly); economic activities may be perceived as a source of the problem, but economic analysis is not considered essential either to the understanding of the problem or to its solution (whatever the problem is thought to be).

Operationally, the important question concerns the way in which the economic aspects of these issues are to be illuminated and the way in which economic intelligence is to be brought to bear. It is certainly appropriate that studies such as the foregoing be framed to explicitly include consideration of economic aspects and issues and, hence, that the scientific groups undertaking these studies include economists. However, the general approach of undertaking large, avowedly comprehensive studies may well be inefficient and, even, counterproductive. When true comprehensiveness may be impossible to achieve, the pretension of comprehensiveness may well lead to a pseudoscientism the biases and excesses of which may well negate the value of the entire activity. This is particularly likely because economists associated with such efforts may become "captives" of an effort dominated by others and may also not be of especially high caliber.

These considerations suggest that the most productive approach under current circumstances may involve a loose, informal interaction between environmental and economic studies, in which the environmental aspects of economic activities are explored as a byproduct of other economic analyses, and *vise versa*. Under this approach major reliance would be placed on cross-fertilization rather than permanent cohabitation. I would suggest that current circumstances are especially favorable for such an approach:

- The analytical excesses and effective pseudoscientism of large, ostensibly comprehensive studies of significant constellations of issues are increasingly being publically recognized, as reflected in the decline in credibility accorded to studies such as *Limits to Growth*, the *Global 2000 Report* and *Energy in a Finite World*.[5]

- Current budgetary realities (especially at IIASA but also in most countries as well) are such that highly ambitious, comprehensive (probably ultimately pseudoscientific) undertakings will be precluded, even if they were still thought to be of value.

---

[5] A substantial part of the blame for the earlier popular regard for these studies must, of course, be placed on members of the scientific community, who perceived benefits in the popular perception that scientific analysis could reach dramatic conclusions of immediate, practical import. Similarly, much of the credit for the declining popular appreciation of these efforts must be accorded to those members of the scientific community (most notably, Julian Simon and Herman Kahn) who refused to be "coopted" by the short-term benefits associated with these analytical excesses.

- Also because of these budgetary circumstances, specific research efforts in economics and in other fields are being subjected to ever more jaundiced examination, motivating *rentier* "scientists" to search for at least apparent justifications for their continued existence and financial sustenance.

- A number of specific studies in economics and environmental sciences, originally undertaken for possibly quite unrelated purposes, are now at a stage at which they might contribute to and benefit from extension and cross-fertilization.

The last three of these considerations are especially relevant with reference to current IIASA efforts in the economics and environmental areas. Analytical excesses are being increasingly perceived in both areas (as reflected in the progressively more skeptical attitude toward ostensible forecasting capabilities), while at least limited capabilities amenable to application to subjects deemed to be of social significance, but not requiring major financial infusions, have been developed. Here attention will be focused on a possible application of the capabilities developed by the IIASA/INFORUM-centered group of national input-output modelling efforts.

3. Multinational Analyses of Secular Change in the Pollution Intensity of International Trade Flows

It seems readily apparent that any meaningful analysis of the environmental implications of international trade must be undertaken at a reasonably high degree of sectoral disaggregation. A "single-commodity" characterization of the global economy would effectively assume away the substance of the issue, i.e., differential pollution-intensities in production and thus the capacity to separate the spatial distribution of pollution generation from the spatial distribution of product utilization. Thus, sectorally-disaggregated input-output models are obvious candidates as the analytical basis for initiating analyses of the environmental implications of international trade. The IIASA/INFORUM models are especially well placed for this role because of the degree of cross-model consistency which they have achieved, specifically the capacity to bridge into a common commodity classification. The following describes a very simple preliminary analysis which could be undertaken on the basis of these models. The objective of this initial modest effort would be simply to document the degree to which changes in patterns of international trade have served to redistribute pollution-intensive production across national economies over the recent past.

In this preliminary phase the focus of the study would be entirely descriptive. That is, it would attempt to identify significant changes over time in patterns of net importation/exportation of pollution-intensive products, but it would not attempt to establish the degree to which pollution-intensity has acted as a *cause* of changes in patterns of trade. Furthermore, because of the qualifications necessarily associated with the data which would be employed, the study would not provide firm evidence concerning, e.g., identities of net importers/exporters of pollution-intensive products; rather, it would attempt to identify significant changes over time in relative importation/exportation of these commodities. In other words, it is concerned with differential trends in the global pattern of pollution-intensive production, as revealed by trends in net importation/exportation of pollution-intensive products.

The analysis of changes over time in directions of international trade in pollution-intensive products will be very simply formulated. For each country (or regional group of countries) vectors of product imports and exports (dimension n *by* 1) are observed over time (t). These are designated y_{mt} and y_{et}, respectively. Exports can be represented as produced subject to a linear Leontief production technology. Thus,

$$x_{et} = (I-A)^{-1}y_{et}$$

where x_{et} represents the vector of outputs required to produce the observed vector of exports, and A is a matrix (dimension n *by* n) of direct requirements from each sector (row) per unit of output of each sector (column).

Sectoral production can be represented as having quantifiable environmental impacts in some finite number of dimensions (q). These can be represented by the effluent matrix F (dimension q *by* n), in which columns represent sectors and rows represent environmental impacts per unit of sectoral output. Thus, the quantitative environmental impacts, u_{et} (dimension q *by* 1), of the production of the vector of exports are be given by

$$u_{et} = Fx_{et} = F(I-A)^{-1}y_{et}.$$

Ignoring transborder flows of pollutants, imports effectively constitute a means by which to avoid the environmental impacts of production. Thus, from the vantage point of the individual economy, the vector of imports is associated with "environmental-impact savings" of

$$u_{mt} = F x_{mt} = F(I-A)^{-1} y_{mt}.$$

The net environmental effect of international trade, for the individual economy, is, then, $u_{bt} = u_{mt} - u_{et}$. If this quantity (i.e., any element $1,\dots,q$ of the vector u_{bt}) is positive, then the environmental impacts avoided through imports exceed the environmental impacts associated with exports, and *vice versa*. More important, for purposes of this study, would be the direction and rate of change over time of this net "environmental balance of trade" for any economy relative to others. Policies which increase the "prices" of "environmental services" in one economy relative to those in others should be reflected in an improvement in its environmental balance of trade as pollution-intensive production is shifted to other economies in which the prices of environmental services are relatively lower.

In the absence of environmental impact matrices for individual countries over time, and on the assumption that lower impacts per unit of output of any commodity (across countries at a point in time, or over time for an individual country) are purchased at a price (higher capital and/or labor inputs per unit of output), a single environmental impact matrix (F) can be employed for indicative purposes. On the basis of U.S. data for 1967,[6] fourteen categories of environmental impacts, measured in physical units (pounds, gallons), can be identified. These are indicated in Table 1. For most purposes these can be grouped into four major categories: (1) air pollutants (pounds), (2) solid waste (pounds), (3) waste water (gallons), and (4) water pollutants (pounds). Thus, a reasonably comprehensive set of indicative indicators of secular change in the "first-round" enviomental implications of international trade could be obtained. In association with other groups, e.g., the IIASA project on transborder flows of pollutants, subsequent "rounds" of this process could then be explored.

---

[6]International Research and Technology Corporation (IRTC), *Effects of Technological Change on, and Environmental Implications of, an Input-Output Analysis for the United States, 1967-2020* (Washington, D.C.: IRTC, 1970).

Code	Effluent	Symbol	Unit
	Table 1. Environmental Impacts (Effluents)		
	Air Pollutants		
1	Particulates	P	
2	Hydrocarbons	HC	Billions
3	Sulfur Oxides	SOX	of
4	Carbon Monoxide	CO	Pounds
5	Nitrogen Oxides	NOX	
6	Solid Waste	SW	Trillion Pounds
	Water Pollutants		
7	Waste Water	WW	Trillion Gallons
8	Chemical Oxygen Demand	COD	
9	Biological Oxygen Demand	BOD	
10	Refractory Organics	RO	Billions
11	Suspended Solids	SS	of
12	Dissolved Solids	DS	Pounds
13	Nitrogen	N	
14	Posphate Compounds	PH	

CHANGES IN THE STRUCTURE
OF THE FINNISH ECONOMY, 1970—1980

Osmo Forssell

Research Institute of the Finnish Economy, Helsinki, Finland

1. INTRODUCTION

The Finnish economy fell from its long-term growth path in the
70's. The average annual growth rate of GDP was annually 4.6 percent
until 1975. In 1976-1983 the growth rate was 2.9 percent. The period
from 1975 until today is too short to justify the conclusion that the
long-term growth rate has also decreased. We can assume that, after a
period of smooth and rapid growth, the Finnish economy was faced with
structural adjustments in connection with the marked changes in the
relative price of oil. How long a period of time will these adjustments
related to overall structural changes in the world economy take? And,
will there be again a period of smooth and rapid growth in the future?
These are interesting questions, but they are hard to answer for the
present.

We can consider that structural adjustments take at least five
years, but we need a longer period in order to identify them. Hence, we
must know the course of the economy almost throughout the 80's before
final conclusions can be drawn. Nevertheless, I will try to analyse the
structural growth and the course of the Finnish economy over the 70's.
My main interest will be in industrial structural changes, which will
be analysed with static input-output models for the years 1970 and
1980. The components of disproportional growth of output in industries
are analysed by studying the effects of the growth and changes in the
structure of final demand categories and the effects of changes in the
input-output technology on the output of industries.

Industrial restructuring or structural adjustment is the search
for a new equilibrium between the demand and supply of industrial
outputs, between the demand and supply of labour, between growing
industries and maturing industries, between exports and imports, and
between saving and investment. The balance within and between different
markets is difficult to determine in practice. Long-run structural
tendencies, short-run cyclical changes and once-for-all incidental
changes have simultaneous effects on economic developments. Transition
from one developmental period to another is often slow, gradual and
indeterminate. It is easy to agree with Schumpeter (1939) in that
industrial change is never a harmonius advance of all elements of the
system actually moving or tending to move in step. Some industries move
on and others stay behind. In different markets. equilibrium conditions

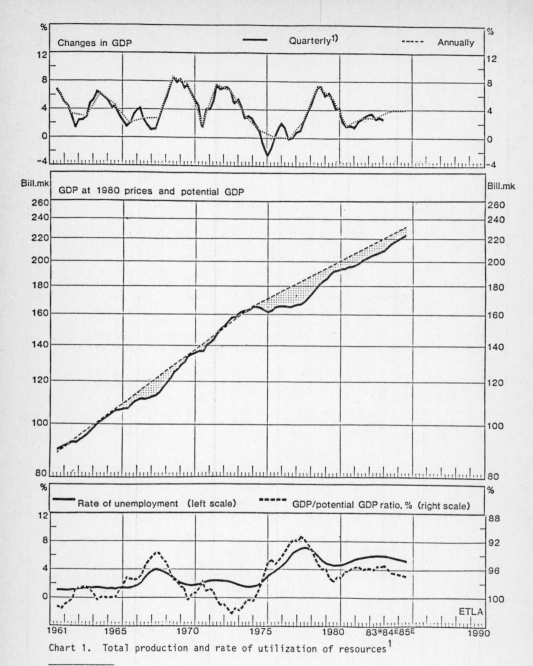

Chart 1. Total production and rate of utilization of resources[1]

[1]The Research Institute of the Finnish Economy, Economic prospects, autumn 1984, Espoo 1984.

can only accidentally be attained in the same year. In cases where it is impossible to observe such a year, it can be determined only by using model simulation.

A full-capacity year can be used as an approximation to an equilibrium year in choosing comparison years for static growth analysis. The years 1960 and 1970 satisfy this condition for the Finnish economy. The actual GDP was the same as the potential GDP and the unemployment rate was only two percent. The next peak year was 1980, but then the actual GDP was only 96 percent of the potential GDP and the unemployment rate was five percent. If we assume, however, that the Finnish economy fell from its growth path in 1975, the potential GDP, in an economic sense, is no longer the same as before. The performance capacity of the Finnish economy diminished. The potential GDP might thus be the same as the actual GDP. The unemployment rate was high, which reveals that the labour market had not adapted itself to the new situation. It may be concluded that the Finnish economy had already partly adapted itself to the new conditions by 1980. Some structural changes had already taken place. It makes sense, then, to analyse these changes by comparing the 1970 and 1980 states of the economy with other. A decisive factor determining the years of comparison is formed by the availability of input-output tables. Fortunately, they exist just for these two years.

Other imbalances typical of a long-wave downswing (van Duijn, 1984) were wage increases which exceeded productivity increases. Further typical imbalances - such as an overabundance of older industries and a relative lack of younger industries, institutional rigidity and a relative increase in the size of debt - were not remarkable features about economic developments in Finland.

2.   CHANGES IN THE FINNISH ECONOMY BETWEEN 1970 AND 1980

A background for the analysis of structural changes is provided by the description of developments in the 60's and the 70's in terms of macro-measures (Table 1). The following observations can then be made.

1. The growth rate of GDP decreased in the 70's.
2. The growth rate of domestic demand failed more than that of exports.
3. The consumption/investment ratio rose all the time. It was 2.24, 2.41, and 2.86 respectively in 1960, 1970 and 1980.
4. Government final consumption expenditure increased at about the same rate both in the 60's and the 70's. Private final expenditure increased clearly less in the 70's than in the 60's.
5. The share of imports in domestic demand increased all the time, but much less in the 70's than in the 60's. In 1960, 1970 and 1980 respectively it was 24 %, 31 % and 33 %.

Economic growth is not a smooth balanced process and it involves a changing relative importance of industries. Hence, a macro economic perspective can only give a background for a disaggregated analysis of structural change. Changes are obvious when the growth rates of various industries for the 70's are examined. Industries are classified in table 2 into four categories according to their growth rates.

TABLE 1   Expenditure on GDP in purchasers' values, 1980 prices

	FIM.mill.	percent-changes 1970/1960	1980/1970	ratio be-tween changes
Gross domestic product in purchasers' values	192556	59.8	42.8	0.72
Final consumption expenditure	138933	65.5	42.0	0.64
-private	104038	65.7	35.3	0.54
-government	34895	64.8	66.8	1.03
Gross fixed capital formation	48638	53.8	19.6	0.36
-private	42537	63.2	19.2	0.30
-government	6101	28.0	22.8	0.81
Domestic demand	194186	63.2	36.9	0.58
Exports of goods and services	63386	102.3	73.9	0.72
Imports of goods and services	65016	111.3	49.4	0.44
Increase in stocks	6287			
Statistical discrepancy	328			

[2]Central Statistical Office, National Accounts, Time series for 1960-1981.

TABLE 2   Growth rates of output by industries 1980/1970, constant prices

I Growth > 1.60

Manufacture of electrical machinery and related products	2.64
Manufacture of chemicals	2.42
Basic metal industries	2.09
Communication	2.04
Electricity, gas and water	1.94
Manufacture of metal products and machinery	1.80
Other real estate, financing, insurance and business services	1.76
Transport	1.70
Sawing, planing and pre-serving	1.62

II 1,60 > Growth > 1.40

Manufacture of paper, and paperboard and of pulp, paper and paperboard articles	1.55
Manufacture of transport equipment	1.55
Other manufacture of wood	1.53
Trade	1.53
Pottery, glass and earthen products	1.52
Petroleum refineries and miscellaneous products of petroleum and coal	1.48
Mining and quarrying	1.45

III 1,40 > Growth > 1.20		IV Growth < 1.20	
Manufacture of chemical,		Private personal and social	
rubber and plastic products	1.34	services	1.14
Printing and publishing	1.34	Other manufacturing indus-	
Food manufacturing	1.33	tries	1.12
Letting and operating of		Restaurants and hotels	1.12
dwellings and use of owner		Forestry and logging	1.01
occupied dwellings	1.31	Other construction	1.00
Textile, wearing apparels		Agriculture, hunting and	
and leather industries	1.31	fishing	0.94
Pulp mills	1.26		
Building	1.25		
Beverage and tobacco in-			
dustries	1.24		

Most of the fastest-growing industries were various engineering and metal manufacturing industries. The traditional Finnish industries, i.e., the forest industries, were among those whose growth rates were in the medium-range. An interesting feature of developments was just the declining share of the forest industries and the growing role of the engineering and metal manufacturing industries. Developments of these industries will be given special attention in the following analyses.

3.   COMPOSITION OF DISPROPORTIONAL GROWTH OF INDUSTRIES

How are the disproportional growth of output of industries affected by differences between the growth rates of final demand categories, by changes in the structure of demand and by changes in input-output technology? This is analysed through calculations as follows:

-growth: $B(0)(\bar{g} - 1)y(0)$
-structure of demand: $B(0)[y(t) - \bar{g}y(0)]$
-input-output technology: $[B(t) - B(0)]y(t)$

where B(0) and B(t) are the inverse matrices $(I - A)^{-1}$ for
1970 and 1980
g is the average growth of final demand gategory between
1980 and 1970: $\Sigma_i\, y_i(t) \,/\, \Sigma_i y_i(0)$

y(0) and y(t) are categories of final demand vectors for
1970 and 1980, $y_i(0)$ and $y_i(t)$ elements of the vectors.

Input coefficients and final demand categories include both imported and domestically produced commodities. Only crude oil, natural gas and coal are treated as non-competitive imports and as primary inputs. The following final demand categories are distinguished: imputed bank service charges, private consumption expenditure, final consumption expenditure of government services, gross fixed capital formation, exports, imports, increase in stocks and statistical discrepancy. All calculations were made at 1970 prices. The results of the calculations are presented in Tables 3-5.

TABLE 3   Effects of average growth of final demand categories,
millions of FIM at 1970 prices

indus- try	private consump- tion	govern- ment con- sumption	capital forma- tion	domestic demand total	exports	imports	total
1	15669	1041	426	17136	7724	−8382	16478
2	1793	262	1039	3093	13176	−1733	14536
3	637	280	1304	2222	3055	−4175	1101
4	18470	1493	140	20103	8352	−5036	23418
5	1706	13	18	1738	367	−342	1763
6	7310	552	449	8362	8923	−8737	8547
7	338	176	696	1210	8221	−605	8826
8	924	47	1192	2162	4968	−684	6447
9	801	280	276	1357	17296	−1259	17394
10	1300	447	442	2189	21549	−1373	22365
11	2446	805	428	3680	1757	−1521	3916
12	3351	711	964	5026	8168	−10177	3018
13	2627	869	919	4415	5205	−5327	4294
14	2300	719	816	3835	2792	−3902	2726
15	724	334	1982	3040	1292	−1575	2757
16	3386	1638	8578	13602	18374	−27832	4144
17	3133	1580	9760	14473	13134	−17797	9811
18	1779	689	2672	5140	3909	−7130	1919
19	2390	325	3403	6118	7463	−9098	4482
20	612	101	71	784	542	−931	395
21	3382	1818	1479	6679	7202	−5451	8430
22	1396	720	14560	16676	663	−570	16770
23	241	2294	5128	7663	350	−162	7852
24	12247	1278	2630	16154	3779	−2052	17881
25	5352	32	105	5489	289	−328	5450
26	4924	1013	2120	8057	13713	−3822	17948
27	1600	506	278	2384	752	−538	2598
28	13319	0	0	13319	0	0	13319
29	3959	819	1358	6136	3204	−2422	6918
30	4945	397	382	5724	1537	−855	6407
Σ	123063	21238	63666	207967	187757	−133815	261909

aThe names of the industries are presented in the appendix.

Table 3 describes how much the output of industries would have
increased if each element in the final demand category under
consideration had increased at the same rate as this category on average.

The total effect on the forest industries (7-10) would then have
been FIM 55032 million, and the growth rate would have been 1.63. The
output of the engineering and metal manufacturing industries (16-19)
increased by FIM 20356 million, giving 1.23 for the growth rate. It may
thus be concluded that the average growth rate of the final demand
categories, without structural changes within the categories, would have
been very favourable for the forest industries.

TABLE 4   Effects of structural changes in final demand categories,
millions of FIM at 1970 prices

indus-try	private consump-tion	govern-ment con-sumption	capital forma-tion	domestic demand total	exports	imports	total
1	-1819	828	-1450	-2442	-6554	5305	-3691
2	2178	437	-226	2390	-8197	43	-5765
3	371	-15	328	683	3001	-1455	2229
4	-632	1604	-145	828	-10288	3548	-5912
5	-496	63	8	-425	304	74	-46
6	-4749	519	127	-4103	8096	-3841	152
7	406	100	-31	475	-122	261	613
8	716	685	-201	1199	-2270	-438	-1508
9	764	194	97	1055	-16921	-625	-16491
10	1332	340	234	1906	-14088	-959	-13142
11	379	-397	117	100	2463	-643	1920
12	1171	453	-38	1586	2518	-2397	1706
13	-537	-44	-53	-634	-1959	-809	-3402
14	150	-554	-150	-554	3473	3643	6563
15	164	-36	-167	-38	2369	-98	2232
16	2103	-206	2756	4653	26930	11100	42683
17	1387	-139	6961	8209	9229	1503	18940
18	2848	-358	1577	4067	10161	-6307	7920
19	836	216	-3068	-2016	-3439	3263	-2192
20	-587	-155	-41	-784	635	-136	-285
21	1933	32	208	2173	-629	1404	2948
22	-18	-178	982	787	-58	95	824
23	214	-2146	-6591	-8523	-82	-18	-8623
24	-5100	489	289	-4322	-85	-1555	-5962
25	-6034	108	4	-5922	59	368	-5495
26	5606	606	-663	5549	-5998	-895	-1345
27	465	374	23	862	207	-336	732
28	1624	-1374	0	250	0	0	250
29	-1423	1026	696	299	3918	-2020	2197
30	-2512	-953	-188	-3653	234	-592	-4011
Σ	740	1518	1394	3652	2904	7482	14039

[a]The names of the name of industries are presented in the appendix.

Table 4 shows how much the output in industries would have changed
if only structural changes had taken place in the various final demand
catagories. A positive figure indicates that the increase in the item
concerned due to structural changes in the final demand category under
consideration would have been greater than the average. A minus-sign
indicates, correspondingly, that the change would have been less than
the average. Imports form an exception to this rule, in that negative
figures indicate greater than average and positive figures smaller than
average changes.

The effects of structural changes on output in the forest industries and in the engineering and metal manufacturing industries are opposite in direction to the effects of growth. Owing to structural changes, the output of the forest industries decreased by FIM 30528 million, whereas output in the engineering and metal manufacturing industries grew by FIM 67356 million. These changes were mainly due to structural changes in export demand. The structural changes in domestic demand had a positive effect on output in both industry groups. The increase in imports of metal and engineering products was also less than the average increase in imports.

TABLE 5   Effects of changes in input-output technology, millions of FIM at 1970 prices

indus-try	private consump-tion	govern-ment con-sumption	capital forma-tion	domestic demand total	exports	imports	total
1	-12495	-725	200	-13020	-2042	3087	-11975
2	-3862	76	373	-3414	-2328	453	-5288
3	-484	-154	-2376	-3014	-3410	3528	-2896
4	11656	724	844	13224	2644	-2849	13018
5	896	88	294	1278	541	-439	1380
6	-2029	-141	4	-2166	-2025	2294	-1898
7	107	78	877	1062	161	-28	1194
8	-322	40	1174	892	51	5	945
9	2104	350	793	3246	2624	-734	5136
10	5133	849	1723	7705	9436	-2527	14614
11	-355	-43	-41	-439	-205	431	-212
12	3126	717	3272	7115	3398	-2427	8087
13	1525	397	1935	3857	1332	-1258	3931
14	-4503	-367	-1646	-6515	-2099	1403	-7211
15	598	66	1478	2143	365	-223	2285
16	-2997	-777	-9481	-13254	-14119	15673	-11701
17	138	112	915	1166	-2515	3409	2060
18	2799	724	6456	9979	3477	-3795	9660
19	-924	-48	-232	-1204	-817	668	-1353
20	13	7	122	141	184	-229	96
21	5481	1323	-238	6566	2693	-562	8697
22	-123	-185	-3673	-3980	-224	426	-3778
23	74	-2	55	127	138	-33	232
24	3262	668	2805	6735	3093	-2981	6847
25	1590	238	728	2555	1524	-787	3292
26	3088	462	1382	4931	1575	-343	6163
27	1282	107	423	1813	478	-329	1962
28	0	0	0	0	0	0	0
29	2708	392	2141	5242	3136	-2784	5594
30	742	27	110	879	-198	-43	638
Σ	18229	5002	10417	33648	6868	9002	49518

aThe names of the industries are presented in the appendix.

Table 5 shows how much the output of the various industries changes owing to changes in the input-output coefficients. Here, positive figures indicate increases and negative figures decreases, except in the case of imports, where the former indicate decreases and the latter increases.

The input-output coefficients related to the demand for forest industry products had increased. The total effect on output was FIM 21889 million. The input-output coefficients related to the demand for metal and engineering products had decreased. The total effect on output was FIM -1334 million. The decrease was particularly notable in the case of the basic metal industries (16).

When the effects outlined above are combined, the following equations are obtained: In 1980 the output of the forest industries was composed of the effects in question as follows: 133891 = 87496 + 55032 - 30528 + 21889. The corresponding composition for the engineering and metal manufacturing industries was 174883 = 88513 + 20353 + 67351 - 1334.

The results indicate how much the output of the various industries changed, in millions of Finnish marks at 1970 prices between 1970 and 1980 owing to the following effects:
1. the growth effect of final demand categories, Table 3,
2. changes in the structure of final demand categories, Table 4,
3. changes in the input-output coefficients between 1970 and 1980, Table 5.
The following Table 6 gives the figures for selected industries.

TABLE 6   Effects of growth, structural change and technological
change[a] in selected industries, millions of FIM at
1970 prices

	Food man-ufac-turing	Pulp mills	Basic metal in-dustries	Trans-port
1. Growth effect	23418	17394	4144	17948
domestic demand	20103	1357	13602	8057
exports	8352	17296	18374	13713
imports	-5036	-1259	-27832	-3822
2. Structural change	-5912	-16491	42683	-1345
domestic demand	828	1055	4653	5549
exports	-10288	-16921	26930	-5998
imports	3548	-625	11100	-895
3. Technological change	13018	5136	-11701	6163
domestic demand	13224	3246	-13254	4931
exports	2644	2624	-14119	1575
imports	-2849	-734	15673	-343
Total increase be-tween 1970 and 1980	30524	6039	35126	22566

[a]The figures do not include the effects of imputed bank services, increases in stocks and statistical discrepancy.

Pulp mills would have increased their output considerably if no structural changes had taken place in the final demand categories. Structural changes played a remarkable role in decreasing the output of pulp mills. Changes in the input-output coefficients had positive effects on the output of pulp mills. Output in the basic metal industries increased mainly because of structural changes, but decreases in the input-output coefficients had negative effects on the output of this industry.

Technological change was finally examined more thoroughly. First the most sensitive coefficients for changes were found out. The following measure was then applied.

$$d_{rs} = 1/a_{rs}(max_i(b_{ir}/x_i)x_s + 0,01b_{sr}) \tag{1}$$

The measure d_{rs} indicates by how many percent an input coefficient a_{rs} may change so that the output of any industry does not change by more than one percent. Final demand is supposed to be constant. The smaller the value of d_{rs} is, the more sensitive the coefficient a_{rs} (b_{ir} and b_{sr} are coefficients of Leontief's inverse matrix $B = (I - A)^{-1}$

The number of coefficients having a d-measure less than 10 was 62. The changes in these coefficients between 1970 and 1980 were determined using the measure:

$$ln(a_{ij}(80 / a_{ij}(70)) = e \tag{2}$$

The distribution of the changes in the coefficients was as follows:

	e >	0.60	4
0.60 >	e >	0.40	7
0.40 >	e >	0.20	8
0.20 >	e >	0.10	8
0.10 >	e >	0.00	7
-0.10 <	e <	0.00	8
-0.20 <	e <	-0.10	9
-0.40 <	e <	-0.20	3
-0.60 <	e <	-0.40	5
	e <	- .60	3
Total			62

We may conclude that the number of very sensitive coefficients was rather small, but the changes in the coefficients were notable. Some of the changes in these coefficients were so great that various classification rules must have been applied to these cases between 1970 and 1980.

From this preliminary study of changes in the industrial structure of the Finnish economy, the following conclusions can be drawn.

1. A simple input-output model is a useful framework for decomposing the different factors conducive to structural changes in an economy.
2. The driving forces behind structural changes in the various final demand categories should be further examined.
3. The input-output coefficients are the links which transmit changes between the industries. The links themselves are related to technological changes and are, thus, an important central area for dynamic analysis of structural changes.

REFERENCES

Central Statistical Office of Finland, National Accounts, Time series for
    1960-1981, Statistical Surveys Nro 75, Helsinki 1984.
van Duijn, J.J. Macro-economic Measures to Implement Structural Change,
    Discussion paper prepared for the IIASA Task Force Meeting on
    Restructuring Interdependent Economies, Albena, Bulgaria, May 8-10, 1984.

Forssell, O. Experiences of Studying Changes in Input-Output Coefficients
    in Finland, in a book Proceedings of the Fourth II ASA Modeling
    edited by A. Smyshlyaev, IIASA Collaborative Proceedings Series
The Research Institute of the Finnish Economy, Economic Prospects,
    spring 1984. CP-83-S5, 1983.

Schumpeter, J.A. Business Cycles Vols. I and II, MacGraw Hill, New York, 1939.

Appendix 1.

The breakdown of the production sectors, by the kind of economic
activity, is as follows (for the codes in brackets, see: Central
Statistical Office, handbooks n:o 4, Standard Industrial Classification
(SIC), Helsinki 1972):

01 Agriculture, hunting and fishing (11,13)
02 Forestry and logging (12)
03 Mining and quarrying (2)
04 Food manufacturing (311,312)
05 Beverage and tobacco industries (313,314)
06 Textile, wearing apparels and leather industries (32)
07 Sawing, planing and preserving (33111)
08 Other manufacture of wood (33113,33119,3312,3319,332)
09 Pulp mills (34111)
10 Manufacture of paper and paperboard and of pulp, paper and
   paperboard articles (34112,34113,3412,3419)
11 Printing and publishing (342)
12 Manufacture of chemicals (351)
13 Manufacture of chemical, rubber and plastic products (352,355,356)
14 Petroleum refineries and miscellaneous products of petroleum and
   coal (353,354)
15 Pottery,glass and earthenware products (36)
16 Basic metal industries (37)
17 Manufacture of metal products and machinery (381,382)
18 Manufacture of electrical machinery and related
   products (383,385)
19 Manufacture of transport equipment (384)
20 Other manufacturing industries (39)
21 Electricity, gas and water (4)
22 Building (51)
23 Other construction (52)
24 Trade (61,62)
25 Restaurants and hotels (63)
26 Transport (71)
27 Communication (72)
28 Letting and operating of dwellings and use of owner-occupied
   dwellings (8311)
29 Other real estate, financing, insurance and business
   services (8312,8313,832,833)
30 Private social and personal services (92,93,94,95)

PATTERNS OF INDUSTRIAL CHANGE IN THE FEDERAL REPUBLIC OF GERMANY. PART I: FLOWS OF MANUFACTURING OUTPUT AND ENERGY INPUT

Claire P. Doblin

International Institute for Applied Systems Analysis,
Laxenburg, Austria

1. GROWTH OF CAPITAL STOCK, OUTPUT, AND ENERGY INPUT IN THE MANUFACTURING SECTOR AS A WHOLE

During the period of economic prosperity ushered in by the reconstruction and development of the FRG following World War II, the value of manufacturing capital stock, measured in constant 1970 prices, expanded at an average annual rate of 7.8% in the 1950s (which was perhaps not a normal period) and 6.9% in the 1960s. The growth of total manufacturing output was unusually high during the 1950s (with an average annual rate of 10.3%) and continued at a somewhat reduced, but still high level during the 1960s (5.5% per annum) (see Table 1). The prime movers behind this development were the expansion of infrastructure and the growth of the chemical, automobile, and electric and electronic equipment industries. The electric equipment industry is traditionally heavily dependent on innovation, and the application of new technologies; much the same applies to a number of chemical goods, such as synthetic fibers, drugs, and pharmaceuticals.

In the 1970s, manufacturing capital stock grew at an average annual rate of no more than 3.3%, while the growth rate for total manufacturing dwindled to an annual average of only 1.8%; this was followed by cutbacks and stagnation of output through 1983, with some recovery expected in 1984. Figure 1 shows the growth of capital stock, output, and final energy demand for the manufacturing sector since 1950, expressed as indexes based on 1970 = 100. The slow growth of capital stock is also reflected in the general slowdown in annual investment and gross fixed capital formation (GFCF) in the manufacturing and other sectors of the economy. It stands to reason that these developments in investment are closely related to the growth of those basic industries, e.g. iron and steel, or stone, clay, and sand (including cement), that are both capital and energy intensive. Consequently, the slowdown in investment in the FRG has largely affected the growth of energy-intensive industries and hence the total demand for final energy by the manufacturing sector. One strong reason for the drying-up of investment in the late 1960s and early 1970s was that by that time the country's need for infrastructure expansion had become saturated. A stage was reached when major construction projects designed to extend networks of communications and transportation (such as roads, bridges, tunnels, underground railways, etc.) largely gave way to maintenance and repair work. The close links between the rise and fall of public sector investment in construction and the energy demand of the manufacturing sector can be seen from Figure 2.

The slowdown in investment imposed an additional constraint on the growth of basic producer and investment goods, e.g. iron and steel and other primary metals (excluding aluminum), stone, sand, and clay (including cement), and also the construction of certain nonelectrical machinery. For a number of reasons, such as the transition to more lightweight materials, these energy-intensive industries had already embarked on a long-term, relative decline. The growth of these industries in

---

*An extended version of this paper is available as Working Paper WP-84-73, IIASA, Laxenburg, Austria.

Table 1. Summary economic indicators of growth in the FRG, 1950—83.

Year	Total economy: gross fixed capital formation		Manufacturing sector		
	Total	Public sector construction	Capital stock	Output (value added)	Final energy input (quantity)
1. Index Numbers 1970 = 100					
1950	24.0	.	24.0	21.9	40.5
1951	25.3	.	25.5	26.4	47.2
1952	27.5	.	27.1	28.3	51.3
1953	32.1	.	28.9	30.5	50.2
1954	36.2	.	30.9	34.9	54.3
1955	43.7	.	33.6	40.8	61.3
1956	47.5	.	36.9	44.2	65.0
1957	47.5	.	40.2	46.1	65.3
1958	49.4	.	43.4	47.5	63.6
1959	55.3	.	46.9	51.6	65.5
1960	64.2	45.7	51.1	58.6	73.5
1961	68.6	50.6	56.0	62.3	74.3
1962	71.4	58.6	61.1	64.7	75.2
1963	72.3	67.6	65.9	66.9	76.7
1964	80.4	82.9	70.5	73.0	82.4
1965	84.3	83.3	75.5	77.4	84.6
1966	85.3	84.2	80.6	78.2	82.1
1967	79.4	76.8	85.2	76.1	81.9
1968	82.3	82.1	89.2	83.3	88.8
1969	91.0	89.0	93.9	94.2	95.5
1970	100.0	100.0	100.0	100.0	100.0
1971	106.2	99.0	106.4	101.6	97.4
1972	108.9	96.0	112.2	105.4	98.8
1973	108.6	94.0	117.2	112.5	104.4
1974	98.2	100.0	121.6	108.0	105.4
1975	93.4	98.0	125.2	102.8	92.7
1976	97.7	95.0	128.2	109.4	98.0
1977	101.5	91.0	130.3	111.8	97.4
1978	106.4	94.0	132.6	113.1	97.9
1979	114.1	98.0	134.9	118.8	100.4
1980	117.8	99.2	137.7	119.0	97.6
1981	112.9	90.6	.	116.4	91.9
1982	107.2	82.5	.	112.9	83.9
1983	110.3	75.9	.	113.5	85.0
2. Absolute values at 1970 prices (10^9 DM)					10^6 TCE
1980	202.7	28.7	575.7	370.1	99.7
1981	194.2	26.2	.	362.7^E	94.1
1982	184.4	23.8	.	351.6^E	85.8
1983	189.7	21.9	.	353.0^E	86.9^{PE}
3. Average annual growth rates (%)					
1950—1960	10.3		7.85	10.54	6.1
1960—1970	4.5	8.145	6.94	5.49	3.12
1970—1980	1.65	−0.08	3.25	1.755	−0.064
1980—1983	−2.169	−8.54	.	−1.565	−4.503

E = estimate; PE = preliminary estimate.

Sources and Notes:
Total Gross Fixed Capital Formation (GFCF) (Anlageinvestitionen) for the economy as a whole includes equipment and construction, by private sector and government.
Data for GFCF total and public sector construction 1960 to 1981 are compiled from *Statistisches Bunesamt. Volkswirtschaftliche Gesamtrechnungen 1960—1981, op. cit.* pp. 57 and 59.
Data for 1981 to 1983 were communicated orally by the *Statistisches Bundesamt,* 12 July 1984 (Data converted from 1976 to 1970 prices).
Data for 1950 to 1960 were compiled from C. Doblin. Capital Formation, Capital Stock and Capital Output Ratios 1950—1975. IIASA Research Memorandum RM-78-70; December 1978.

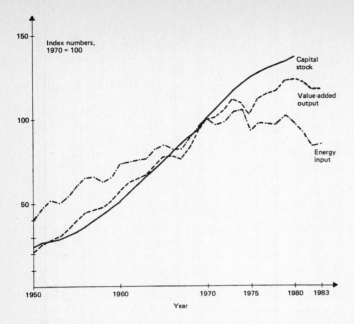

Figure 1. Total manufacturing in the FRG. The growth of capital stock, output, and final energy input since 1950. Index numbers, 1970 = 100.

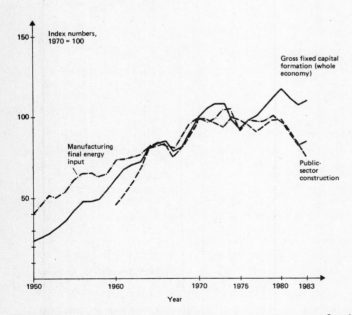

Figure 2. The growth of the whole economy's gross fixed capital formation, total and public-sector construction, and the manufacturing sector's demand for final energy input in the FRG since 1950.

absolute terms was soon eclipsed by the expansion of industries less demanding in energy and yielding a higher proportion of value added. This trend was already apparent in the structural changes of industry after 1950, and became especially marked from the 1960s onward. In the 1970s and early 1980s, the slower than average growth of the basic producer- and investment-goods industries turned into no growth and the outputs of some of the industries (e.g. steel and basic chemicals) that are most energy intensive, actually fell in terms of absolute physical quantities.

The analysis of the structural changes of manufacturing in the FRG shows that there has been a long-term trend for the energy input per unit of output of the manufacturing sector as a whole to decrease. Progressive improvements in energy productivity, during periods of generally decreasing energy prices, were mainly due to two factors. Machinery and equipment embodying better technologies and with higher efficiency of fuel utilization routinely came on stream through either the normal replacement of retired equipment or the expansion of production facilities. During the recession years of the 1970s and early 1980s, overall energy productivity was further enhanced by disinvestment, or the shutdown of older equipment that was less efficient in fuel utilization. Throughout the entire period studied, starting with the 1950s, the efficiency of fuel utilization was progressively improved by interfuel substitution, the displacement of coal by oil and natural gas, and the increasing use of electricity.

The confluence in the late 1960s and early 1970s of the three trends described above, namely the slowdown of infrastructure investment, the continued displacement of basic, energy-intensive industries, and the long-term trend toward energy saving in manufacturing, explains in large measure the widening of the gap between energy input and manufacturing output in the FRG (see also Figure 1). Thus, the recessions brought on by the oil price shocks of the 1970s seem merely to have accelerated, rather than caused, the process known as the "breaking of the energy coefficient" (i.e. the observation that total primary energy demand and GDP no longer follow the same growth rates, as they did over a long period from the end of World War II until the first oil price shock of 1973).

2. MAJOR TRENDS WITHIN THE MANUFACTURING SECTOR

The analysis concentrated on the patterns of structural change within the manufacturing sector of the FRG since the 1950s. For this purpose, the sector was disaggregated into 20 groups that roughly correspond to the groupings at the 2-digit level of the US Standard Industrial Classification (SIC). In order to broaden the analysis, we supplemented the 20 groups with 60 indexes of gross and net production and with data on physical quantities for selected industries.

The index of production for the manufacturing sector as a whole indicates what may be considered as national average growth. Deviations from this average indicate whether an industry is fast growing or slow growing. The differences in growth behavior are also reflected in the structure of the percentage shares of the various industries in total manufacturing over a period of time. Depending on whether their percentage shares in total manufacturing have been consistently rising or falling since 1950 or only since the 1970s, the industries were grouped into three categories: slow-growth industries, fast-growth industries, and former fast-growth industries.

The slow-growth category, which also includes the no-growth industries, saw its share in total manufacturing output decrease from 43% in 1950 and 35% in 1960 to 29% in 1980. The most prominent "losers" were the iron and steel industry, foundries and castings, other primary metals (except aluminum), and constructional steel. To some extent, the relative decrease in the share of these industries was due to the displacement of heavier materials by those of lighter weight. In the case of steel, for example, this meant the use of more concrete in highway bridges, more plastic in cars, and less steel in the manufacture of refrigerators, washing machines, and beer and other cans.

Major users of steel and other heavy metals such as nonelectrical machinery and construction have themselves become slow-growth industries, while some steel-using activities have ceased to grow at all, such as shipbuilding, or gone out of style, as for instance railroads.

One very strong reason for the decline of the primary metals (except aluminum) as well as the stone, sand, and clay group (including cement) was that the demand for investment goods became depressed as the requirements for infrastructure building receded. This was true not only for the FRG, but for other industrialized countries, such as the United States, as well.

Besides the investment-goods industries mentioned above, there were other relative losers as the structure of industry in the FRG changed, for a variety of reasons. These included the lumber and sawmill industry (including pulp and raw paper), some of whose products may have been displaced by imports, the textiles industry, whose secular decline has long been a feature of other developed economies, and the food industry (including beverages and tobacco). The growth of food production usually lags behind growing prosperity, as it did in the FRG until the recession of the 1980s, when the sector regained some of its former relative importance. Finally, there are a number of miscellaneous consumer goods, excluding food, whose development was stunted to some extent by the inroads of foreign products into the domestic market (clothing, gloves, shoes) and/or the competition of foreign producers on the world market (optical and precision instruments, clocks and watches, toys, etc.).

The fast-growth industries increased their share in total output from 15.56% in 1950 to 31.84% in 1980. This group comprises the electric and electronic equipment industry; its share in the total *manufacturing* output of the FRG increased from 6.53 to 14.35% over the same period. For the energy requirements analysis, this industry had to be lumped together with optical and precision instruments; this combination is not very helpful because of the opposing growth trends of the two industries. Thus, electric and electronic equipment manufacture taken alone would have followed an even higher growth path. However, not all branches of the electric and electronic equipment industry experienced the same degree of growth. For instance, during the 1970s, the manufacture of cables and other infrastructural elements connected with electric equipment experienced relative and sometimes even absolute declines. This clearly indicates the connection that exists with the construction industries. A decline was also observed for certain household appliances, such as washing machines and refrigerators, whose markets had become almost saturated. But the regression of these industries was more than compensated by the spectacular expansion of the growth industries *par excellence* that embody the application of new technologies, such as the manufacture of computers and other electronic equipment.

The chemicals and allied industry increased its share in total manufacturing output from 6.68% in 1950 to 12.44% in 1980. The chemicals group includes a variety of industries, associated with three types of product: some of these are primary or basic materials such as inorganic and organic chemicals; others are intermediate products like fertilizers, dyestuffs, and synthetic fibers; and others again are final consumer goods such as pharmaceuticals, cosmetics, paints, etc. Each of these groups differs in its energy requirements and potential for value added, with energy demand decreasing and value added increasing as we move from basic materials to final consumer goods.

Based on the FRG's census-type periodical *The Survey of Employment, Turnover, and Energy Consumption*, it is estimated that 13.3% of the final energy demand of the entire manufacturing sector in 1980 was absorbed by basic and intermediate chemicals. Bearing in mind that the quantitative output of a significant group of basic chemicals, including synthetic ammonia, methanol, and phosphate fertilizers, had ceased to grow by the early 1970s and even decreased in the late 1970s and early 1980s, it is estimated that the slow and at times negative growth of the energy-intensive basic and intermediate chemicals industry as a whole played a major role in the "breaking of the energy coefficient."

The growth in the chemical industry's production of final consumer goods was echoed in the expansion of another fast-growth industry, namely the processing of plastic and synthetic goods, whose share in total manufacturing output increased from 0.22% in 1950 to 2.81% in 1980. This development was undoubtedly due to innovation. The same seems to have been true for the recent rapid growth of the fine ceramics group, which manufactures some of the components for the computer industry. Fine ceramics (which also includes glass production and processing) was a slow-growth industry in the earlier decades, when its share in total output fell from 2.31% in 1950 to 1.31% in 1970, but subsequently its share advanced to 2.29% by 1980.

In contrast to former slow-growth industries that later became fast-growth, there are a few former fast-growth industries that seemed to lose their momentum for expansion under the impact of the oil price explosions of the 1970s. These are mineral oil refining, rubber, and asbestos (including automobile tires), and possibly the vehicles industry (including automobiles). The combined share of these groups in total manufacturing output rose from 5.68% in 1950 to 13.62% in 1970; but by 1980 the share of these industries was no higher than 13.70%.

The first and second oil price explosions had some impact on the production of distillate fuel oil; 1980 output, after a few oscillations during the preceding decade, was only 8% above the 1970 figure. More direct and serious was the impact on residual fuels production; this fell continuously after 1974, so that by 1980 it was nearly 40% below the 1970 figure. More recent data are so far unavailable for distillate and residual fuels. In any case their development sharply contrasts with that of gasoline — where 1980 output was still 55% above the 1970 level, followed by a minor dip in 1981, recovery in 1982, and stagnation in 1983. At the same time, tire production for automobiles in 1980 was no higher than in 1970; it subsequently dropped to below the 1970 figure in 1983.

The impact of the oil price explosion on automobile production is not yet completely clear. In the 1950s and 1960s this industry expanded at about the same, high rate as total chemicals and the production of electric and electronic equipment. The latter industries continued on essentially the same growth path throughout the 1970s with only a minor disturbance in 1975 — thanks mostly to the growth of pharmaceuticals and other chemical consumer goods, and the revolution in the computer industry. However, automobile production grew only very little in the early 1970s, and in the recession years it fell to a level that was slightly below that of 1970. But since the slump of 1975 output has somewhat recovered. By 1983 the net production index (1970 = 100) for vehicles serving as investment goods had climbed to 136.9, while the gross production index (1970 = 100) for private-use vehicles stood at 121.5.

What is really in store for FRG automobile production — if the approaching saturation of the domestic market should happen to coincide with growing constraints on exports — only time will tell.

ON MODELING STRUCTURAL CHANGES IN SECTORAL WAGE DISTRIBUTION IN A MODERN INPUT—OUTPUT MODEL

Cristina Raffaelli

Faculty of Political Science, University of Florence, Florence, Italy

1. INTRODUCTION

In an Input-Output model used for forecasting structural changes, special attention must be paid to the time pattern of technical coefficients. Among them, labor inputs requirements deserve a specific analysis, being labor one of the primary inputs. Furthermore, on developing price-formation mechanism, the determination of the amount of labor per unit of output is at the basis of wage distribution among sectors together with the sectoral wage per unit of labor.

This paper deals with the analysis of wage equations of INTIMO (Interindustry Italian Model) within the analytical framework of the income side of an INFORUM-type model.

The wage equations consider the effect on wages per worker due to indexation and to the impact of changes in output (as cycle determinant) and in employment (as labor market determinant).

In Section 2 we present the time pattern of the ratio of sectoral wages over sectoral value added and the time pattern of the ratio of sectoral wages over sectoral costs of production. Section 3 deals with the anlytical forms of sectoral wage equations which have been adopted to make our estimates; also the results of the estimates are shown in Section 3.

(*) This research has been supported by a C.N.R. grant, contratto N. 83.02360.53.

TABLE 1 Rate of sectoral wage over sectoral value added

Sectors		1975	1979	1983
1	agriculture, for., fishery	0.26	0.29	0.32
2	coal	0.67	0.53	0.61
3	coke, petroleum, refining	0.22	0.16	0.14
4	electricity, gas, water	0.47	0.38	0.41
5*	nuclear fuels	0.00	0.00	0.00
6	ferrous, non ferrous ores	0.50	0.50	0.69
7	non metal min., min. prod.	0.48	0.46	0.47
8	chemical products	0.49	0.48	0.45
9	metal products	0.49	0.51	0.55
10	agric. & indus. machinery	0.47	0.48	0.53
11	office, precis., opt. instr.	0.51	0.47	0.40
12	electrical goods	0.54	0.54	0.55
13	motor vehicles	0.54	0.58	0.53
14	other transport equipment	0.59	0.60	0.49
15	foods	0.42	0.41	0.38
16	tobacco	1.01	0.94	2.17
17	textiles & clothing	0.53	0.48	0.51
18	leather & footwear	0.41	0.38	0.44
19	wood & furniture	0.42	0.38	0.40
20	paper & printing prod.	0.50	0.45	0.47
21	rubber & plastic prod.	0.49	0.52	0.52
22	other manufac. prod.	0.40	0.36	0.40
23	construction	0.43	0.44	0.41
24	recovery & repair serv.	0.37	0.43	0.47
25	trade	0.23	0.24	0.27
26	hotels & restaurants	0.26	0.31	0.30
27	inland transport	0.44	0.39	0.40
28	sea & air transport	0.53	0.38	0.35
29	transport services	0.34	0.31	0.30
30	communication	0.50	0.61	0.55
31	banking & insurance	0.34	0.35	0.33
32	other services	0.46	0.47	0.50
average		0.41	0.42	0.45

TABLE 2 Rate of sectoral wage over sectoral production costs

1975	1979	1983	Sectors
0.15	0.17	0.17	1
0.46	-0.33	-0.41	2
0.01	-0.03	-0.21	3
0.26	0.22	0.21	4
0.00	0.00	0.00	5*
0.14	0.16	0.12	6
0.24	0.21	0.21	7
0.16	0.13	0.07	8
0.21	0.19	0.22	9
0.20	0.18	0.22	10
0.27	0.19	0.12	11
0.26	0.22	0.22	12
0.19	0.22	0.18	13
0.26	0.23	0.20	14
0.14	0.16	0.16	15
0.89	0.81	1.96	16
0.22	0.20	0.21	17
0.17	0.20	0.22	18
0.19	0.17	0.17	19
0.20	0.16	0.13	20
0.20	0.18	0.16	21
0.17	0.15	0.20	22
0.25	0.25	0.25	23
0.20	0.20	0.24	24
0.16	0.17	0.19	25
0.13	0.15	0.18	26
0.27	0.26	0.28	27
0.21	0.17	0.16	28
0.23	0.22	0.20	29
0.38	0.45	0.41	30
0.05	0.04	0.04	31
0.36	0.38	0.41	32
0.22	0.21	0.23	average

*There are not any data for sector 5 because in Italy there is not internal production of nuclear fuels.

2. WAGES, VALUE ADDED AND PRODUCTION COSTS: TIME PATTERN OF THEIR RELATIONS.

A first outline of the time evolution of the weight of sectoral wages over sectoral value added and over sectoral costs of production, is presented in Table 1 and Table 2. The first table shows the ratio between the total amount of sectoral wages and the sectoral value added at factors cost; the second table shows the ratio between sectoral wages and the values of sectoral production. Thus, the coefficients which are shown in Table 2 can be utilized to study the changes of weight of wages in the production costs structure which occurred in the Italian economy from 1975 up to 1983.

Looking at the values shown in these two tables it can be noted that, generally, the changes in the ratio of wages over value added are more remarkable than the changes in the ratio of wages over the total cost of production (during the observed period, the average value of the first index has been increasing, while the average value of the second one has been almost constant).

This fact may lead to the conclusion that the largest part of the increases in total amount of wages is due to a redistribution of income rather than to general structural changes of the main items of the costs of production which carried out a larger utilization of the labor factor. More precisely we can argue that the cycle effect of the costs of production is mainly located in the "risultato lordo di gestione" which in the Italian statistics includes interests, replacements and profits. Now, assuming that interests behaves like the compensation of the other primary factor (labor), we think that profits and the "strategic" replacements pay the role of the buffer component of the revenue for unit of output.

In addition, we can observe that, in order to minimize the weight of labor cost over the total cost of production, firms succeeded in keeping it constant, by doing a production reorganization whose effect has essentially been a reduction of workers employed.

The tables we have just presented are useful to analyze the behavior of sectoral wages as a whole. But, in order to obtain information about the behavior of sectoral wages which could be utilized within the income side of a multisectoral model, it is necessary to make a more detailed analysis of the time pattern of sectoral wages with regard to the number of workers employed and to sectoral output.

3. THE SECTORAL WAGE EQUATIONS: ANALYTICAL FORMS AND RESULTS OF THE ESTIMATE.

According to the scheme which is used in the INFORUM-type models to define sectoral wages, in this work it was first of

all specified an aggregate equation describing the average wage
of industrial sectors (not including constructions) and then
some relative equations describing the behavior of sectoral
relative wages over time.

The use of relative equations, which describe the shifting
aside from the average of sectoral wages, can be justified in
many ways.

Using relative equations we can consider that the wage
bill of each sector depends on the wage bills of some leading
sectors. Actually, we can observe that the relative structure
of sectoral wages is determined by what we call an "imitative
process".

Another important reason advises the use of relative
equations: if we define an aggregate equation for the average
wage and some relative sectoral equations, it is possible to
separate the causes of secular increase in wages (which
influences the average wage) from the causes of specific
sectoral increase in wages. Otherwise, if we had only
sectoral equations, we had to be sure that the causes of the
general increase in wages would not change the relative
structure of sectoral wages (see Almon C., 1984).

We will first consider the aggregate equation.
Looking at the explanatory variables which are included in the
behavioral equations for wages, the level of prices can be
found both in macroeconomic and disaggregated models.

In fact, one can realistically assume that whenever prices
increase, wages will try to rise in order to preserve their
real value.

So we first specified a simple equation relating the level
of wages to the level of prices, to obtain a "row" estimate of
the influence of prices over the wage bill.

The data used are the sectoral time series (from 1970 up
to 1983 included) of gross wages and salaries (1), the ones of
the amount of workers employed, and the time series of private
consumption expenditure (current and constant prices).

The analytical form of the equation is:

$$\log WGG^t = a + b \log P^t \tag{1}$$

where, defining WG as the amount of wages for industry, and
E as the amount of employees of industry, we have

$$WGG^t = (WG^t/E^t) / (WG^{75}/E^{75}) \tag{2}$$

namely the index of wage per worker (time t), taking 1975 as
the base year.

The consumer price index at time t, P^t, was obtained
as the implicit deflator of private consumption expenditure,

----
(1) Making the sectoral time series, Italian Statistical
Office (ISTAT) does not distinguish wages from salaries. So
that one must bear in mind that, even if we will continue
speaking of "wages", our dependent variable is in fact "wages
and salaries".

```
           COEFFICIENT   T-STAT
CONST        0.003       0.183
P(T)         1.181      49.193
RBARSO       0.995       RHO        0.739    RSO       0.995   IW      0.522


   YEAR          PREDICTED     OBSERVED
                   ( + )         ( * )
    71           -0.624        -0.709      1
    72           -0.579        -0.605      2
    73           -0.413        -0.387      3
    74           -0.189        -0.188      4
    75            0.003         0.0        5
    76            0.199         0.211      6
    77            0.396         0.456      7
    78            0.539         0.598      8
    79            0.704         0.760      9
    80            0.922         0.943     10
    81            1.130         1.133     11
    82            1.316         1.276     12
    83            1.481         1.397     13
                                             -1.050   -0.700   -0.350   0.000   0.350   0.700   1.050   1.400   1.750
```

Fig. 1. Aggregate wage - eqn. (1).

```
           COEFFICIENT   T-STAT
CONST       -4.189      -1.621
PP(T)        1.054      11.932
PROD(T)      0.677       1.725
PROD(T-1)    0.225       0.513

RBARSO       0.995       RHO        0.743    RSO       0.996   DW      0.514


   YEAR          PREDICTED     OBSERVED
                   ( + )         ( * )
    71           -0.649        -0.709      1
    72           -0.569        -0.605      2
    73           -0.377        -0.387      3
    74           -0.161        -0.188      4
    75           -0.047         0.0        5
    76            0.179         0.211      6
    77            0.383         0.456      7
    78            0.539         0.598      8
    79            0.725         0.760      9
    80            0.948         0.943     10
    81            1.145         1.133     11
    82            1.311         1.276     12
    83            1.460         1.397     13
                                             -1.050   -0.700   -0.350   0.000   0.350   0.700   1.050   1.400   1.750
```

Fig. 2. Aggregate wage - eqn. (3).

```
           COEFFICIENT   T-STAT
CONST       -5.457      -5.558
P(T)         0.824      17.618
P SCALHO     0.184       7.355
PROD(T)      0.857       5.923
PROD(T-1)    0.323       2.017

RBARSO       0.999       RHO        0.153    RSO       1.000   DW      1.694


   YEAR          PREDICTED     OBSERVED
                   ( + )         ( * )
    71           -0.704        -0.709      1
    72           -0.619        -0.605      2
    73           -0.396        -0.387      3
    74           -0.170        -0.188      4
    75            0.009         0.0        5
    76            0.239         0.211      6
    77            0.437         0.456      7
    78            0.575         0.598      8
    79            0.748         0.760      9
    80            0.958         0.943     10
    81            1.136         1.133     11
    82            1.275         1.276     12
    83            1.397         1.397     13
                                             -1.050   -0.700   -0.350   0.000   0.350   0.700   1.050   1.400   1.750
```

Fig. 3. Aggregate wage - eqn. (7).

still 1975 remaining the base year.
    The results of the estimations of equation (1) are shown
in Table 3 and the graph is shown in Fig. 1.

TABLE 3 Results of the estimate of equation (1)

      Const.   Price coeff.

      0.003   1.181
     (0.016)   (0.024)

    As a first remark, we can see that the value of price
coefficient is significantly greater than one. This means that
in spite of the remarkable increase in the price level, wages
have not only preserved but increased their real value over the
last fourteen years. Furthermore, the value of the coefficient
shows that during the same period the income distribution has
changed in favour of wages (as we observed in the first part of
this work, looking at the evolution of the average rate
of total amount of wages over total value added).
    From an economic point of view however, these results are
not very satisfying - notwithstanding the high value obtained
for the R-square coefficient. In fact, they seem to show that
as the price level rises, the wage rate rises more than prices
themselves - as if it had an autonomous trend to grow up -
with no regard to any other economic factor.
    In other words it seems that, for istance, if the price
level rises with the productivity of labor being constant, the
wage rate will increase more than prices.
    But what is really important for us, is to know something
about the evolution of income distribution according to the
pattern of total production and labor productivity. That is
why we need to add some others explanatory variables in our
wage behavioral equation for taking account of labor
productivity.
    The new analytical form of the equation is:

$$\log WGG^t = a + b \log PP^t + c \log \pi^t + d \log \pi^{t-1} \qquad (3)$$

where π is indicative of labor productivity index (current and
lagged one period) defined as:

$$\pi^t = (X^t / E^t) \; / \; (X^{75} / E^{75}) \qquad (4)$$

$$\pi^{t-1} = (X^{t-1}/E^{t-1}) \; / \; (X^{75}/E^{75}) \qquad (5)$$

where X is total production (constant   prices) of industry.
This index of productivity is thus a per worker productivity
index in terms of total amount of real production.
    But another remark about the price index PP^t is needed.
A further step consists in trying to consider more exactly how
do prices influence the wage bill.

We have to remind that in Italy an institutional factor links the wage bill to the price level. The level of wages in fact, is automatically adjusted when the price level increases by means of a mechanism which is called "scala mobile".

The latest form of automatic indexation of wages was defined in 1974 (2) by means of an agreement between Trade Unions and Employers' Unions, and it began to work during 1975.

Every three months wages are automatically revised looking at the changes which, in the course of the same period, came about in a specifically constructed index of the consumer price level: a fixed amount of money has to be added to the previous wage level for each point of increase in the price index, which is put equal to 100 in the base-quarter.

The quarters utilized from this index to record the annual increase in prices, do not coincide with the standard ones; in fact a quarter overlapps the year because it includes November and December of the past year and January of the current year.

On relating wages with prices we must consider this peculiar way to construct the annual price index - due to the agreement on "scala mobile" - to make possible to compare the annual increase in wage level with the annual increase in price level; and, moreover, to consider that the wage increases take place at the end of each quarter, when the change in price index has already been recorded.

This is the reason why we decided to construct the consumer price index, PP^t, of equation (3) in this way:

$$PP^t = (.8\ P^t + .2\ P^{t-1})\tag{6}$$

where the weights approximate the effect of the overlapping quarter.

The estimate of the coefficients of equation (3) gave us the results which are shown in Table 4, while the graph can be seen in Fig.2.

TABLE 4   Results of the estimate of equation (3)

        Const.   Price.

        -4.189   1.054   0.677   0.225
        (2.584) (0.088) (0.392)   (0.438)

The price coefficient is smaller than the one which was

----
(2) In order to try to reduce the still high rate of inflation, at the beginning of 1984 this mechanism was partially revised by a government bill - Trade Unions did not at all agree among themselves.

obtained in the previous regression - even if it is still
greater than one - while the new two variables related to the
labor productivity seem to be rather important to determine the
dynamics of wages.

We preferred to keep separate the contribution of π^t from
the one of π^{t-1} - in spite of the risk of multicollinearity
between these two variables - to make clear both the direct
effect of an increase (decrease) in per worker productivity and
the one that the same increase (decrease) spreads over the
future. This form of equation provides a good fitting and, from
an economic point of view, it is more satisfactory than the
previous one; but by introducing some others alterations it
could be made even better.

We were not sure that the specification of equation (3)
was correct, because of the price coefficient P^t. The
idea was that it should have been better to disjoin the
contribution of prices to the dynamic of wages passing through
the "scala mobile", from the one which acts by means of other
factors, essentially through the bargaining. Our fears about
a specification error which might be committed in
formulating equation (3), was confirmed by a residual
analysis and by the level of the Durbin-Watson test. The
value was actually rather low: 0.51.

Talking about the effects on wages due to the "scala
mobile", it is important to point out that these effects have
not been constant over time.

To make clear this very important point we must stress
that the amount of money which has to be added to the previous
wage level for each point of increase in the price index is a
"fixed" amount. It is this fixed amount that defines the wage
which would have been - and it had been - totally protected
from inflation. Lower wages will have taken advantage of
extra increase, while higher wages will have turned to be
penalized in real terms.

Unfortunately, the wage distribution among workers was not
enough well known to guarantee a final balance between the
gifted and penalized equal to zero; we can only observe that
after the introduction of the "scala mobile", which works
using this "fixed point", inflation has been followed by a
remarkable increase in per worker wage.

This result may lead to the conclusion that, in the
given wage distribution, the standard wage totally protected
was rather higher than expected. Anyway, we cannot ignore that
besides the "scala mobile", individual and/or firm bargaining
took place; his effect, as the time went on, was a
progressive reduction of the level of wage totally protected.

Looking at the per cent increase in wage level which every
year can be ascribed to the "scala mobile" and at the increase
in consumer price level in the same year, it is possible to
define what we use to call the "degree of coverage" of
automatic wage indexation compared with the price inflation.
Because of the increase in the bargained wage, given a fixed
value of wage compensation for each point of inflation, this
"degree of coverage" has been falling down from 1975 up to
now; therefore this is the reason why we said before that the

effects of the "scala mobile" have not been constant over time. Thus, in the latest specification of the wage equation, there are two explanatory variables that take in account the effects of prices over the wage bill. The first one refers to the effect of the "scala mobile" and the second to the secular trend due to those effects which pass through the bargaining. The first one was constructed by multiplying the consumer price index P by the coefficient of the "degree of coverage" related to the same year t.

During these last years researchers did a lot of studies to determine the several values which the coefficient of the "degree of coverage" undertook as the years were setting by (see Dell'Aringa C., 1982; CER, 1984). Therefore doing our work, we did not carry out a new specific study to determine this coefficients but we decided to use the suggestions arising from the available works (3).

The analytical form of the equation which, for the moment, has given the best results is:

$$\log WGG^t = a + b \log P^t + c \log(SCALMO^t \times P^t) + d \log \pi^t + e \log \pi^{t-1} \quad (7)$$

where $SCALMO^t$ is the coefficient of the "degree of coverage" at time t.

The results of the estimation of equation (7) can be seen in Table 5 and the graph is shown in Fig. 3.

TABLE 5 Results of the estimate of equation (7)

Const.	Price	Scalmo-price	π^t	π^{t-1}
-5.457	0.824	0.184	0.857	0.323
(0.982)	(0.047)	(0.025)	(0.145)	(0.160)

Making a residual analysis, it seems that the misspecification error, which was found out in the previous equation, had been removed from equation (7). The level of the Durbin-Watson test is greater than the one obtained for the previous equation - now its value is equal to 1.69 - giving value to our belief. Looking at the graphs shown in Fig. 2 and Fig. 3 it can be seen that

----

(3) In his work Dell'Aringa states that the coefficient of the "degree of coverage" has essentially been less than one from 1970 up to 1975 (during these years another kind of "scala mobile" was working); in 1975, and for a couple of years later, it has been equal to one (or near to) and then it began to fall down to about 0.5 in 1982-83. To define our coefficients of the the "degree of coverage" we chose a trend like the one which was suggested by Dell'Aringa.

equation (3) tends to over-estimate the wage level during the last years of the observed period, while equation (7) fits well in those years too; this can be considered as a very useful property whenever one likes to use this wage equation in a simulation exercise with prediction purposes.

Another remark can be done about the values of the coefficients of the two price variables. Prices seem to spread the most part of their effects over the wage level through the non-automatic channel.

Labor productivity - both current and lagged - becomes more important; the most part of an increase in labor productivity seems to be converted into an increase in wage level in the course of the same year.

Finally, if we do accept the basic hypoteses which are required to make the Student test, rather high values will be obtained.

Examining the sectoral wage equations, it may be useful to remind that they are relative equations. So, the dependent variable has been constructed as the rate between the per worker sectoral wage index, W_i (time t), and the per worker industrial wage index, WGG (time t), where the base year is 1975 for both of them. The first two explanatory variables are sectoral specific and refer to the sectoral employment pattern, E_i, and to the evolution of the sectoral total production, X_i; the third explanatory variable is a time trend.

We tried out several analytical forms to describe the dynamics of sectoral wages; at last, we decided for two kinds of equations, each of them have been chosen for those sectors in which they showed the best results.

Thus, the sectoral wage equations are:

$$(W_i^t/WGG^t) = \alpha + \beta [(E_i^t - E_i^{t-1})/E_i^{t-1}] + \gamma [(X_i^t - X_i^{t-1})/X_i^{t-1}] + \lambda t$$
$$(i = 1,2,\ldots,36) \tag{8}$$

$$(W_i^t/WGG^t) = \alpha + \beta [(E_i^t/E_i^{75})/(E^t/E^{75})] + \gamma [(X_i^t/X_i^{75})/(X^t/X^{75})] + \lambda t$$
$$(i = 1,2,\ldots,36) \tag{9}$$

where t is the time trend, WGG is defined by (2) and, denoting WG_i as the amount of sectoral wages, W_i^t is defined as

$$W_i^t = (WG_i^t/E_i^t) / (WG_i^{75}/E_i^{75}) \qquad (i = 1,2,\ldots,36) \tag{10}$$

The data which have been used to make the estimations of the sectoral wage equations are the same time series (from 1970 up to 1983 included) used to estimate the aggregate wage equation.

Concerning this subject, it is worth while pointing out that the available sectoral time series for the wage levels (all of them provided by ISTAT) have a different classification for the branches of services with respect to the ones of IO table. Thus, it is necessary to reorganize the data in order to match the 36 sectoral wage data with the 45 sectoral total production data. The 36th branch of sectoral wage data refers to those services supplied by the Public Administration and others private sectors; so we ascribed to

TABLE 6   Results of the estimate of sectoral wage equations.

	SECTORS	CONST.	EMP.	X-SECT.	TREND	TYPE N.
1	AGRICULTURE, FOR., FISHERY	1.29371 (0.6512)	-1.00684 (0.2304)	0.15843 (0.1570)	0.00736 (0.0063)	2
2	COAL	2.80066 (0.3173)	-0.21980 (0.1380)	-0.05821 (0.0162)	-0.02009 (0.0031)	2
3	COKE	0.77376 (0.8254)	0.03359 (0.3570)	0.38517 (0.3043)	-0.00250 (0.0069)	2
4	PETROLEUM, GAS, REFINING	1.34575 (0.4401)	-0.55881 (1.0491)	-0.15326 (0.2097)	-0.00582 (0.0056)	1
5	ELECTRICITY, GAS, WATER	3.68359 (0.3516)	1.24094 (1.0268)	-1.46320 (0.6246)	-0.03298 (0.0129)	2
7*	FERROUS, NON FERROUS ORES	1.81680 (0.1779)	-0.49106 (0.2325)	0.20245 (0.1929)	-0.00715 (0.0027)	2
8	NON METAL MIN., MIN. PROD.	1.19823 (0.9960)	-1.01231 (0.5921)	0.1690 (0.3381)	0.00835 (0.0032)	2
9	CHEMICAL PRODUCTS	1.02445 (0.4046)	0.31136 (0.1842)	0.33421 (0.2815)	-0.00936 (0.0065)	2
10	METAL PRODUCTS	1.55797 (0.7804)	-1.29565 (0.7167)	0.25600 (0.1842)	0.00672 (0.0052)	2
11	AGRIC. & INDST. MACHINERY	1.48154 (0.2386)	-1.65098 (0.6809)	0.25466 (0.1494)	0.01217 (0.0058)	2
12	OFFICE, PRECIS., OPT. INSTR.	-0.52748 (0.4714)	0.43919 (0.3220)	-0.06006 (0.0426)	0.01510 (0.0042)	2
13	ELECTRICAL GOODS	1.39381 (0.1330)	-0.35962 (0.1036)	0.22559 (0.1172)	-0.0331 (0.0013)	2
14	MOTOR VEHICLES	2.28772 (0.3553)	0.03070 (0.1064)	0.43276 (0.1827)	-0.02309 (0.0023)	2
15	OTHER TRANSPORT EQUIPMENT	1.81925 (0.2465)	-0.22159 (0.2653)	0.13541 (0.0567)	-0.00959 (0.0070)	2
16	MEAT	-0.69156 (0.3264)	0.71728 (0.4149)	0.59088 (0.3075)	0.00524 (0.0051)	2
17	MILK	0.00853 (0.4776)	0.01059 (0.7389)	0.18860 (0.2678)	0.00986 (0.0064)	2
18	OTHER FOODS	1.73707 (1.0886)	-2.50426 (1.1877)	0.66187 (0.7005)	0.01403 (0.0072)	2
19	NON ALCOHOL, ALCOH. BEVERAGES	0.82255 (0.5461)	-0.71100 (0.4496)	-0.11192 (0.1495)	0.01242 (0.0030)	2
20	TOBACCO	2.83206 (0.3770)	-0.67309 (0.2559)	0.01230 (0.3248)	-0.02437 (0.0049)	1
21	TEXTILES & CLOTHING	0.44998 (0.0749)	-0.00042 (0.3056)	0.04158 (0.0432)	0.00756 (0.0010)	1
22	LEATHER & FOOTWEAR	-1.50396 (0.3802)	0.27428 (0.2321)	0.24555 (0.1697)	0.02640 (0.0015)	1
23	WOOD & FURNITURE	0.20867 (0.3733)	0.04381 (0.3864)	0.18578 (0.1120)	0.00755 (0.0026)	1
24	PAPER & PRINTING PROD.	1.57637 (0.3059)	-0.01578 (0.3294)	0.21584 (0.0786)	-0.01044 (0.0010)	1
25	RUBBER & PLASTIC PROD.	0.43316 (0.2341)	1.05381 (0.3233)	0.13419 (0.0926)	0.00802 (0.0030)	1
26	OTHER MANUFACT. PROD.	0.90002 (0.1800)	-0.15307 (0.2795)	-0.09116 (0.0635)	0.00143 (0.0023)	1
27	CONSTRUCTION	0.81487 (0.2410)	-0.51702 (0.1610)	0.38187 (0.1591)	0.00429 (0.0026)	2
28	RECOVERY & REPAIR SERVICES	0.19044 (0.1951)	-0.30884 (0.0927)	0.26122 (0.2182)	0.01128 (0.0027)	2
29	TRADE	0.08133 (0.1996)	-0.34165 (0.1755)	0.61379 (0.2493)	0.00832 (0.0030)	2
30	HOTELS & RESTAURANTS	-0.86934 (0.2900)	0.01539 (0.2598)	0.30696 (0.2581)	0.02042 (0.0047)	2
31	INLAND TRASPORTS	2.12862 (0.4662)	-2.44775 (2.2623)	-1.07900 (0.7115)	-0.01350 (0.0057)	1
32	SEA & AIR TRANSPORTS	1.28513 (0.3257)	2.27572 (0.2542)	0.48984 (0.1983)	-0.04103 (0.0026)	2
33	TRANSPORT SERVICES	1.08627 (0.1446)	0.13708 (0.3013)	-0.59832 (0.2259)	-0.00146 (0.0018)	1
34	COMMUNICATION	1.94159 (0.5144)	2.18532 (1.0057)	1.11773 (0.7985)	-0.01365 (0.0064)	1
35	BANKING & INSURANCE	6.73634 (2.0054)	0.86219 (0.6850)	0.24254 (0.4364)	-0.09142 (0.0330)	2
36	OTHER SERVICES	7.31808 (1.3966)	4.00200 (0.9902)	-0.81241 (0.5588)	-0.12702 (0.0276)	2

*There are no data for sector 6 because there is no production of nuclear fuels in Italy.

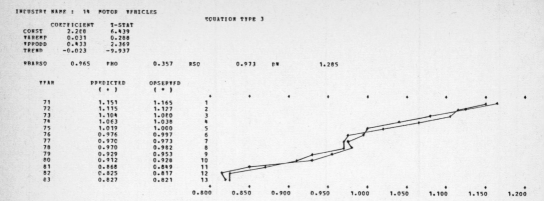

INDUSTRY NAME : 14 MOTOR VEHICLES

EQUATION TYPE 3

	COEFFICIENT	T-STAT
CONST	2.208	6.439
VAREMP	0.031	0.288
YPRODD	0.433	2.369
TREND	-0.023	-9.937

RBARSQ	0.965	RHO	0.357	RSQ	0.973	DW	1.285

YEAR	PREDICTED (+)	OBSERVED (*)	
71	1.151	1.165	1
72	1.115	1.127	2
73	1.104	1.080	3
74	1.063	1.038	4
75	1.019	1.000	5
76	0.976	0.997	6
77	0.970	0.973	7
78	0.970	0.982	8
79	0.929	0.953	9
80	0.912	0.928	10
81	0.868	0.849	11
82	0.825	0.817	12
83	0.827	0.821	13

Fig. 4a.   Sectoral wages - motor vehicles.

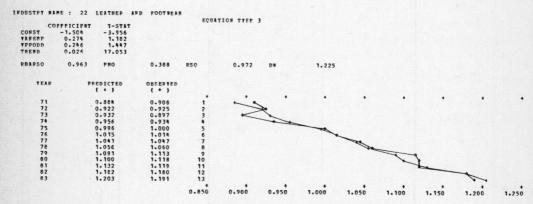

INDUSTRY NAME : 22 LEATHER AND FOOTWEAR

EQUATION TYPE 3

	COEFFICIENT	T-STAT
CONST	-1.504	-3.956
VAREMP	0.274	1.182
YPRODD	0.246	1.447
TREND	0.026	17.053

RBARSQ	0.963	RHO	0.388	RSQ	0.972	DW	1.225

YEAR	PREDICTED (+)	OBSERVED (*)	
71	0.884	0.908	1
72	0.922	0.925	2
73	0.932	0.897	3
74	0.956	0.934	4
75	0.996	1.000	5
76	1.015	1.014	6
77	1.041	1.047	7
78	1.056	1.060	8
79	1.091	1.113	9
80	1.100	1.118	10
81	1.132	1.119	11
82	1.182	1.180	12
83	1.203	1.191	13

Fig. 4b.   Sectoral wages - leather and footwear.

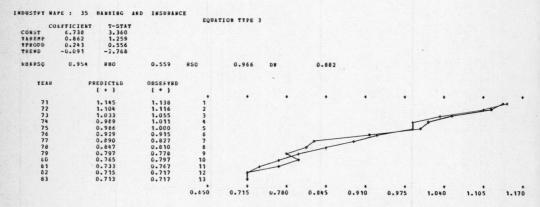

INDUSTRY NAME : 35 BANKING AND INSURANCE

EQUATION TYPE 3

	COEFFICIENT	T-STAT
CONST	6.738	3.360
VAREMP	0.862	1.259
YPRODD	0.243	0.556
TREND	-0.091	-2.768

RBARSQ	0.954	RHO	0.559	RSQ	0.966	DW	0.882

YEAR	PREDICTED (+)	OBSERVED (*)	
71	1.145	1.138	1
72	1.104	1.116	2
73	1.033	1.055	3
74	0.989	1.011	4
75	0.986	1.000	5
76	0.929	0.915	6
77	0.890	0.827	7
78	0.847	0.810	8
79	0.797	0.778	9
80	0.765	0.797	10
81	0.733	0.767	11
82	0.715	0.717	12
83	0.713	0.717	13

Fig. 4c.   Sectoral wages - banking and insurance.

this branch the total production coming from the 36th branch up to the 45th, the ones which, in IO classification, refer to Public Administration and other sectors which supply services.

Having a look at the explanatory variables included into the industrial wage equation and into the sectoral wage equations, it can be noted that, as previously stated, in the aggregate equation there are variables useful to determine only the pattern of wage dynamics as a whole; while in the sectoral equations the variables are related to the peculiar state of each branch as regards to the average, in order to explain the deviation of sectoral wage trend from the whole industry.

Concerning the expected signes of the coefficients, it is important to remind that our sectoral equations are "relative" equations, they show changes in relative sectoral wage structure and then the coefficients should take either the positive and the negative sign to guarantee that if some relative wages rise, some others will fall down (4).

In addition, the imitative mechanism which takes part in determining the sectoral wage level could breed different reactions to the same economic event from one to the other sector.

The results of the estimations are shown in Table 6 and some of the graphs are shown in Fig. 4.

The analytical form which has been chosen for each sector is denoted as "Type 1" or "Type 2" when, respectively, equation (8) or (9) has been adopted. As a first remark we can note that the coefficients have - as we expected they had - either positive and negative sign. Then relative sectoral wages react to changes in sectoral employment or sectoral total production in different ways (either for the intensity and for the direction).

In the case of the variables related to the sectoral employment trends, the number of positive signes is essentially equal to the one of negative signes (there are 19 negative signes); while the number of variables related to the sectoral production trends which have positive sign is rather higher than the ones having negative sign (there are 26 positive signes).

We would try to suggest a possible explanation for this last result; in other words, to expound why usually, as the sectoral production increases (decreases) the sectoral wage level tends to increase (decrease) too. It is reasonable to relate this result to what could be called the "power to pay" of a firm. In fact firms are surely more inclined to grant a wage increase in the course of a period of economic expansion than in a period of crisis.

Also the time trend coefficients have either positive or negative sign: the negative ones are 17. This result agrees with what we said before about the role played by the time trend to record the relative movements of sectoral wages.

The value of R-square coefficient is rather high in

----

(4) The sign of the time trend will give an important contribution to guarantee this balance.

various sectors: its value is between 0.80 and 0.99 in 20
sectors, and only in 9 sectors it is lower than 0.60. To
comment on the values of R-square, it must be reminded once
again that we are dealing with "relative" equations; this
means that our sectoral equations have to explain the
observed range of the value of relative wage index as regards
to the value which the relative wage index had in the base year
(1975). In those sectors where this value has been essentially
constant over time - showing that these sectors have been
keeping their "status" in the sectoral wage structure - the
behavioral equations have to explain a narrow range of the
dependent variable; this leads to the well known effects on the
R-square value.

Among the sectors where the R-square is rather low (lower
than 0.60) it is possible to find at least four of them where
the situation we have just described unfolds; these are the
sectors 10, 11, 26 and 33. On the contrary it can be
stressed that there are three sectors where, despite the
narrow range of the dependent variable, the R-square values
are rather satisfactory (included between 0.73 and 0.88);
these sectors are 13, 21, 28.

To have the total view of the relations between the range
of dependent variable and the R-square coefficient in each
sector, the required data have been transcribed in Table 7.

Some interesting remarks can be made looking at the
changes occurred in the wage structure in the course of the
observed period.

To make a very deep analysis of the pattern of each
sectoral wage and to find all the reasons (5) why the changes
in sectoral wage levels took place, a specific knowledge of
the economic situation of each sector would be necessary.
But it could be equally interesting, using the information
coming from the data, to point out some sectors whose wage
level changes into the wage structure have been very
remarkable; and, when it is possible to us, to suggest an
explanation for what happened.

Table 8 shows the sectors whose relative wage indices had
a considerable variation between the first and the last year
of the observed period.

In some of the sectors indicated in Table 8 (like in
sectors 1, 5, 14, 19, 20 and 22) the dependent variables
change according to a continuous increasing (or decreasing)
trend which can be found out since the beginning of the
observed period.

In the left over sectors indicated in Table 8 (and in some
others not belonging to the ones shown in Table 8) the changes
are not continuous but they started, or they became more
intense, since 1975. It is useful to remind that the agreement
on the "scala mobile" began to work in the course of 1975 too.
This "coincidence" leads us to suppose the agreement was one

----

(5) Beside those represented by the first two explanatory
variables which have been used; the remaining ones are
represented, but not explained, by the time trend.

of the causes - probably the most important one - of this sudden change in the wage structure.

TABLE 7 Range of observed dependent variable and R-square values

Sector	Min-observed	Max-observed	R-square
1	0.75	1.19	.98
2	0.88	1.06	.83
3	0.85	1.03	.48
4	0.81	1.00	.13
5	0.86	1.23	.87
7*	0.91	1.06	.94
8	0.91	1.06	.88
9	0.89	1.00	.74
10	1.00	1.08	.40
11	0.98	1.05	.80
13	0.99	1.06	.83
14	0.82	1.16	.97
15	0.98	1.10	.82
16	0.92	1.09	.89
17	0.82	1.02	.64
18	0.80	1.05	.83
19	0.84	1.01	.83
20	0.85	1.22	.88
21	0.99	1.07	.88
22	0.90	1.20	.97
23	0.97	1.09	.86
24	0.95	1.06	.93
25	1.00	1.12	.57
26	0.95	1.04	.41
27	0.95	1.00	.55
28	0.93	1.00	.73
29	0.90	1.00	.64
30	0.85	1.17	.92
31	0.94	1.15	.41
32	0.82	1.23	.98
33	0.91	1.00	.44
34	0.87	1.28	.71
35	0.72	1.14	.97
36	0.91	1.23	.78

* There are not any data for sector 6 because in Italy there is not internal production of nuclear fuels.

Many sectors could be taken as examples to show what we used to call the "wage flattening" which is, as we noted before, one of the direct effects of the agreement for the wage indexation. In fact they are exactly the lower (higher) wage levels which had the largest increases (decreases) with regard to the industrial wage level. That is the case, for example, of sector 17 or 18 whose relative wage index was equal to 0.84 in

1974 and to 1.00 in 1975, after which it went on increasing until 1982 when it reached its maximum value, equal to 1.05; we could point out also the sectors 32, 35 and 36 which had begun to fall down before 1975, but their fall became more intense since this year.

TABLE 8   Sectors with remarkable changes in the value of the dependent variable between the first and the last year of the observed period

Sectors	Value of dependent variable	
	1971	1983
1	0.75	1.19
5	1.20	0.87
14	1.16	0.82
17	0.87	1.01
18	0.80	1.04
19	0.84	1.00
20	1.17	0.86
22	0.91	1.19
30	0.85	1.17
32	1.23	0.82
34	1.28	0.97
35	1.14	0.72
36	1.23	1.02

To simplify the remarks about the results of our analysis we studied only the sectors where the behavior of relative wages was particularly revealing of the changes in the wage structure - which are, after all, structural changes in the production costs of each branch.

REFERENCES

Almon, C. (1984) The Conceptual and Accounting Basis of the Price-Income-National Accounts Part of INFORUM Related Models. Paper presented at The INFORUM-Type Model Users' Meeting. IIASA, Laxenburg, Austria, 22-24 May 1984.
CER (1984) Lo stretto sentiero della ripresa. Rapporto n.3. Centro Europa Ricerche, Rome.
Dell'Aringa, C. (1983) Prezzi e redditi. Frammenti di un modello econometrico disaggregato. Bologna, Il Mulino.

ON MODELING FOREIGN TRADE IN AN INPUT—OUTPUT MODEL OF AN OPEN ECONOMY

Marco Barnabani and Maurizio Grassini

Faculty of Political Science, University of Florence, Florence, Italy

1. INTRODUCTION

The new estimates of imports and exports equations for Italy have been done for providing the Interindustry Italian Model (INTIMO) of a suitable set of equations since the model has expanded including besides the original real side (Grassini,1982) the blocks of the price equation and the income side. An input—output model with real and price sides integrated requires in fact a careful definition of the prices influencing the final demand components of the real side in order to preserve the simultaneity among the variables determined inside its blocks; this implies a clear link between the producers' prices determined in the price side of the model and the prices considered as explanatory variables in the imports and exports equations.

Furthermore, after the end of the Bretton Woods agreements, the bilateral exchange rates have marked changes which have been emphasized by the oil crises which took place during the seventies. These changes have continuosly redefined the competitiveness of each country in the world market. Because of the differences in the market areas for imports and exports and for each traded commodity, the use of a unique effective exchange rate or even an effective exchange rate specific for imports and exports can introduce a bias on the estimation of price elasticities. If one can be content with an approximate estimate of exports and imports equations using global effective exchange rates, when the model is used for simulating the effect of a devaluation or a revaluation of a foreign currency, it is for sure that the forecasts will turn out to be unsatisfactory.

In this paper we present the procedure for computing sectoral effective exchange rates and present the results obtained in the italian model foreign sector by using them.

A brief presentation of the used data is done in section 2; in section 3 the analytical structure of the equations of the foreign sector of the model is reminded; the contruction of sectoral exchange rates is described in section 4 followed by some remarks on the estimation procedure in section 5; section 6 contains the presentation of and comments on the new

---

(*) This research has been supported by a C.N.R. grant, Contratto n. 83.02360.53. We thank INFORUM Project for having made available the necessary international trade data.

imports and exports equations.

2. THE DATA.

As it is known, IO table for Italy, as for all EEC countries, has sectors defined according to the NACE/CLIO classification; this European Comunity Standard code for building input-output tables makes the comparison among multisectoral models of EEC countries easier but the official statistics and sources related to such a classification are not self-sufficient for building up modern input-output models. In fact, besides the IO table only a few time series of variables linked or linkable with the input-output sectors are available. Then, some variables, such as imports and exports in the italian model, require a specific reconstruction of their time series.

The italian model foreign block uses informations coming from UN statistics on foreign trade (on commodities); these data follow the Standard International Trade Code, SITC, which identifies each commodity together with its destination (for exports) or origin (for imports), and its value and quantity traded. Unfortunatly, during the sample period (1963-1980), this code has been submitted to modifications which arises problems concerning the intertemporal homogeneity of the statistical informations available. These problems have been tackled with the construction of bridges connecting the elementary records at 4-digit detail (but for some records even the 5-th digit has been considered) for the different code structures introduced during the sample period. Furthermore, bridges between SITC and NACE/CLIO codes have been specifically designed. Some remarks on the time series on imports and exports obtained for the italian model have been already presented in Grassini (1983); theory, procedures and technical problems are described in Barnabani (1983).

3. THE MODEL

Although the standard analytical structure of the foreign trade equations of the INFORUM type models (and among them the italian one) is well known, we think that it deserves to be reminded for having a convenient notational reference in order to make clear the comment we are going to do in this piece of research on the italian foreign trade block.

The analytical structure of the imports and exports equations has the following form

$$y = (a + b*x)*p^n$$

a,b and n are parameters; y is alternatively the volume of imports of a given good or the volume of exports of a given good; x is a variable which represents the demand component; it is the domestic demand in the imports equations defined as total output plus imports (that is to say, the total sectoral resources) minus exports; it is the foreign demand (as index number) in the exports equations. While the domestic demand is country specific (it is determined by the national model builder using sectoral data on total production, imports and exports), the foreign demand comes from the INFORUM trade model which makes the link of the input-output type models possible (Nyhus, 1975).

p is a price term. It preserves homogeneity of degree zero on prices of the imports and exports equations; infact, only relative prices are considered. For imports (of each good) the relative price is given by the ratio of import price, pm, over the domestic price, pd; for exports the relative price is a ratio between the export price, pe, and the price in the world market, pw. The price term is analitycally defined giving the structural equations the characteristic of demand functions: demand for imports and demand for exports; an increase in the relative price (higher imports price with respect to domestic price and higher exports price with respect to world market price) would decrease imports and exports.

In the general equation, y,x and p have an index t denoting time. The demand component, x, influences the dependent variable at time t with no lag effect; the impact of the (relative) price on imports or exports is distributed over time. The price term is in fact put equal to

$$ p_t = \sum_l w_l (pm_{t-1}/pd_{t-1}) $$

for imports, with l=0,1,....L, and

$$ p_t = \sum_l w_l (pe_{t-1}/pw_{t-1}) $$

for exports.

The maximum lag considered, L, covers 6 years. Hence, it is assumed that modifications on imports and exports due to prices take a relative long time interval. The shape of the lag structure does not follow a smooth simple curve but is based upon the methodology proposed and applied by Nyhus (1975). These weights, are assumed, at first, as structural characteristic of every traded commodity and afterwards they are submitted to a check based on the goodness of fit with respect to weights coming from simpler and/or shorter distributed lag forms.

The relative price is determined by a ratio between a domestic price and a foreign price (pm for imports and pw for exports). The foreign prices are derived from the international trade model data set; there, the domestic prices index numbers available for many commodities for each country are aggregated in order to match the italian input-output sectors; this is done by means of a bridge code which connects the specific italian NACE/CLIO sectors with the given international model commodity classification. The foreign prices are now comparable with the domestic prices at sectoral level; using matrices MS and ES, which will be described in the next section, these foreign prices are then packed into the global indexes pm and pw.

The relative price, which now represents the "effective differential inflation index", is then multiplied by the exchange rate index to make the domestic price and the foreign price comparable. The exchange rate used - as a first approximation - is assumed to be equal to the effective exchange rate of the economy as a whole. In so far, we have used the effective exchange rate provided by the Bank of Italy following a procedure described in Ulizzi (1979).

4. THE EFFECTIVE AND REAL SECTORAL EXCHANGE RATE

Using the data bank on imports and exports of the italian model, imports and exports share matrices have been built. The elementary information available for each traded good records the partner country (destination of exports and origin of imports), the quantity, the value and the SITC code; for each year, the values are then arranged in arrays; such arrays display the values of the traded flows with respect to a set of countries or group of countries and to the input-output sectors producing tradable goods. These arrays of values are converted into market share matrices; the shares are obtained dividing the flow of a good going to or coming from a country by the total flow (respectively of exports or of imports) of the good; let us call these market share matrices MS and ES respectively for imports and exports. In general, we can assume that each matrix has elements w_{ij}, with j indicating the country and i indicating the good, with $\sum_{j} w_{ij} = 1$.

The country or group of countries considered are: Canada, United States, Japan, Belgium, France, FRG, The Netherlands, Great Britain, Rest of the World; the goods are classified according to the input-output sectors following the bridges between SITC codes and NACE/CLIO classification as described in Barnabani(1983).

Besides the time series on italian producers' prices (which is part of the italian model data set), time series on producers' prices from the above countries for goods matching the italian input-output sectors have been produced from the INFORUM data base.

Finally, the current bilateral exchange rates of Italy with the above countries complete the set of informations used. Let us call c_{jt} the exchange rate with country j at time t and c_{j0} the exchange rate at the base year; c_{jt}/c_{j0} will be the index used in order to mantain the price term in the structural equations as an index number.

The sectoral exchange rates are, then, defined as follows

$$sc_{it} = \prod_{j} (c_{jt}/c_{j0})^{w_{ij}}$$

They differ from the effective exchange rate for the whole economy because the averaging procedure adopted for it uses market shares determined on the total commodities flows to and from market areas (or countries). Sometimes, the market shares are modified according to the vehicle currency used in the transactions; this makes such an exchange rate interesting for evaluating the effects of sudden variations on bilateral exchange rates in the short run; for long run economic analyses such a mix between country market areas and vehicle currency areas is inadequate.

Once a sectoral effective exchange rate is determined , one can compute the sectoral relative price - a component of the price term in the structural equations - as follows (for imports)

$$pr_{it} = \prod_j (pm_{ijt}/pd_{it})^{w_{ij}}$$

where pm_{ijt} is the price index of good i in country j at time t, and pd is the domestic producers' price for good i at time t.

TABLE 1. The effective sectoral exchange rates (1970 = 100)

Sectors	EXPORTS		IMPORTS	
	1975	1980	1975	1980
1 Agriculture	131	199	116	159
2 Coal	108	147	118	171
3 Coke	110	149	131	193
4 Oil	116	165	109	147
5 Electricity,water,gas	108	147	122	178
6 Nuclear fuels	115	163	120	176
7 Ferrous/non ferrous ores	115	162	123	176
8 Nonmetal, mineral products	125	183	123	178
9 Chemical products	119	170	129	196
10 Metal products	119	169	130	197
11 Agric. & indust. machinery	115	160	128	195
12 Office,prec., optic. instr.	121	176	125	186
13 Electrical goods	122	177	129	196
14 Motor vehicles	119	169	140	213
15 Other transp. equipment	115	159	116	165
16 Meat	125	182	128	191
17 Milk and Dairy	117	161	141	224
18 Other foods	122	176	121	172
19 Nonalcoh. & alcoh. beverages	126	182	124	179
20 Tobacco	130	184	150	252
21 Textiles & clothing	132	203	119	168
22 Leather & shoes	127	190	114	158
23 Wood & fornitures	127	187	112	155
24 Paper & printing products	125	181	115	158
25 Rubber & plastic products	122	176	137	211
26 Other manufact. products	121	175	121	175
Total	121	174	120	173

Applying the sectoral exchange rate, sc_{it}, to the sectoral relative price, pr_{it}, we obtain the so called sectoral real exchange rate. We prefer to mantain the distinction between the relative price component (which is computed from the producers' prices recorded in each country) and the exchange rate (which is based upon nominal exchange rates) in order to distinguish competitiveness due to variations on production costs from the component due to variations on bilateral exchange rates.

5. SOME REMARKS ON THE ESTIMATION PROCEDURE

The nonlinear structure of the standard equation leads to an estimation procedure based upon the scanning of one parameter: the parameter n of the price term. It is assumed that the researcher is able to make a guess about the price elasticity of sectoral imports and exports demand. The scanning procedure proceeds as follows: given the guess on price elasticity, np (prior elasticity), the interval (-2np,0) is investigated by inspection for equally spaced steps. On carrying on the first estimate of imports and exports equations, the researcher must give a guess for every (prior) elasticity; when, as it is the present case, the estimation of the equations follows previous studies from which an estimate of price elesticities have been already obtained, these can conveniently represent the new guesses for initializing the estimation procedure.

Now, theoretical constraints imply only negative value of price elasticities; when under these theoretical constraints the price term does not give evidence of any explanatory power, the parameter n turns out to be equal to zero. Since the definition of the interval to be scanned, when the previous estimate of the price elasticity is equal to zero or is relatively low, the researcher must insist on guessing values higher than those coming from previous estimates.

Furthermore, the estimation procedure relies upon soft constraints (Almon,1983) which establish a trade off between the prior elasticity and the goodness of fit; the trade off is measured in term of how many points in goodness of fit we are ready to give up in order to move not too far from the guessed prior elasticity.

The weights of the lag structure have been submitted to a first check; simpler and shorter lag structures have not given better results except for textiles and clothing, leather and shoes and wood and furnitures. It seems that there is some evidence on a quicker response to price for the exports of these commodities. The results are not conclusive, but the destinations of such goods (final consumption) can give a rational to a shorter lag structure of their price term.

6. RESULTS AND COMMENTS

First of all, we give a brief picture of the differences between the

global effective exchange rate and the sectoral exchange rates specifically
constructed for the present research. The idea about the differences
implied by using the two kinds of exchange rates is given by comparing
their values recorded in the years 1975 and 1980 taking 1970 as the base
year. The global exchange rate has value 118 in 1975 and 173.3 in 1980; the
sectoral exchange rates for imports and exports - presented in Table 1 -
show a wide range around the mean value (which is not far from the global
exchange rate previously used). In 1980 we notice a minimum value for coal
and electricity of 147 and a maximun of 203 for textiles and clothing among
exports and a minimum of 147 for oil and a maximum of 252 for tobacco among
imports.

TABLE 2.   Imports equations

| Sectors | ELASTICITIES | | | |
| | PRICE | | DEMAND | |
	old	new	old	new
Agriculture	0.50	0.50	1.14	1.25
Coke (*)	1.10	2.20		
Oil	0.30	0.20	1.06	1.50
Ferrous/non ferrous ores	0.00	0.20	0.92	0.98
Nonmetal, mineral products	0.00	0.20	1.52	1.58
Chemical products	1.00	0.80	1.27	1.24
Metal products	0.00	0.00		
Agric. & indust. machinery	0.00	3.40	1.66	1.37
Office,prec., optic. instr.	0.20	0.40	1.11	1.13
Electrical goods	0.00	0.00	1.50	1.51
Motor vehicles	1.00	1.00	1.70	1.71
Other transp. equipment	0.00	2.00	0.99	1.17
Meat	0.35	0.50	1.29	1.38
Milk and Dairy	0.50	0.45	1.16	0.94
Other foods	0.55	0.45	1.34	1.37
Nonalcoh. & alcoh. beverages	0.90	0.50	1.00	1.86
Tobacco	0.00	0.00	4.05	3.81
Textiles & clothing	1.70	3.00	2.32	1.90
Leather & shoes	1.50	1.50	1.41	1.49
Wood & fornitures	0.10	1.00	0.97	1.09
Paper & printing products	0.00	1.00	1.15	1.24
Rubber & plastic products	1.00	1.00	1.57	1.58
Other manufact. products	0.00	0.00	0.95	0.97
Total	0.46	0.75	1.24	1.39

(*) When the demand elasticity is not recorded, a simpler
equation with trend and relative price has been adopted (see
Grassini,1983).

A closer look at the matrices MS and ES for year 1975 can give a hint to understand the different levels reached by the sectoral exchange rates, and then the importance of considering the market shares on simulating the effect of variations in one or more bilateral exchange rates. Matrices ES and MS are shown in the Appendix; the values in the tables give the percentage of the flows of a given good respectively going to or coming from the countries considered.

In Table 2 and Table 3 the values of price and demand elasticities obtained with the global effective exchange rate (old) and with sectoral exchage rates (new) are presented.Firts of all, we notice that three commodities - ferrous and non ferrous ores, non metal mineral products and agricultural and industrial machinery - have no longer price inelastic

TABLE 3. Exports equations

| Sectors | ELASTICITIES | | | |
| | PRICE | | DEMAND | |
	old	new	old	new
Agriculture	0.50	0.55	1.027	1.088
Coal		0.75		1.345
Coke	1.50	0.75	1.481	1.577
Oil	0.0	0.00	0.868	0.866
Ferrous/non ferrous ores	0.0	0.00	1.678	1.670
Nonmetal, mineral products	0.00	2.00	1.886	1.900
Chemical products	0.40	0.80	1.043	1.092
Metal products	2.00	2.60	1.037	1.278
Agric. & indust. machinery	2.00	0.00	1.503	1.388
Office,prec., optic. instr.	0.40	2.00	1.447	1.248
Electrical goods	0.80	1.00	1.496	1.472
Motor vehicles	2.00	2.00	1.141	1.424
Other transp. equipment	0.20	1.00	1.321	1.479
Meat	0.50	0.50	2.398	2.208
Other foods	0.65	0.75	1.551	1.510
Nonalcoh. & alcoh. beverages	1.00	1.00	1.907	1.954
Textiles & clothing	0.00	1.50	2.337	2.951
Leather & shoes (*)	2.42	1.11		
Wood & fornitures	0.00	1.00	1.840	1.859
Paper & printing products	1.00	1.00	1.830	1.704
Rubber & plastic products	1.00	1.00	1.280	1.298
Other manufact. products				
Total	0.96	1.04	1.390	1.492

(*) see footnote table 2

imports. The aggregate price elasticity for imports is remarkably higher than before moving from 0.46 to 0.75, and so the aggregate demand elasticity which records 1.39 with respect to the previous 1.24. On one side, these results contradict who understates the price effect on imports, on the other side the higher demand elasticity emphasizes the balance of payments constraint imposed by imports when a fast growth of domestic demand takes place.

Sectoral exchange rates in the exports equations give a higher value of the aggregate price elasticity which still remains lower the values usually obtained on estimating aggregate exports equation for macromodels. These new estimate give price elasticities not equal to zero for textiles and clothing and for wood and fornitures; a successful performance of these two sectors together with leather and shoes – which belong to the so called "fashion system" – is usually attributed to the importance of a Made in Italy label (namely, the design), assuming that what matters is mainly the demand. This assumption is confirmed by the high values of the demand elasticities, but even prices seem to play an important role for exports of goods belonging to the fashion system.

If the increase in the aggregate price elasicity is not very high, the aggregate demand elasicity, which goes from 1.38 to 1.49, confirms the high dependence of the italian economy from the dynamic of the world market.

REFERENCES

Almon, C. (1984) Building Models for Economic Forecasting. Text Material for Economics 402. University of Maryland, USA.
Barnabani, M. (1983) Un'analisi del commercio con l'estero italiano disaggregato per branca produttiva. Tesi di laurea. Facolta' di Economia e commercio. Universita' di Firenze, Italy.
Grassini, M. (1982) A National Scenario for a Regional Model. WP-82-131. IIASA, Laxenburg, Austria.
Grassini, M. (1983) Structural Changes in Italian Foreign Trade. In A. Smyshlyaev (Ed.),Proceedings of the Fourth IIASA Task Force Meeting on Input-ouput Modeling, CP-83-S5, IIASA, Laxenburg, Austria.
Nyhus, D.E. (1975) The Trade Model of a Dynamic World Input-output Forecasting System. INFORUN Research Report no. 14. Department of Economics, University of Maryland, College Park, Maryland.
UN (1975) Standard International Trade Classification. Revision 2. Statistical Papers, Series M N, 34/ Rev. 2. United Nations, New York.
Ulizzi, A. (1979) Metodologia di calcolo del tasso di cambio effettivo della lira e delle altre principali valute. Bollettino della Banca d'Italia, oct.-dic.(4).

APPENDIX

MATRIX ES

	CANADA	U.S.A.	JAPAN	BELGIUM	FRANCE	FRG	NEDERL.	U.K.	R.O.W.
1	0.17	2.04	0.57	3.30	17.29	39.52	2.99	3.78	30.34
2	0.0	0.0	0.0	0.0	0.65	0.65	0.0	0.11	98.59
3	0.0	4.37	0.0	0.0	6.13	1.44	0.0	0.01	88.05
4	0.00	7.49	0.39	1.29	5.20	6.92	13.21	6.35	59.14
5	0.0	0.0	0.0	0.0	1.41	0.01	0.0	0.0	98.58
6	0.19	2.04	0.00	1.36	3.66	14.14	1.72	3.48	73.21
7	0.47	4.50	0.02	1.47	9.07	11.94	1.64	3.34	67.54
8	1.60	6.65	0.74	4.01	19.81	25.63	2.37	2.92	36.27
9	0.64	5.02	1.19	4.95	11.83	13.44	5.06	4.43	53.45
10	1.08	4.69	0.28	3.56	14.93	13.89	3.01	2.14	56.41
11	1.19	4.51	0.57	2.13	11.32	8.41	1.90	3.96	66.02
12	1.33	9.26	2.72	3.01	15.04	20.01	3.81	6.30	38.52
13	0.78	2.28	0.42	3.84	13.22	18.55	7.10	6.50	47.31
14	1.14	14.04	0.29	3.64	12.93	15.49	3.52	5.15	43.80
15	1.01	6.97	0.18	2.07	11.76	8.15	2.09	3.46	64.31
16	0.70	0.96	0.11	6.96	25.64	20.99	1.49	3.84	39.31
17	11.70	18.71	0.20	4.77	16.58	11.08	1.51	5.05	30.39
18	0.85	3.92	0.22	3.61	16.23	21.06	3.31	9.72	40.88
19	2.43	12.17	0.16	2.77	33.57	23.57	1.45	7.49	16.38
20	0.0	0.51	3.38	5.07	55.91	4.39	10.81	0.0	19.93
21	1.13	4.56	3.13	4.59	15.55	38.94	5.49	4.00	22.61
22	2.12	17.54	1.53	5.37	11.26	32.58	4.77	5.01	19.82
23	0.63	4.55	0.55	4.93	20.86	25.27	5.33	3.25	34.64
24	0.36	2.56	0.43	3.88	24.41	21.76	3.32	6.60	36.66
25	0.97	6.34	0.21	4.61	15.34	17.90	5.64	3.97	44.82
26	2.30	11.52	2.48	3.28	11.58	20.63	3.89	4.52	39.79

MATRIX MS

	CANADA	U.S.A.	JAPAN	BELGIUM	FRANCE	FRG	NEDERL.	U.K.	R.O.W.
1	5.25	19.40	0.48	1.32	17.37	7.66	3.64	1.68	43.19
2	0.0	32.73	0.0	0.00	0.21	28.24	0.01	0.14	38.66
3	0.0	0.0	0.0	0.02	38.57	34.65	0.01	16.01	10.74
4	0.13	0.68	0.11	0.37	0.95	0.30	0.67	0.37	96.41
5	0.0	0.41	0.0	0.04	2.19	0.73	35.69	0.67	60.28
6	0.22	48.05	0.01	2.46	3.73	32.70	0.27	5.62	6.93
7	3.50	5.69	2.52	5.58	20.36	17.50	2.88	3.54	38.42
8	4.46	6.76	0.87	6.48	19.45	22.45	1.34	8.71	29.49
9	0.22	10.62	1.70	5.81	17.73	29.25	9.99	5.85	18.83
10	0.29	10.04	1.20	5.64	16.34	36.63	3.42	6.87	19.56
11	0.46	12.91	2.40	4.91	13.38	38.06	2.40	9.78	15.69
12	1.39	16.36	5.69	1.45	15.76	26.51	7.57	9.38	15.88
13	0.34	17.31	3.66	3.64	12.08	36.22	6.13	6.07	14.55
14	0.01	0.75	0.25	11.21	43.93	36.81	1.64	3.90	1.51
15	0.71	31.17	5.17	1.57	8.18	13.94	3.51	4.20	31.54
16	0.01	1.31	0.03	4.41	14.15	14.80	23.74	1.20	40.33
17	0.0	0.00	0.0	3.30	22.20	52.91	6.52	0.41	14.65
18	0.07	5.70	0.04	1.87	22.04	11.84	7.62	1.05	49.79
19	0.18	0.72	0.03	0.74	31.80	11.61	16.16	24.42	14.33
20	0.0	0.74	0.04	2.08	3.36	37.09	56.11	0.21	0.35
21	0.10	8.28	0.88	4.91	17.03	12.08	2.78	4.22	49.72
22	0.04	1.82	2.68	0.96	15.29	6.01	1.02	5.09	67.09
23	0.85	6.29	0.24	0.38	5.03	7.51	0.42	0.67	78.62
24	13.45	17.14	1.10	3.29	7.98	11.15	2.41	1.65	41.85
25	0.10	4.17	0.58	9.94	27.16	37.25	7.68	4.95	8.17
26	0.35	6.73	7.89	2.55	19.20	17.82	1.28	6.98	37.19

CHANGES IN FACTOR INPUT COEFFICIENTS
AND THE LEONTIEF PARADOX

Arvid Stentoft Jakobsen

Denmarks Statistik, Copenhagen, Denmark

1984 marks the 30'tieth anniversary of probably one of the most controversial input-output analysis, and of one of the most persistent paradoxes in economic theory. The analysis referred to is the one carried out by Leontief in his 1954 article "Domestic Production and Foreign Trade; the American Capital Position Re-examined"[1], an analysis that presented America as a net exporter of labour services, and a net importer of capital services. Since the Hecksher-Ohlin theory - at least at that time the predominant trade theory - holds that the comparative advantage of individual goods increases monotonously when they are ranked according to their intensity in the relatively cheap factor, and since the American wage interest ratio was generally agreed not to be surpassed by any of her trading partners, such results were paradoxical indeed.

The method adopted by Leontief rests on an application of the industry technology assumption, not only to inputs of primary products, but also to inputs of primary factors, and to coverage of not only actual domestic production, but also hypothesised domestic production of actual competitive imports. Based on these assumptions, computation of the amounts of capital and labour embodied in exports and in competitive imports, is a relative straightforward matter, and comparison of the results will prove whether the economy in question is a capital or a labour exporter; however, the purpose of this paper is to show that the assumption of an industry technology is hard to defend in the present context.

The Industry Technology Assumption in Relation to Factor Coefficients of Exports, Imports and Total Domestic Production

In the strict version, adaption of an industry technology assumption requires that all individual goods produced by any particular industry have identical input structures (= identical factor intensities in the present context). In practice this requirement seems unlikely to be fulfilled, and accordingly, an adaption of the assumption normally is justified by presuming, that the composition of goods in an analysed change in industry output, is the same as the composition of goods in total industry output. As is to be shown, however, Leontief's test has to be based on the assumption that the strict version of the industry technology assumption is valid, since the alternative assumption of equal composition of goods in total industry output and in change in industry output, would gravely violate the conclusions of the theory tested.

To illustrate this, fig. 1 and 2 - in schematic outline - presents an economy in which the strict version of the industry technology assumption is not applicable.

---

[1]"Economica Internationale", Vol. VII. No. 1

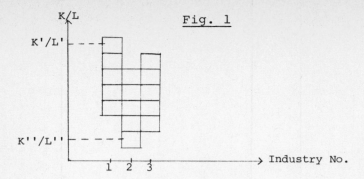

Fig. 1

Fig. 1 is intended as map of all goods produced in a given economy, according to the industry in which they are produced, and the factor intensity with which they are produced (i.e. the three industries in the that economy produce five different goods each, and the factor intensity in the production of these fifteen different goods spans the interval $K'/L'-K''/L''$).

To validate adaption of Leontief's test to the economy in fig. 1, it is required that the composite factor-intensity of total exports from, total imports competing with, and total domestic production in, each industry, are all identical. Presuming this to be the case - and the economy in fig. 1 to be labour expensive - Leontief's test will confirm the H-O theory if imports competing with industry 2 are greater, and exports from the same industry smaller, than those of industries 1 and 3.

As previously mentioned, equality of composite factor-intensity requires equal composition of goods in both total exports from, total imports competing with, and total domestic production in, any particular industry, and to assume this gravely violates the conclusions of the theory tested, since - according to the H-O- theory - competing imports would be concentrated among the labour intensive goods, and exports among the capital intensive goods in each industry. It thus follows that unless industry technology is perceived in the strict sense, the fundamental assumption whereupon Leontief's test rests, is contradicted by the theory it seeks to test.

Further, it can also be shown that the conclusions derived from Leontief's test are very sensitive to violations of the strict version of the industry technology assumption.

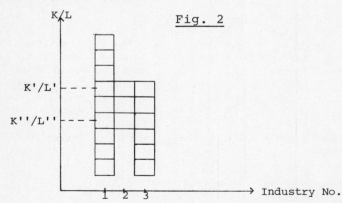

Fig. 2

Fig. 2 illustrates the same general relationships as fig. 1, only this time the output structures of the three industries have changed.

Using the predictions of the H-O theory it follows that exports are concentrated among the capital intensive goods, and that imports are concentrated among the labour intensive goods. According to this, an industry that on the one hand is a substantial exporter, but on the other hand is isolated from import competition, would - in large outline - present itself much like industry 1, since this industry has substantial production above K'/L' (= substantial production of exportables) and at the same time has substantial production below K''/L'' (= importables are produced at home instead of abroad). Similiary industry 2 with no production above K'/L' (= insignificant production of exportables) or below K''/L'' (= importables are actually imported) represents an industry with little exports but with substantial competition from imports, and finally industry 3 with no production above K'/L', but substantial production below K''/L'', represents an industry that neither exports nor is exposed to competition from imports.

The composite capital-intensity of industries 1 and 2 appears to be the same, however, and greater than that of industry 3. Application of Leontief's method to the economy in fig. 2 would therefore indicate that both exports and imports were capital intensive.

If Leontief's method is applied to an economy where the H-O theorem is valid, but the industry technology assumption violated - strict version - both exports and imports tend to be relatively intensive in the relatively cheap factor, since both import penetration and increased production of exportables move the industry in question towards intensity in the relatively cheap factor.

In relation to this, the information contained in Leontief's analyses can be summarized as follows:

Ratio of capital to labour embodied in total exports	14.0
Ratio of capital to labour embodied in total competitive imports	18.2
Ratio of capital to labour embodied in an output vector with equal deliveries from all industries	11.3

This implies that according to Leontief's method both exports and imports are revealed as capital intensive, only exports less so than imports, and following the preceding argumentation this leaves two possible conclusions, either, based on the assumption of an industry technology, to infer that the H-O theorem is violated, since imports are capital intensive, or, based on an application of the H-O theorem, to infer that the industry technology assumption - either version - is violated, since import penetration leads to increased capital intensity of the remaining domestic production.

The present writer holds the latter possibility to be the more likely, and the rest of the paper concerns an attempt to verify this in the case of Denmark through demonstrating that

1) the factor intensity of individual industries moves towards intensity in what is perceived as the relatively cheap factor - capital - when exports increase their shares of domestic production, and when imports

increase their shares of domestic use; this simultaneously implies the validity of the H-O theorem and the violation of the industry technology assumption - either version.

2) a traditional analysis of the factor content of Danish foreign trade, reveals roughly the same relative factor content of exports and imports; on the basis of 1) this only reflects that as imports penetrate labour intensive domestic production, the composite factor-intensity of the remaining domestic production moves towards greater capital intensity.

Relating Changes in Industry Output Composition to Changes in Industry Factor Coefficients

The composite output of each industry is classified in the following five "individual goods"

M_i^+ Domestic production for domestic use which is penetrated by imports (= losing market shares to imports)

M_i^- Domestic production for domestic use which penetrates imports markets (= gains market shares from imports)

D_i Other domestic production for domestic use

X_i^+ Production for export which increases its share of total exports

X_i^- Production for export which has a decreasing share of total exports

and it is assumed that

M_i^+ is produced with labour intensity L^{M+}

M_i^- - " - L^{M-}

D_i - " - L^{D}

X_i^+ - " - L^{X+}

X_i^- - " - L^{X-}

Subscript "i" indicates industry number, and to be noticed is that - using the H-O theory - the individual factor intensity of each of these five "goods" is identical in all industries.[2]

---

[2] The applied classification in five "individual" goods is intended to be a classification of all goods according to their revealed competitiveness (X^+ and M^- being the most competitive and M^+ the least competitive). Since - according to the H-O theory - the competitiveness of individual goods is determined solely by their factor intensity the equality of each of the five individual factor intensities in all industries thus follows.

Defining $C_i = M_i^+ + M_i^- + D_i$ (= domestic production for domestic use) and $Y_i = C_i + X_i^+ + X_i^-$ (domestic production) the composite labour-intensity, L_i^{COM}, can be written as

(1) $\quad L_i^{COM} = (M^+/Y)_i L^{M+} + (M^-/Y)_i L^{M-} + (D/Y)_i L^D + (X^+/Y)_i L^{X+} + (X^-/Y)_i L^{X-}$

and taking first order differences and rearranging terms one obtains[3]

(2) $\quad dL_i^{COM} = dL + (L^{M+}-L^D)(C/Y)_i d(M^+/C)_i + (L^{M-}-L^D)(C/Y)_i d(M^-/C)_i$

$\qquad + (L^{X+}-L_i^C)d(X^+/Y)_i + (L^{X-}-L_i^C)d(X^-/Y)_i$

where L_i^C is the composite labour-intensity in the production of C_i (i.e. $L_i^C = L^{M+}(M_i^+/C_i) + L^{M-}(M_i^-/C_i) + L^D(D_i/C_i))$, dL is the – negative – increase in labour intensity, which is not due to changes in output-composition[4], and $d(M^+/C)_i$, $d(M^-/C)_i$, $d(X^+/Y)_i$ and $d(X^-/Y)_i$ are changes in the respective market shares.

L^{M-} and L^{X+} both represent labour intensity of domestic production that increases its market share at the expense of foreign production. Since labour is perceived as the relatively expensive factor, it follows that according to the H-O theorem L^{M-} and L^{X+} should be small compared to L^D and L_i^C, which both represent some average labour intensity in domestic production for domestic use; i.e. according to the H-O theorem, the following inequalities should hold

$(L^{M-} - L^D) < 0$

$(L^{X+} - L_i^C) < 0$

and in the estimation procedure it is further assumed that

$(L^{M-} - L^D) = (L^{X\circ} - L_i^C)$

These two differences are called (L^+-L^0) and represent the difference in labour intensity between "domestic production, competitive in relation to foreign production" and "other domestic production for domestic use".

---

[3] The derivation of (2) on the basis of (1) is treated in more detail in appendix B.

[4] In the present analysis labour intensity is measured as the ratio of "total physical amount of labour used" to "total factor income generated" in the final product of each individual industry; dL reflects therefore – apart from inflation – the general increase in labour productivity.

Again, according to the H-O theorem, the following inequality should hold

$$(L^+ - L^0) < 0$$

Similarily, according to the H-O theorem

$$(L^{M+} - L^D) > 0$$

since L^{M+} is the labour intensity in domestic production of importables; while the sign of the difference $(L^{X}-L^C)$ is impredictable[5].

It thus follows that when (2) is rearranged as

$$(3) \quad dL^{COM}_i = dL + (L^{M+}-L^D)(C/Y)_i d(M^+/C)_i \quad + \quad (L^{X-}-L^C_i)d(X^-/Y)_i \quad + \quad (L^+-L^0)$$
$$\left[(C/Y)_i d(M^-/C)_i + d(X^+/Y)_i\right]$$

and the changes in market shares and composite labour intensities are calculated, the differences $(L^{M+}-L^D)$, $(L^{X}-L^C_i)$ and (L^+-L^0) can be estimated on a cross-sectional basis. If these differences have the expected sign, both the validity of the H-O theory and the invalidity of either version of the industry technology assumption - and hence of Leontief's test are confirmed.

TABLE I

All Industries	Estimated Coefficient	t-statistic
dL	-11.8	9.3
$L^{M+} - L^D$	-7.3	0.5
$L^{X-} - L^C$	-28.1	1.6
$L^+ - L^0$	-39.3	3.8

r-squared = 0.26

Number of observations = 46

---

[5]Still, in industries where $d((X^-/Y)_i$ is positive, L^{X-} should be smaller than L^C, since X must be considered an exportable in such cases. If $d(X^-/Y)_i$ is positive, industry "i" is an industry whose export production decreases its share of total exports, but increases its share of industry domestic production. At first glance this might appear contradictory, but due to a marked increase in the international division of labour, this type of production actually does increase its share of domestic production in most instances.

Estimation Results

If all changes are calculated as $dQ = Q_{72}-Q_{66}$ (i.e. as change in variable from 1966 to 1972) the differences shown in table I can be estimated.

First, it appears that the difference L^+-L^0 is negative and highly significant, thus implying that production - both for domestic use and for export - which is able to increase its market share at the expense of foreign production, is indeed relatively capital intensive.

Secondly, it appears that also the difference $L^{X-}-L^C$ is negative and significant at the 90 per cent level. This implies that even export production which has a decreasing share of total exports is capital intensive; in connexion with footnote 5) this also supports the H-O theorem at the expense of the industry technology assumption.

Thirdly and fourthly however, the difference $L^{M+}-L^D$ has the wrong sign - though small and insignificant - and r-squared is probably somewhat smaller than desirable, even for a cross-section analysis.

Both these latter shortcomings might be due to a violation of the assumption that the factor intensities L^{M+}, L^{M-}, L^D, L^{X-} and L^{X+} each are identical in all industries. More specifically, it appears likely that the most labour intensive industries are generally more protected against import penetration; if this is the case, a substantial amount of "domestic production for domestic use" in such industries, might be able to sustain its market share, not because it is capital intensive enough to be competitive, but because it is protected against competition from imports. In the present context the effect of this is, that domestic production of importables, "M^+"production, will be classified as domestic production, competitive in domestic use, "D"production, if, due to restrictions on imports, it is able to sustain its market share. When import restrictions are concentrated in labour intensive industries, this means that a relatively large amount of "M^+"production will be classified as "D"production in these industries, which again means that L^D, and hence $L^{X-}-L^C$ and L^+-L^0, will be larger, while $L^{M+}-L^0$ will be smaller, or even zero, in these labour intensive industries.

If industries are grouped according to their labour intensity, and the differences are estimated separately for labour-intensive, neutral and capital-intensive industries, r-squared should increase, and at least in the neutral group of industries the difference $L^{M+}-L^0$ should turn out positive and significant.

The results of such separate estimations are shown in table II (labour intensive industries), and table III (neutral industries)[6].

TABLE II

Labour-intensive Industries	Estimated Coefficient	t-statistic
dL	-12.8	3.9
$L^{M+} - L^D$	-21.6	1,0
$L^{X-} - L^C$	-44.8	1.3
$L^+ - L^0$	-63.3	3.2

r-squared = 0.51

Number of observations = 17

TABLE III

Neutral Industries	Estimated Coefficient	t-statistic
dL	-14.1	3.0
$L^{M+} - L^D$	-9.5	1.6
$L^{X-} - L^C$	6.2	.9
$L^+ - L^0$	-11.8	2.6

r-squared = 0.46

Number of observations = 15

To be noticed is first, that in both cases the difference L^+-L^- still has the expected sign and is significant, that r-squared increases to a satisfactory level, and that the numerical values of differences are substantially greater in the labour-intensive industries, thus indicating that L^D and L^C are greater - and trade restrictions more concentrated - in these industries. Further, the fact that L^X-L^C changes from negative to positive, is still in accordance with the H-O theorem, since it turns out that in the labour intensive industries the share of "X^-"production in domestic production increases in all instances (an effect of a marked import penetration in these industries), while in the neutral group of industries this share changes either way.

---

[6] In practice, estimations are not carried out for the group of capital intensive industries, since in these industries all domestic production tends to be competitive, and no systematic influence on composite labour-intensity can therefore be expected from changes in market shares.

Rather less satisfactory, however, is the fact that $L^{M+}-L^D$ still has the wrong sign, and in the neutral group of industries – where it primarily was expected to be positive and significant – this estimated negative difference even becomes significant at the 90 per cent level; still, also this shortcoming might be explained and remedied.

As mentioned previously the composite labour-intensities of individual industries are measured as the ratio of "total[7] physical amount of labour used" to "total[7] factor income generated" in the final product of each industry.

Total generated factor income will be a correct measure of total factor use, only if all factors are rewarded their competitive factor price. This can generally be assumed to be the case when production capacity is expanding. However, when profits are squeezed and production capacity is contracting, fixed capital will be rewarded less than its competitive factor price, and in such cases the ratio of labour to factor income will overestimate labour intensity.

In the present context this means that during a period in which imports penetrate domestic production of importables in a given industry, there will be two offsetting effects on measured change in composite labour-intensity of that industry: one is the real decrease in composite labour-intensity we seek to estimate, which is due to a lower weight to production of importables in total industry product; the other is the effect of the profit squeeze on domestic production of importables remaining at the end of the period, the measured labour-intensity of this production will now have increased, this leading to an increase in measured composite labour-intensity.

This offsetting effect might be avoided, if the change in composite labour intensity alternatively is measured as the ratio of "total physical amount of labour used" to "total production generated" in the final product of each industry. This has been done for the group of neutral industries where the posibility – and need – to find a positive $L^{M+}-L^D$ is greatest, and the results obtained are shown below in table IV.

TABLE IV

Neutral Industries	Estimated Coefficient	t-statistic
dL	-1.8	12.1
$L^{M+} - L^D$	3.2	1.7
$L^{X-} - L^C$	2.6	1.3
$L^+ - L^0$	-2.6	1.8

r-squared = 0.64

Number of observations = 15

As is seen, $L^{M+}-L^D$ now has the expected sign, and is significant at the 90 per cent level, while L^+-L^0 remains negative and significant, though now

---

[7]Direct and indirect.

only at the 95 per cent level[8].

Traditional Analysis

If alternatively a traditional analysis is carried out on the same industries as the analysis presented in table I the following results are obtained:

	1966	1971
Ratio of labour to factor income embodied in exports from 46 industries	35.5	20.6
Ratio of labour to factor income embodied in imports competing with 46 industries	34.5	20.0

As is seen, this analysis reveals no significant difference between labour intensity of exports and of competitive imports.

Conclusion

The results of the regression analysis are of course influenced by the fact that input-output tables do not contain the required amount of information on changes in market shares, and that accordingly the data sources applied are of less than desirable quality[9]. Whether or not this in fact adds to the reliability of the results obtained is perhaps less clear, but then the important question is not as much whether the results obtained are reliable in an absolute sense, but whether they are more reliable than the results obtained through a traditional analysis.
Considering here

1) that the traditional analysis is heavily dependent on the unlikely event that the strict version of the industry technology assumption is valid

2) that if this assumption is abandoned, the results obtained by Leontief are more easily interpreted as a verification of the H-O theorem than as the opposite

and

3) that the analysis carried out concerning the connection between changes in output composition and changes in coefficients of factor use, relatively unambiguously supports the validity of the H-O theorem at the expense of the industry technology assumption.

the conclusion emerges that the weight of the empirical evidence has shifted in favour of the H-O theorem.

---

[8]This decrease in significance should be expected, since the factor intensities L^{X+} and L^{M-} concern expanding production, where this alternative measure of change in labour intensity must be considered inferior.

[9]The construction of applied data sources is dealt with in appendix A.

Appendix A

Construction of Data Sources

1) Exports

In industries where

$$(X_i/X_{TOT})_{1972} - (X_i - X_{TOT})_{1966} > 0$$

X_i = total export from industry i

$$X_{TOT} = \sum_i X_i$$

$d(X^+/Y)_i$ is calculated as $(X_i/Y_i)_{1972} - (X_i/Y_i)_{1966}$

and $d(X^-/Y)_i$ is assumed to equal zero.

Similarily in industries where

$$(X_i/X_{TOT})_{1972} - (X_i/X_{TOT})_{1966} < 0$$

$d(X^+/Y)_i$ is assumed to equal zero, and

$d(X^-/Y)_i$ is calculated as $(X_i/Y_i)_{1972} - (X_i/Y_i)_{1966}$

2) Imports

In industries where

$$\left[C_i/(C_i+M_i) \right]_{1972} - \left[C_i/(C_i+M_i) \right]_{1966} < 0$$

M_i = total imports competing with industry i

C_i = total domestic production for domestic use in industry i

$d(M^+/C)_i$ is approximated as this difference and $d(M^-/C)_i$ is assumed to equal zero.

Similarily in industries where

$$\left[C_i/(C_i+M_i) \right]_{1972} - \left[C_i/(C_i+M_i) \right]_{1966} > 0$$

$d(M^+/C)_i$ is assumed to equal zero and $d(M^-/C)_i$ is approximated as the difference.

It thus follows that in practice these changes in market shares are measured net instead of gross. Net and gross changes in market shares are of course positively correlated, and significant coefficients can therefore still be estimated. However, the numerical values of coefficients ($\sim$ the "differences") estimated on such net changes will be upwards biased, and it is for this reason that the estimated differences in labour intensity between exportables and importables have not been compared to average composite labour-intensity ; had the estimated differences been unbiased, such comparisons would reveal quantitative information concerning the trade patterns, to supplement the qualitative information from the sign of the differences.

Subset of Industries Included in the Analysis

The method applied in the regression analysis requires in general three assumptions to be fulfilled : 1) that specific factors of production (e.g. natural resources) do not affect the comparative advantages, 2) that industry output is composed of different goods (different in respect to labour intensity), and 3) that sufficiently large shares of industry output are traded internationally.

Out of a total of 117 industries in the Danish input-output tables, the analysis therfore is confined to the 46 industries that make up ISIC major division 3 - manufacturing - when division 31 - food and beverages - and major groups 342 - printing and publishing - and 353 - petroleum refineries - are excluded.

Definition of Period

The period 1966-1972 was chosen because it appeared to be a period of divergence between what could be learned about the structure of trade using Leontief´s method and what was in general perceived to be the structural changes in the economy, caused by international trade.

More specifically it was the period where the socalled "Newly Industrialized Countries" [9] emerged and to a substantial extent were able to penetrate the international markets for labour intensive goods; yet traditional calculations of the factor contents of trade revealed no clue to such changes.

Alternative definitions of period have not been tested.

9) E.g. Hongkong,, Singapore, South Corea and Taiwan.

Appendix B

Derivation of the Estimation Equation

From (1) we have.

$$L^{COM} = L^{M+}(M^+/Y) + L^{M-}(M^-/Y) + L^D(D/Y) + L^{X-}(X^-/Y) + L^{Y+}(X^+/Y)$$
$$\Updownarrow$$
$$L^{COM} = \left[L^{M+}(M^+/C) + L^{M-}(M^-/C) + L^D(D/C)\right] C/Y + L^{X-}(X^-/Y) + L^{X+}(X^+/Y)$$

Taking first order differences we obtain

$$dL^{COM} = dL^{M+}(M^+/Y) + dL^{M-}(M^-/Y) + dL^D(D/Y) + dL^{X-}(X^-/Y) + dL^{X+}(X^+/Y)$$

$$+d(C/Y) \left[L^{M+}(M^+/C) + L^{M-}(M^-/C) + L^D(D/C)\right]$$

$$+(C/Y) \left[L^{M+}d(M^+/C) + L^{M-} d(M^-/C) + L^D d (D/C)\right]$$

$$+ L^{X-} d (X^-/Y)$$

$$+ L^{X+} d (X^+/Y)$$

Assuming that $dL^{M+} = dL^{M-} = dL^D = dL^{X-} = dL^{X+} = dL$

and utilizing that $d(C/Y) = - \left[d(X^-/Y) + d(X^+/Y)\right]$

and $d(D/C) = - \left[d(M^+/C) + d(M^-/C)\right]$ this can be written as

$$dL^{COM} = dL + \left[(L^{M+}-L^D) d(M^+/C) + (L^{M-}-L^D) d(M^-/C)\right] C/Y$$

$$+ (L^{X-}-L^C) d (X^-/Y) + (L^{X+}-L^C) d (X^+/Y)$$

where $L^C = L^{M+}(M^+/C) + L^{M-}(M^-/C) + L^D(D/C)$, as previously.

SOME EXPERIENCE IN THE PLANNING OF INPUT COEFFICIENTS

Rolf Pieplow

University of Economics, Berlin, GDR

1. INTRODUCTION

One of the most complicated problems in using input-output models for plan calculations is the planning of input coefficients. The accurate planning of input coefficients is very important for the usefulness of the results of input-output calculations. The exactness of planned input coefficients in the national economic planning has to reach such a level that the results of these calculations can be used in the process of preparing planning decisions.

The planning of input coefficients in the GDR is faced with different requirements because input-output models are applied to diverse planning decisions. They differ, first of all, as to the periods of planning and the degree of aggregation. The extent of work and the exactness of planning input coefficients also depends on the stage of preparing planning decisions with the help of input-output calculations, e.g. the stage of the first project for the Five-Year-plan or the Annual plan, the stage of preparing the state plan tasks for elaborating the plan projects on the level of ministries, combines and enterprises or the stage of coordinating the plan projects of all economic organisations and of finishing the plan on the level of the central management organs. We consider input-output calculations to be only one part of preparing planning decisions. These decisions are never made on the basis of input-output calculations only. The input-output models, even if they are very detailed, cannot reflect all significant details of preparing planning decisions. This refers, for instance, to details in changes of the structure of production, exports and imports, materials, technologies or to the availibility of manpower and construction capacity in a certain region of the country. Such details are planned on the basis of balances of materials, equipment and consumer goods or on the basis of regional construction capacity balances. That means the planning of input coefficients and input-output calculations is included in a whole system of balancing and plan calculations from which several links to the input-output models arise.

We also have to take into consideration that there exists a deal of uncertainty in the process of accurate planning input coefficients, too, due to the possibilities of forecasting the factors co-influencing the changes of coefficients. Our experience shows that a successive approach to the planning of input coefficients is necessary.

2.   TYPES OF INPUT COEFFICIENTS

Different input-output models are used in the national economic planning of the GDR (aggregated input-output models, the so-called use-value and value input-output table, partial input-output models - for details, see Köhler et al 1981). Therefore different types of input coefficients are to be planned. These are:

1. More or less aggregated coefficients in price units, e.g. input and output in their quality as material flows are reflected in price terms;

2. Coefficients in physical units, e.g. input and output are reflected in a more or less aggregated manner in physical terms;

3. Coefficients in which the numerator is expressed in money units (depreciations, wages, net income, prime cost) and the denominator in price or physical units;

4. Mixed coefficients in which input is reflected in physical units and output in price units or vice versa. Such coefficients appear in the use-value and value input-output table and in partial input-output models. Manpower input is expressed, as a rule, in the number of persons.

The type of input coefficients influences the choice of methods of their planning. When planning input coefficients in price units the influences of price changes must be taken into account. Even if the planning of input coefficients is started with constant prices the price changes have to be calculated in preparing planning decisons. That will be done on the basis of special price input-output models.

3.   ANALYSIS OF THE CHANGES IN INPUT COEFFICIENTS

An essential prerequisite for the planning of input coefficients is the careful analysis of their development and changes in the past. This is to be seen not only in the sense of a general prerequisite for each kind of planning but also in the sense of the first step of planning, because analysis will result in the formation of some groups of coefficients as the starting point of their further planning.

The extensive analysis of input coefficients includes their changes in the temporal development and the causes of their changes. This analysis uses several statistical methods. Their use, however, depends on the existing comparable statistical data basis. The analysis of input coefficients can be subdivided into some steps. These steps are not only made one after the other but also simultaneously or in another sequence.

1. The analysis of the trends of input coefficients with the aim to find a classification of the temporal changes of input coefficients which consists of three groups at least:
a) Coefficients which are relatively constant in certain periods;
b) coefficients changing more or less dynamically in periods, but the changes are following a definable trend;
c) coefficients changing irregularely in periods.

In all these cases an analysis of reasons for temporal reactions of input coefficients takes place. When analysing the changes the attempt is made to determine the quantitative influence of reasons by means of factor analysis. In this context it is very important to discover the reasons for irregular changes of input coefficients which are based in many cases on structural changes in production and foreign trade or in the substitution of materials.

An analysis of deviations between input coefficients planned in former periods and the actual coefficients also belongs to the analysis of the temporal reactions of input coefficients.

2. The analysis of linearity between input and output. Input coefficients express the consumption or the use of a ressource per unit of production. The calculations by means of the above-mentioned input-output models assume a linear dependency between the development of production and the consumption or the use of ressources. It is well known that in reality the dependency is not linear in each case. Non-linearity can be observed in such processes as the consumption of energy and other auxiliary materials, in the use of manpower or in the use of equipment and constructions. The information about linearity or non-linearity between input and output is necessory, above all, for planning desaggregated input coefficients in physical terms.

3. The analysis of stability of input coefficients, i.e. the analysis of the impacts of changes in input coefficients on the results of the input-output calculation. This analysis is an integrated part of the working process with input-output models in preparing planning decisions. This procedure makes it possible to defino the most important input coefficients. Within the use-value and value input-output table of the GDR these coefficients comprise about 10-20 percent of all input coefficients (see Köhler at al. 1981). The remaining input coefficients are considered to be less important input coefficients. Their changes have only a limited influence on the results of calculation.

The analysis of input coefficients is relatively time consuming. These expenditures are necessary. A careful analysis of changes of input coefficients in the past is an indispensable prerequisite of their planning. But this analysis puts high demands on the information basis. The difficulties lie in the fact that in the process of model construction the necessary information is only partly available in many cases. It happens that we cannot analyse time series of input coefficients. Therefore, planning of input coefficients has to take into account the uncertainty of basic information and sometimes the small knowledge about the coefficient changes in the past.

For the purpose of planning on the basis of the analysis we can arrange the input coefficients in the following group:

1. The most important coefficients which are of great importance for the structure of national economy having the main influence on the results of input-output calculations. Their changes require a very accurate planning especially of those coefficients which have been changed in the past dynamically and irregularely.

2. The less important coefficients with small influences on the results of input-output calculation and with regular changes in the past. These coefficients can be planned by simple methods partly, by time series extrapolation for example. If less important coefficients have been changed irregularely in the past special estimates are to be made.

3. The input or use of ressources (or the part of input or use) not having linear links to the output. The influence of nonlinear consumption on changes of input coefficients has to be calculated seperately.

4. PLANNING METHODS OF INPUT COEFFICIENTS

The planning methods of input coefficients are multifarious. They are based on the analysis of their changes in the past and on prognoses of processes and factors causing their changes in the plan period. Essentially, we can distinguish four main groups of methods being suitable for planning input coefficients.

1. Time series extrapolations (trend extrapolations). Their use for planning input coefficients, however, presumes not only the existence of statistical time series but also relativly regular changes of the input coefficients. All kinds of time series extrapolation in every case presume the estimation by experts whether the given trend would continue in the future or not. First of all, the possible changes in the impulses from the factors influencing the development of the input coefficient have to be estimated. If divergencies between the results of extrapolation and the effects of factors can be estimated then it would be possible to correct the extrapolated trend. In other cases the question arises whether to follow the trend or to correct something based on the estimates by experts. Time series extrapolation can be used for planning all groups of input coefficients but for planning of the most important coefficients the extrapolation can be only one of the methods of their planning which is to be completed by other methods, by desaggregation for example.

The problem of time series extrapolation shall be outlined by an example - the development of the input coefficient "Electricity consumption per production unit in chemical industry" (see Table 1). The chemical industry is one of the main consumers of electricity in the national economy of the GDR. In 1982, it consumed 19,4 percent of all the electricity produced. Therefore, this input coefficient belongs to the most important coefficients of the input-output models.

TABLE 1   Electricity consumption per production unit in
          chemical industry

Year	kWh/Mark
1970	0,9932
1971	0,9037
1972	0,8442
1973	0,7935
1974	0,7349
1975	0,6741
1976	0,6323
1977	0,6006
1978	0,5741
1979	0,5644
1980	0,5519
1981	0,5396
1982	0,5159

SOURCES: Statistical Yearbooks of the GDR 1983, 1981, 1980,
         1979, 1978, 1977, 1976, 1974, Berlin (Tables on
         industrial production per sector and the balance of
         electricity)

It is possible to find a trend function reflecting the
curve of consumption in a sufficiently precise manner. In the
case of the time series presented in Table 1 the selection of
the base year has a great influence on the capability of the
trend function for extrapolation. On the other hand, the data
of decreasing consumption per unit show that trend functions
cannot be used for extrapolation without estimates by experts
and desaggregation of the coefficient, hence the structure of
production strongly influences electricity consumption in
chemical industry. The deceleration of consumption decrease
beginning in 1979 probably reflects this fact.

2. The extrapolation of analysed connections between
the development of input coefficients and the factors of
their changes (the extrapolation of regressions analysis for
example). The use of this group of planning methods also
presumes the existence of time series or acceptable assumptions
on the relations between coefficients and the impulses of
their development. It is difficult to evaluate the usefullness
of these methods for planning. They also need in each case
estimates by experts. Moreover, the usefullness of these
methods for planning depends on the type of coefficient and
the degree of aggregation. The test of several methods of
this type (for example the method RAS) in planning input
coefficients in the GDR shows that none of these methods can
be taken alone as a basis for the accurate planning of input
coefficients. This is true for all more or less global methods
for changing input coefficients of the matrix A completely.
The necessary assumptions for using such methods often diverge
from the actual economic processes too widely. The extrapolation of a regression function for one input coefficient
only is more promising, provided that one can estimate the

common tendency of the effect of the calculated factors. Naturally, the working expense for the calculation of such regression functions is much higher than in the case of global methods. Although giving preference to regression analysis the use of global methods should not be rejected generally as they are not suitable as the only ones. But calculations of input coefficients with their help (with modified methods RAS for example) can provoke the experts to check assumptions, extrapolations and estimations in planning input coefficients.

3. The desaggregation of aggregated input coefficients. Input-output models covering the whole national economy include many highly aggregated input coefficients. Even if we try to summarize as many as possible homogeneous technologies in the process of determining the nomenclature of input-output models we have to take into cousideration the more or less strong influence of structural changes in input and output on the changes of coefficients. Besides, at a high degree of aggregation of national economic input-output models a large part of material consumption is included in only one coefficient, the a_{ij} where i = j, i.g. the self-consumption of materials of the sector. Table 2 reflects some examples of consumption in an input-output table of the GDR with 29 sectors in 1966. This situation has not been changed fundamentally up to now.

TABLE 2   The share of self-consumption of materials in the whole material consumption of some sectors

Groups of products	Share in percent	in the sector
Energy products	59	Energy
Metals	46	Metallurgy
Chemical products	49	Chemical industry
Machinery	25	Machinery construction
Transportation equipment (without ships)	30	Transportation equipment industry (without Ship building)
Electrical goods	47	Electrotechnical industry
Textiles	57	Textile industry
Food and Bererages	48	Food and beverages industry

SOURCE: Statistical Yearbook of the GDR 1968, Berlin 1968, p. 46/47

The changes of these coefficients and other most important but also highly aggregated coefficients influence the results of model calculation significantly. Therefore, these coefficients have to be examined very carefully by des-aggregation. True, the highly aggregated coefficients without changes in their methical construction, as a rule, do not change erratically. Estimates by experts leant on extra-polation methods might find the real tendency of their changes. But the high influence on results requires decomposition of these coefficients as much as possible. This is also important for aggregated input coefficients in physical terms, for instance, in the use-value and value input-output table or in partial input-output models. In that case we try to decompose the input coefficients into so-called elementary coefficients. In the case of national economic input-output models we try to reduce the degree of aggregation also by means of the less aggregated input-output tables which include in detail the main technologies reflected by the aggregated input coefficient. The way of desaggregation is used not only in the sense of planning more detailed input coefficients according to the special features of different technologies but also for estimates of structural changes in production and inputs of energy and materials. The last-mentioned is to be linked with the planning of structure changes in the final product of the national economy, with the planning of the availability of raw materials, the substitution of materials and the objectives for saving energy and materials. These changes often influence anly a part of the aggregated coefficient (for example, the substitution of fuel oil by lignite in energy or the quickly increasing use of integrated chips in the electronic industry). The desaggregation of such input coefficients is an important prerequisite for their sufficiently precise planning.

4. The estimates by experts (connected with possible heuristic methods). The use of the methods described above showed that no method of planning input coefficients can be applied without estimates by experts. This has been confirmed by all experience. But the estimates by experts have their own importance for the planning of input coefficients. For changing input coefficients, the main reasons as technological progress and its influence on products and technologies, the processes of substitution, the rationalization of production, structural changes in production and foreign trade, in the availability of ressources, changes in the specialization of production and others must be evaluated in terms of quality and quantity by experts. This is the main field of planning before calculating or estimating plan data.

The diversity of reasons requires to involve experts from different branches in planning input coefficients. This is guaranteed in the planning process in the GDR, for example, by including the planning works at the plan Science and technique, the investment plan and at other parts of the national economic plan in the planning of input coefficients. Moreover, in the planning of input coefficients experts of all branches of production are included. Therefore the planning of input coefficients is not only based on the work done by specialists in modeling.

The planning of input coefficients in the GDR is not only a process covering input coefficients. The use-value and value input-output table and the partial input-output models contain coefficients which belong to a system of fixed normatives of the energy and material consumption. These normatives are plan targets and must be kept or reached. Therefore, a part of input coefficients has not only the

character of a model indicator but also a directive character
as a state plan task. On the one hand, this stimulates the
exactness of planning these coefficients. On the other, the
reliability of reachingthe planned coefficients is approximately high.

Further, the estimates by experts have the function to
prove the probability or nonprobability of the development
of calculated or estimated input coefficients. This does not
only mean to check the assumptions and results of calculated
coefficients by the means of different methods. It is also
a complicated process of taking the links beetween different
input coefficients into consideration. From these connections
conclusions can be made being important for an accurate estimation of the development of input coefficients. For example,
as it is reflected in Table 3, the whole material consumption
of an aggregated sector changes slowly over several years.
These coefficients are relatively stable in the tendency of
their changes. That can be used to plan at first those

TABLE 3   Material consumption per unit of industrial
          production (Mark/Mark, constant prices 1975)

Industrial sector	1977	1978	1979
Energy	0,531	0,541	0,546
Chemical industry	0,525	0,523	0,522
Metallurgy	0,727	0,728	0,727
Construction materials industry	0,563	0,564	0,572
Machinery and transportation equipment industries	0,575	0,574	0,572
Electric and electronic industries	0,506	0,506	0,504
Light industry	0,557	0,555	0,553
Textile industry	0,559	0,556	0,554
Food and beverages industry	0,770	0,769	0,769

SOURCE: Statistical Yearbooks of the GDR 1979, 1980, 1981
        Berlin 1979, p. 115, 1980, p. 117, 1981, p. 123

input coefficients which can be estimated in a sufficiently
exact manner. Then it is possible to determine the range of
changes of those coefficients which can be estimated with
great difficulties only. In such a way we can estimate, for
example, the changes of the coefficients of self-consumption
of materials of the sectors (i=j) if it is too difficult to
plan them in another way. We can also check their planning
with the help of other methods in this way.

The estimates by experts are also very significant when
the development of input coefficients is closely connected
with the objectives of the economic policy, with the well
known availibility of ressources and the targets for
structural changes in the final product of the national
economy. This concerns, above all, the input coefficients of
manpower, capital stocks, wages, cost and net income. The

target in the development of the national income, for example, directly influences the coefficients of labour productivity (manpower intensity per unit production) under the condition of a strongly limited addition of manpower per sector. Targets for the development of individual consumption are linked with the development of income (wages) where it is to consider additionally that the increase of average wages has to be slower than increase in productivity. The increase of net income is directly connected with the decrease of cost coefficients, first of all, with the decrease of materials and wages per unit production. Another exemple ist the investment ment policy and their consequences for the planning of capital stocks, energy and material coefficients.

When summarizing our experience in planning of input coefficients it shall be underlined that their sufficiently accurate planning for preparing decisions by means of input-output calculations is possible only by careful analysis and well-organised team work of experts from different branches. The use of special methods in planning input coefficients can support the work of experts but not replace it. The calculation of variants of input coefficients and iterative calculations of the input-output models can improve the exactness of planned coefficients because the assumptions of their planning partly can be checked by the results of the input-output calculations. Experience shows, that the exactness of planning input coefficients, both aggregated and desaggregated ones, first of all, depends on the accuracy of determining the factors of their changes in terms of quality and quantity.

REFERENCES

Autorenkollektiv (1978). Die Erprobung der Natural-Wert-Verflechtungsbilanz im Planungsprozeß. Wirtschafts-wissenschaft (Berlin), 3: 283-295.

Köhler, G., Fülle, H., and Pinkau, K. (1981). Materialle Bilanzierung, Berlin, part. 5.

Matthes, B. and Müller, J.A. (1977). Extrapolation von Zeit-reihen. Wissenschaftliche Zeitschrift der Hochschule für Ökonomie 'Bruno Leuschner', Berlin, 4: 48-70.

STABILITY OF IMPORT INPUT COEFFICIENTS

Joachim Schintke and Reiner Stäglin

German Institute for Economic Research, Berlin (West)

1. INTRODUCTION

Input coefficients play a central role in input-output analysis. For that reason many criteria and definitions have been developed to examine the problem of significant resp. important input coefficients. One criterion is the consideration of the absolute figure of the input coefficient, another the volume of the intermediate transaction value by itself. A third criterion aims at the single transaction cell as share of total sectoral intermediate input.

In this paper an additional definition of important input coefficients is given taking into account the method of 'tolerable limits'. The measurement of important coefficients follows the theory of error analysis within linear systems. Special inconsistent error simulations within the open static Leontief model will be used to define the significance of input coefficients and their change on sectoral gross output. This results in a distinction of important and unimportant input coefficients.

The degree of coefficients' sensitivity will be calculated on the basis of three enterprise-based and three commodity-based input-output tables for the Federal Republic of Germany. Two evaluations are feasible: An intertemporal analysis of the stability of important input coefficients and a corresponding comparison between the different types of input-output tables.

2. THE DATA

The three selected input-output tables based on enterprises as statistical units are compiled by the German Institute of Economic Research (DIW). They refer to the years 1967, 1972, 1976 and consist of 56 industries (respectively 60 industries for 1976). The intermediate input of the governmental sector is shown as final demand component.

The comparable input-output tables classified according to the commodity groups are compiled by the Federal Statistical Office (FSO) for the years 1970, 1974, and 1975. They distinguish 60 branches and include the governments' intermediate input as production sector.

Both types of input-output tables reflect domestic intermediate transactions, i.e. imported goods and services are excluded. The transaction values are expressed at current prices.

3. THE METHOD

To determine the importance of input coefficients, sectoral production effects will be calculated on the basis of fictive errors in individual coefficients. This method of 'tolerable limits' was first introduced by Sekulić (1968) and Jilek (1971) but extended for selected input coefficients by Schintke (1976, 1979, 1984). The measurement of the significance of coefficients follows the theory of error analysis within linear systems. The input coefficients as well as the corresponding columns or rows of the intermediate transaction matrix are classified according to their influence on sectoral gross output.

Assuming an 'errorless' empirical input-output table, inconsistent error simulations will be performed for input coefficients fictively being changed. The simulations refer to the well-known open static Leontief model

$$x = (I-A)^{-1} \cdot y = C \cdot y, \tag{1}$$

wherein $x = $ vector of gross output resp. production

$y = $ vector of final demand

$A = (a_{ij}) = $ matrix of input coefficients

$C = (c_{ij}) = $ matrix of inverse coefficients

with $i, j = 1, ..., n = $ number of industries resp. production sectors.

The concentration on single coefficients makes it possible to formulate the following thesis with respect to error analysis: If the absolute amount of the percentage error of an input coefficient $a_{ij} = x_{ij}/x_j \neq 0$ $(1 \leqslant i, j \leqslant n)$ is limited by $r_{ij}(p) = 100 \, p/W^{(ij)}(p)$ for $p > 0$ with

$$W^{(ij)}(p) = a_{ij}(c_{ji}p + 100 \, \text{Max} \, c_{ki}x_j/x_k) = a_{ij}(c_{ji}p + 100c_{ii}x_j/x_i), \tag{2}$$
$$k = 1, ..., n$$

no relative errors of more than p per cent will occur in any sectoral gross production x_k (k=1, ..., n). In the formula (2) $W^{(ij)}(p)$ represents the degree of importance and $r_{ij}(p)$ represents the sensitivity of a_{ij}.

Each input coefficient a_{ij} can be characterized by the degree of importance $W^{(ij)}(p) \geqslant 0$ with p>0 reflecting the coefficients' influence on sectoral gross output. Supposing that p is positive and considerable smaller than 100 per cent the degree of importance can be calculated approximately by

$$W^{(ij)}(p) \approx o_{ij} c_{ii} (\delta_{ij} p + 100) \approx 100 \ o_{ij} \ c_{ii}, \tag{3}$$

using the output coefficient $o_{ij} = x_{ij}/x_i$ and $\delta_{ij} = 1$ for i = j and in other respects zero.

Hence it follows: The importance of an input coefficient within one row is approximately proportional to the corresponding output coefficient or the inter-mediate transaction value. It reflects the significance of sector j as purchasing industry for sector i as supplier.

The considerations presented in this section result in a distinction of important and unimportant cells. An intermediate transaction value, not being zero, or the corresponding input coefficient will be defined important if a percentage error in this cell of less than 100 per cent - i.e. the degree of sensitivity is $r_{ij}(p) < 100$ per cent - induces a pre-specified change of p per cent in at least one sectoral gross output. In this case the constant final demand has to be "errorless", too. All other intermediate cells or input coefficients being characterized by an acceptable error interval or a high degree of sensitivity $r_{ij}(p) \geqslant 100$ per cent will be classified unimportant. The error limits p can be specified according to the aggregation of the input-output table referring to the proposals of Schintke (1976) and Katzenbeisser (1979). Empirical analysis proves it advisable to use a percentage for p which permits that all important cells include about 90 per cent of total domestic intermediate transactions.

4. THE RESULTS

On the basis of DIW and FSO input-output tables sensitivities $R = (r_{ij})$ were calculated. The results were analyzed in different manner and summarized in TABLES 1 and 2.

The degrees of sensitivity $r_{ij}(p)$ permit a classification of input coefficients according to their influence on sectoral gross output; the resulting order seems to be mostly independent from the pre-specified error limits p(cf. formula (3) and Schintke (1976)). The use of p = 0.5 per cent guarantees that in the input-output

TABLE 1   Important and unimportant input coefficients in the DIW input-output tables for the Federal Republic of Germany 1967, 1972, and 1976

(Error limits p= 0.5 per cent for sectoral gross production)

Interval of sensitivity for a_{ij} $r_{ij}(p)$ in p.c. [c]		1967[a]		1972[a]		1976[b]	
		Quantity in p.c.	Interm.-input quota in p.c.	Quantity in p.c.	Interm.-input quota in p.c.	Quantity in p.c.	Interm.-input quota in p.c.
	0 - 10	138 6.2	51.8	146 6.5	50.7	128 4.2	52.3
	10 - 20	106 4.8	15.1	116 5.1	16.2	122 4.0	13.2
	20 - 30	110 4.9	8.9	100 4.4	9.6	107 3.5	7.4
	30 - 40	79 3.5	4.8	73 3.2	4.2	93 3.0	4.7
Important coefficients	40 - 50	52 2.3	2.4	60 2.7	2.6	80 2.6	2.9
classified according to	50 - 60	49 2.2	1.9	44 1.9	1.5	80 2.6	2.9
10 groups of significance	60 - 70	40 1.8	1.2	49 2.2	1.7	73 2.4	1.9
	70 - 80	57 2.6	1.3	56 2.5	1.2	68 2.2	1.4
	80 - 90	58 2.6	1.5	52 2.3	1.8	79 2.6	1.7
	90 -100	40 1.8	1.3	43 1.9	1.0	49 1.6	1.1
All important coefficients	from 0 - 100	729 32.7	90.3	739 32.7	90.4	879 28.7	89.5
Unimportant coefficients	above 100	1501 67.3	9.7	1524 67.3	9.6	2182 71.3	10.5
All positive coefficients	above 0	2230 100.0	100.0	2263 100.0	100.0	3061 100.0	100.0

[a] Input-output tables with 56 industries.-- [b] Input-output table with 60 industries.-- [c] Incl. lower limit.
Source: Input-output accounting of DIW.

TABLE 2

Important and unimportant input coefficients in the FSO input-ouput tables for the Federal Republic of Germany 1970, 1974, and 1975

(Error limits p= 0.5 per cent for sectoral gross production)

Interval of sensitivity for a_{ij} $r_{ij}(p)$ in p.c. [a]		1970 Quantity in p.c.	1970 Interm.input quota in p.c.	1974 Quantity in p.c.	1974 Interm.input quota in p.c.	1975 Quantity in p.c.	1975 Interm.input quota in p.c.
0 - 10		159 6.2	61.0	165 6.4	62.8	155 6.2	61.3
10 - 20		121 4.7	11.7	118 4.6	9.9	134 5.3	12.3
20 - 30		128 5.0	7.6	110 4.3	7.7	114 4.5	7.1
30 - 40		83 3.2	3.6	91 3.6	3.9	95 3.8	4.2
Important coefficients 40 - 50		72 2.8	2.5	79 3.1	2.5	73 2.9	2.4
classified according to 50 - 60		70 2.7	1.9	70 2.7	2.1	64 2.5	1.8
10 groups of significance 60 - 70		71 2.8	1.5	62 2.4	1.3	62 2.5	1.3
70 - 80		52 2.0	0.8	51 2.0	1.2	58 2.3	0.9
80 - 90		58 2.3	0.9	38 1.5	0.6	45 1.8	0.8
90 - 100		48 1.9	0.8	45 1.8	0.5	42 1.7	0.6
All important coefficients	from 0 - 100	862 33.6	92.4	829 32.4	92.4	842 33.4	92.7
Unimportant coefficients	above 100	1704 66.4	7.6	1731 67.6	7.6	1678 66.6	7.3
All positive coefficients	above 0	2566 100.0	100.0	2560 100.0	100.0	2520 100.0	100.0

a Incl. lower limit.
Sources: Input-output tables of FSO and compilations of DIW.

tables with 56 and 60 sectors the important coefficients constitute nearly one third of all positive cells. They also include about 90 per cent of total domestic intermediate transactions.

TABLE 1 shows the number of important, unimportant and all positive coefficients in the three enterprise-based DIW input-output matrices whereas TABLE 2 shows the corresponding cells for the three commodity-based FSO matrices. It can be proved that the DIW tables contain between 729 and 879 important input coefficients. In the FSO tables the important cells fluctuate from 829 to 862. A certain error of less than 100 per cent in any input coefficient would induce a maximum percentage error of $p = 0.5$ in one sectoral gross output.

The important coefficients are classified according to their importance into ten groups of significance. Each group reflects an interval of sensitivity of 10 per cent. TABLE 1 shows for example that in 1976 128 coefficients are included in the first group of significance $0 \leqslant r_{ij}(0.5) < 10$ covering already 52.3 per cent of total domestic intermediate inputs. From TABLE 2 the corresponding figures for 1975 can be derived: 155 input coefficients, i.e. 6.2 per cent of all positive coefficients, cover 61.3 per cent of domestic intermediate transactions. Within the first group of significance there are about ten coefficients being extremely important with degrees of sensitivity less than one per cent. These coefficients represent intra-sectoral transactions (for example within the iron and steel industry) or describe high dependent intersectoral relationships (as for example between building materials and construction). The great importance of intrasectoral coefficients in the main diagonal cells had been found out also by Skolka (1983) evaluating the important input coefficients in austrian input-output tables.

An analysis of TABLES 1 and 2 produces a wide conformity in the results. Excluding the DIW table 1976 where the diverging figures might be caused by new sectoral classification and conceptionally revised national accounts data, a cross-section comparison of the enterprise-based and the commodity-based input-output matrices yields a high stability in the shares of all important and unimportant coefficients. This also applies to the percentage distribution of the important input coefficients according to the ten groups of significance.

The important intermediate transaction values - not to be shown here - vary from 8 to 37779 millions of DM in the DIW table 1976 and from 11 to 70695 millions of DM in the FSO table 1975. The corresponding input coefficients range from $2 \cdot 10^{-4}$ to $7 \cdot 10^{-1}$ resp. from $5 \cdot 10^{-5}$ to $8 \cdot 10^{-1}$. Only 62 important coefficients in 1976 and 59 important coefficients in 1975 are minor 10^{-3}. The smallest input coefficient within the first group of significance amounts to $2 \cdot 10^{-3}$ in the DIW table and to 10^{-3} in the FSO matrix. In comparison with these degrees of importance the largest unimportant coefficient amounts to $5 \cdot 10^{-2}$ resp. $8 \cdot 10^{-2}$, i.e. their volumes exceed the size of more than 80 per cent of all important coefficients.

TABLES 3 and 4 offer a disaggregation of the important and unimportant coefficients for 1976 and 1975 already shown in TABLES 1 and 2 according to their size. It becomes obvious that 773 of the 2182 unimportant coefficients in 1976 were most unimportant with sensitivities of above 1000 per cent. The comparable results for 1975 prove 654 of the 1678 unimportant coefficients most unimportant. All unimportant cells with $r_{ij}(0.5)$ above 100 per cent range from $8 \cdot 10^{-6}$ to $8 \cdot 10^{-2}$ being concentrated in the sizes of 10^{-4} to 10^{-2}.

Analyzing the distribution of important input coefficients according to the ten groups of significance on the one hand and according to the sizes of coefficients on the other, a high concentration can be perceived. About 40 per cent of all important coefficients in 1976 resp. 48 per cent in 1975 belong to the first three groups of significance with sensitivities between 0 and 30 per cent. In both years 88 per cent of the important coefficients is to be found in the two size classes $10^{-3} - 10^{-2}$ and $10^{-2} - 10^{-1}$. TABLES 3 and 4 show that in each case 35 input coefficients represent the size class $10^{-1} - 1$ where an error of less than 10 per cent would induce a maximum percentage error of 0.5 in one of the sectoral gross outputs. Excluding the sensitivity groups 1 and 2 in 1976 such as the groups 1 and 3 in 1975 it can be derived that in all other groups of significance the largest amount of important coefficients appears in size class $10^{-3} - 10^{-2}$.

Summarizing the presented results and some others not explicitly shown, a high temporal stability in the importance of coefficients can be pointed out. This follows the consideration that the significance of an input coefficient can not be determined only according to its size which, by the way, varies more than the degree of sensitivity.

An intertemporal comparison of the different input-output tables reveals a steady importance of nearly 90 per cent of input coefficients in all years. About one third of positive coefficients proved important in at least one of the selected years. Even the very important coefficients with $r_{ij}(0.5) < 1$ per cent remain extremely stable reflecting variations in the corresponding degrees of sensitivity of at most ± 0.3 per cent (cf. also Erdmann (1982)). Most of the coefficients show an importance which changes only for one group of significance from year to year. Wider fluctuations are recognized in the degrees of sensitivity for the unimportant coefficients. The amount of at least 80 per cent of positive coefficients being steadily important or unimportant over the years observed confirm the intertemporal stability of coefficients' importance. The degree of this stability increases with decreasing percentages of sensitivity.

TABLE 3

Important and unimportant input coefficients in the DIW input-output table
for the Federal Republic of Germany 1976 classified according to sensitivities and sizes of coefficients

(Error limits p = 0.5 per cent for sectoral gross production)

Interval of sensitivity for input coefficients a_{ij} $r_{ij}(p)$ in p.c.		Sizes of input coefficients[a]						total
		10^{-6} - 10^{-5}	10^{-5} - 10^{-4}	10^{-4} - 10^{-3}	10^{-3} - 10^{-2}	10^{-2} - 10^{-1}	10^{-1} - 1	
0 - 10		-	-	-	21	72	35	128
10 - 20		-	-	3	46	68	5	122
20 - 30		-	-	4	53	50	1	107
30 - 40		-	-	8	50	34	1	93
Important coefficients classified according to 10 groups of significance 40 - 50		-	-	9	45	26	1	80
50 - 60		-	-	7	48	24	1	80
60 - 70		-	-	9	49	15	-	73
70 - 80		-	-	5	47	16	-	68
80 - 90		-	-	11	43	25	-	79
90 - 100		-	-	6	27	16	-	49
All important coefficients	from 0 - 100	-	-	62	429	346	42	879
Unimportant coefficients	from 100 - 1000	2	31	485	796	95	-	1409
Most unimportant coefficients	above 1000	-	147	427	193	6	-	773
All unimportant coefficients	above 100	2	178	912	989	101	-	2182
All positive coefficients	above 0	2	178	974	1418	447	42	3061

a Incl. lower limit.
Source: Input-output accounting of DIW.

TABLE 4

**Important and unimportant input coefficients in the FSO input-output table
for the Federal Republic of Germany 1975 classified according to sensitivities and sizes of coefficients**

(Error limits p = 0.5 per cent for sectoral gross production)

Interval of sensitivity for input coefficients a_{ij} $r_{ij}(p)$ in p. c.		Sizes of input coefficients [a]						total
		$10^{-6} - 10^{-5}$	$10^{-5} - 10^{-4}$	$10^{-4} - 10^{-3}$	$10^{-3} - 10^{-2}$	$10^{-2} - 10^{-1}$	$10^{-1} - 1$	
Important coefficients classified according to 10 groups of significance	0 - 10	-	-	-	38	82	35	155
	10 - 20	-	-	3	72	54	5	134
	20 - 30	-	-	6	49	57	2	114
	30 - 40	-	-	6	53	34	2	95
	40 - 50	-	-	9	35	29	-	73
	50 - 60	-	-	5	38	21	-	64
	60 - 70	-	-	6	38	18	-	62
	70 - 80	-	1	12	35	10	-	58
	80 - 90	-	-	5	27	13	-	45
	90 - 100	-	-	6	28	8	-	42
All important coefficients	from 0 - 100	-	1	58	413	326	44	842
Unimportant coefficients	from 100 - 1000	-	19	340	551	114	-	1024
Most unimportant coefficients	above 1000	3	142	339	164	6	-	654
All unimportant coefficients	above 100	3	161	679	715	120	-	1678
All positive coefficients	above 0	3	162	737	1128	446	44	2520

[a] Incl. lower limit.
Sources: Input-output tables of FSO and compilations of DIW.

In addition to the measurement of the importance of single input coefficients, also rows and columns can be classified according to their influence on sectoral gross production. These calculations and the resulting rank orders of important rows and columns prove the thesis of temporal stability, too.

5. CONCLUSION

The information on important and unimportant input coefficients can be used in the process of compiling, updating and forecasting input-output tables (cf. also Tomaszewicz (1983)), and for their integration into econometric systems. Although input-output computations are relatively insensitive to many errors in coefficients, a great deal of empirical work should be concentrated on the compilation of important intermediate relationships, especially on input coefficients with a high influence on sectoral gross output. The degree of importance which should be evaluated also by intercountry comparisons offers a measure for distributing small resources available for the compilation of input-output tables on the most significant cells and sectors. Often it is easier to collect complete sectoral input and output pattern. For that reason the information on important or unimportant rows and columns can be taken into account rather than the information on single coefficients.

6. REFERENCES

Erdmann, E.(1982). Die Sensitivität der Input-Koeffizienten des ZENCAP/D-Modells. Working Paper Nr. 12, Center of Economic Research, Swiss Federal Institute of Technology Zurich.

Filip-Köhn, R. (1974). Input-Output-Tabelle für die Bundesrepublik Deutschland 1967. Vierteljahrshefte zur Wirtschaftsforschung, Heft 1, pp. 69-73.

Jilek, J. (1971). The selection of most important input coefficients. Economic Bulletin for Europe, Vol. 23, No. 1, p. 86 ff.

Katzenbeisser, W. (1979). Ein Vergleich von Methoden zur Bestimmung von Schlüsselsektoren. Jahrbuch für Nationalökonomie und Statistik, Bd. 194, Heft 3, pp. 280-291.

Lorenzen, G. (1980). Fehlerrechnung in Input-Output-Analysen. Schweizerische Zeit schrift für Volkswirtschaft und Statistik, 116. Jg., Heft 2, pp. 195-203.

Maaß, S. (1980). Die Reagibilität von Prognosen mittels Input-Output-Modellen auf Fehler im Datenmaterial; gezeigt am Beispiel des statischen offenen Leontief-Modells. Volkswirtschaftliche Schriften, Heft 297, Duncker & Humblot, Berlin-München.

Pischner, R., Stäglin, R. and Wessels, H. (1975). Input-Output-Rechnung für die Bundesrepublik Deutschland 1972. Beiträge zur Strukturforschung, Heft 38, Duncker & Humblot, Berlin.

Schintke, J. (1976). Sensitivitätsanalysen im statischen offenen Leontief-Modell. Beiträge zur Strukturforschung, Heft 42, Duncker & Humblot, Berlin.

Schintke, J. (1979). Der Einfluß von Input-Koeffizientenänderungen auf die sektorale Bruttoproduktion. In: J. Seetzen, R. Krengel, G. v. Kortzfleisch (Eds.),

Makroökonomische Input-Output-Analysen und dynamische Modelle zur Erfassung technischer Entwicklungen. Interdisciplinary Systems Research, Vol. 69, Birkhäuser, Basel-Boston-Stuttgart, pp. 127-144.

Schintke, J. (1984). Fehlersimulationen mit Input-Output-Tabellen des Statistischen Bundesamtes. Vierteljahrshefte zur Wirtschaftsforschung, Heft 3.

Sekulić, M. (1968). Applications for Input-Output Models to the Structural Analysis of the Yugoslav Economy. Fourth International Conference on Input-Output Techniques, Geneva.

Skolka, J. (1983). Important Input Coefficients in Austrian Input-Output Tables for 1964 and 1967. In M. Grassini and A. Smyshlyaev (Eds.), Input-Output Modeling, Proceedings of the Third IIASA Task Force Meeting, Laxenburg, Austria, pp. 409-436.

Stäglin, R. (1981). Input-Output-Tabelle für die Bundesrepublik Deutschland 1976. Vierteljahrshefte zur Wirtschaftsforschung, Heft 1, pp. 5-19.

Stahmer, C. (1983). Input-Output-Rechnung des Statistischen Bundesamtes. Wirtschaft und Statistik, Heft 8, pp. 601-609.

Statistisches Bundesamt (1981a). Fachserie 18, Volkswirtschaftliche Gesamtrechnungen, Reihe 2, Input-Output-Tabellen 1974, Kohlhammer, Stuttgart und Mainz.

Statistisches Bundesamt (1981b). Fachserie 18, Volkswirtschaftliche Gesamtrechnungen, Reihe 2, Input-Output-Tabellen 1975, Kohlhammer, Stuttgart und Mainz.

Tomaszewicz, L. (1983). Variations in Input-Output Coefficients: The Application of Estimation and Forecasting Techniques for the Case of Poland. In A. Smyshlyaev (Ed.), Proceedings of the Fourth IIASA Task Force Meeting on Input-Output Modeling, Laxenburg, Austria, pp. 207-218.

CHANGES IN INPUT COEFFICIENTS IN THE GERMAN ECONOMY

Rudi Rettig

Rheinisch-Westfälisches Institut für Wirtschaftsforschung,
Essen, FRG

1. INTRODUCTION

The analysis of change of the industrial structure frequently is based on Leontief's famous input-output model. This instrument shows the inter-industry flows through a system of linear equations, the structural characteristics of the industries being expressed by the numerical values of the inter-industry-flows coefficients.

In short-run observations, it is quite justifiable to assume a constant structure of coefficients and to employ, therefore, the statically open classic Leontief model. The analysis of change of the industrial structure, however, requires the input-output model to be dynamized by introducing a variable structure of inter-industry flows. It is this possibility of variable inter-industry-flow coefficients that permits shifts in the industrial structure. Processes of substitution which took place in the past - e.g. in the energy sector - require to abandon the premise that the input coefficients are constant in respect of time. In order to test the hypothesis of the variability of the inter-industry-flow coefficients, however, it is necessary to have a number of input-output tables covering quite a long period. Such tables are the basis of analyzing the development of the input coefficients in respect of time - at least for those matrix fields of inter-industry flows that are filled with original statistical data.

2. BASIS OF DATA

The analysis of the development of the input coefficients in the course of time is based on the input-output tables for the Federal Republic of Germany prepared by the RWI[1]. These tables are available in a very far-reaching disaggregation for 52 industries, for the period 1960 to 1981. They are adjusted to the input-output tables of Statistisches Bundesamt[2] for the year 1970. Due to partial insufficiencies in the procurement of the data, it is, of course, not possible to determine originally all the fields of the tables. This applies in particular to a number of industries

---

[1] B. Hillebrand, Input-Output-Tabellen für die Bundesrepublik Deutschland 1960 bis 1981. (RWI-Papiere Nr. 12.) Essen, published shortly.

[2] Statistisches Bundesamt (ed.), Input-Output-Tabellen 1974 (Fachserie 18: Volkswirtschaftliche Gesamtrechnungen, Reihe 2), Stuttgart und Mainz 1981.

of the service sector. For the major part of the industries of the manufacturing sector on the other hand it is possible to fill the fields of the
input-output table with data. Furthermore, the data basis could be determined originally also for all the energy sectors of the input-output table.
This will be taken into account later on when selecting the estimation
approach for the input coefficients.

For industries the data of which could not be determined originally,
the fields have been filled with data by means of a modified MODOP procedure. As already mentioned, this mainly applies to branches of the service
sector. Although the MODOP procedure completes the data fields against the
background of industrial substitutability and rationalization effects,
several restrictions have to be made when interpreting the developments in
the course of time of the values of these fields thus estimated. This has
to be taken into account when making, farther below, the analysis of the
variation and of the course of the trends of these inter-industry-flow coefficients. In this respect, a special investigation into the econometric
possibilities to estimate input coefficients should concentrate only on
such field values that have been determined originally.

3. DISTRIBUTION OF THE INPUT COEFFICIENTS

There are various ways to examine the development of the inter-industry-flow coefficients. Projecting and analysing are certainly justified
for input-output tables containing only a small number of inter-industry-
flow fields and therefore being very highly aggregated. In this place,
however, a higher aggregation has been renounced in favour of the very detailed present matrices of inter-industry flows, in order not to be forced
to drop the information on the development in the course of time of some
very special coefficients, for instance of the energy sector. When examining an input-output table comprising 52 industries, consequently only
statistical indices could be used that summarize a special aspect of a time
series. In order to obtain a rough idea of the size of the real input coefficients, the mean value was calculated for each coefficient over the
period 1960 to 1981.

Table 1 shows the distribution of the coefficients. Of the 2,704 maximum possible fields, 2,206 i.e. about 82 p.c. of all the field values have
altogether been occupied. It is interesting to note that the major part is
very small in value. Almost 30 p.c. of all coefficients are smaller than 1
p.m., and half of the 2,206 coefficients are smaller than 0,25 p.c. For
the estimation and calculation of the field values of an input-output table
it is probably important to know that in the present farreaching disaggregation almost 4/5 of all the inter-industry-flow coefficients are smaller
than 1 p.c. This can, of course, not be decisive for the "importance" of a
coefficient, it may, however, signalize that only relatively few input coefficients by their values can be considered as relatively big and therefore may have the priority when setting up an input-output table.

TABLE 1   Frequency distribution of
          average input-coefficients

No.	group (per cent)			abs.	frequency rel.	cum.
1	0.00	-	0.10	693	31,4	31,4
2	0.10	-	0.25	422	19,1	50,5
3	0.25	-	0.50	318	14,4	65,0
4	0.50	-	1.00	304	13,8	78,7
5	1.00	-	2.50	265	12,0	90,8
6	2.50	-	5.00	103	4,7	95,4
7	5.00	-	10.00	56	2,5	98,0
8	10.00	-	20.00	26	1,2	99,1
9	20.00	-	30.00	13	0,6	99,7
10	30.00	-	40.00	1	0,0	99,8
11	40.00	-	50.00	1	0,0	99,8
12	50.00	-	60.00	2	0,1	99,9
13	60.00	-	70.00	1	0,0	100,0
14	70.00	-	80.00	1	0,0	100,0
15	Total			2206	100,0	

TABLE 2   Frequency distribution of
          variation-coefficients

No.	group (per cent)			abs.	frequency rel.	cum.
1	0.0	-	10.0	137	6,2	6,2
2	10.0	-	20.0	592	26,8	33,0
3	20.0	-	30.0	439	19,9	52,9
4	30.0	-	40.0	302	13,7	66,6
5	40.0	-	50.0	212	9,6	76,2
6	50.0	-	60.0	155	7,0	83,3
7	60.0	-	70.0	105	4,8	88,0
8	70.0	-	80.0	77	3,5	91,5
9	80.0	-	90.0	72	3,3	94,8
10	90.0	-	100.0	43	1,9	96,7
11	100.0	-	112.5	32	1,5	98,2
12	112.5	-	125.0	20	0,9	99,1
13	125.0	-	150.0	12	0,5	99,6
14	150.0	-	200.0	7	0,3	100,0
15	200.0	-	300.0	1	0,0	100,0
16	Total			2206	100,0	

In order to make the extent of the timely dispersion of the input co-efficients apparent, the respective variation coefficients have been calculated for the values of the inter-industry flow. Table 2 shows the distribution by sizes of these dispersion parameters: 1/3 of all the coefficients varies within a range of up to 20 p.c., a further third of up to 40 p.c. Almost 3/4 of all the values have a dispersion range of up to 50 p.c. With 97 p.c. of all the coefficients the variation range in its maximum comprises their average values. Insofar, the variation range of input coefficients remains within justifiable limits. The average variation coefficient obtained on the whole for all dispersion values was about 37 p.c. From this can be concluded that a relatively high disaggregation leads to relatively greater variations of the coefficients. This can certainly be explained by the fact that with great differentiation of the industries substitution effects have an inter-industrial influence rather than an intra-industrial one, thus increasing the extent of the variation of the co-efficients.

TABLE 3   Cross-tabulation:
            Average input-coefficients and variation coefficients
            (per cent)

		average input-coefficients						
		1	2	3	4	5	6	7
No.	variation-	0.00	0.10	0.25	0.5	1.0	2.5	
	coefficients	-	-	-	-	-	-	Total
		0.10	0.25	0.50	1.0	2.5	80.0	
1	0.0 - 10.0	19	19	17	21	19	42	137
2	10.0 - 20.0	172	78	74	91	94	83	592
3	20.0 - 30.0	126	90	64	61	64	34	439
4	30.0 - 40.0	81	61	45	52	39	24	302
5	40.0 - 50.0	61	53	36	36	18	8	212
6	50.0 - 60.0	54	38	28	18	12	5	155
7	60.0 - 70.0	44	28	14	8	5	6	105
8	70.0 - 80.0	37	16	15	5	4	0	77
9	80.0 - 90.0	38	16	10	4	4	0	72
10	90.0 - 100.0	16	13	7	5	1	1	43
11	100.0 - 112.5	20	3	4	2	2	1	32
12	112.5 - 125.0	13	3	2	0	2	0	20
13	125.0 - 150.0	7	2	1	1	1	0	12
14	150.0 - 200.0	4	2	1	0	0	0	7
15	200.0 - 300.0	1	0	0	0	0	0	1
16	Total	693	422	318	304	265	204	2206

Beside the size of the table, the variation range of the coefficients will also depend on the value of the individual coefficients. Table 3 shows a cross-tabulation by mean values and variation coefficients of the inter-industry-flow values. It clearly shows that there exists a negative relationship: the smaller a coefficient, the wider is its range of variation. The reason for this is certainly the fact that with small coefficients measuring and rounding errors have a larger influence, and that substitution processes between individual input commodities make themselves felt in percents with smaller coefficients rather than with larger coefficients.

TABLE 4 Significant trends of input-coefficients

| t-Values | Prob. | frequency | | |
		abs.	rel.	cum.
1. Negative trend				
< -2.83	99	518	23,5	23,5
-2.08 till -2.83	95	76	3,4	26,9
2. Positive trend				
> +2.83	99	830	37,6	64,5
+2.08 till +2.83	95	107	4,9	69,4
3. No significant trend				
-2.08 till +2.08	95	675	30,6	100,0
4. Total		2206	100,0	

Having characterized the distribution by size and the ranges of dispersion of the input coefficients, the analysis will now be made of the development of the inter-industry-flow values in the course of time. In the simplest case, the production coefficients can be represented by a time variable. Table 4 shows the results for a linear trend approach by different classes of size of the coefficients and different classes of significance for the inclination measures of the trend variables. In the first and third class, the regression coefficients have a level of significance of 99 p.c., in the classes 2 and 4, however, only of 95 p.c. The fifth class covers all the input coefficients for which statistically secured results cannot be provided. It can be seen that of all the 2,206 production coefficients almost 70 p.c. are subject to a trend. Three fifth of these have a positive inclination and two fifth a negative one. Therefore, it is an important finding that for the majority of production coefficients a more or less continuous increase or decrease through time cannot be denied, particularly since more than 60 p.c. of all the trend courses of the production coefficients are secured with a level of significance of 99 p.c.

Yet this approach can only be considered as a description of the development of the input coefficients in the course of time, whereas an explanation rather ought to present economic variables in order to reveal the determinants, e.g. substitution processes as a result of a change in price relations.

4. ESTIMATION FUNCTIONS OF ENERGY COEFFICIENTS

Table 5 shows the ex post substitution processes in the energy sector. Electricity and gas have at the expense of coal, gained a growing market share in the inter-industrial sector. The less secured coefficients in the oil sector are probably due to the U-shaped curves of the corresponding energy coefficients. For this sector, increasing values can be observed empirically up to the mid-seventies, and decreasing ones again for the years thereafter. This development can, of course, only insufficiently be represented by a linear trend for which reason this shall be done by an adequate explanatory approach that contains important economic variables such as, for instance, price relations.

TABLE 5   Substitution processes by sources of energy 1960-1981: Number of secured trends (95 p.c.) of the input coefficients

Serial No.	Industry	Trend	
		positive	negative
2	Electricity	44	7
3	Gas distribution	35	7
5	Coal mining	0	49
7	Oil production	2	2
9	Mineral oil refining	23	5

Starting point for the estimation to be made here of the functions of the production coefficients is the specification of a production function and its differentiation to the profit maximizing function of the production factors:

$$G_j = P_j X_j (X_{1j}, X_{2j}, \ldots, X_{nj}) - \sum_{i=1}^{n} P_i X_{ij} \rightarrow max!. \tag{1}$$

If for instance a Cobb-Douglas production function is assumed the optimal volume of factor inputs is:

$$X_{ij}^* = d_{ij} \cdot \frac{P_i}{P_j} \cdot X_j \tag{2}$$

and for the optimal input coefficients:

$$\frac{X_{ij}^*}{X_j} = a_{ij} = d_{ij} \cdot \frac{P_i}{P_j}. \tag{3}$$

This function, therefore, shows the production coefficients dependent on the input-output price relation.

Nevertheless, the simple estimation of equation (3) does not seem to be sufficient, as besides shifts in the price relations other factors, too, will influence the production coefficients. In particular, the technological progress has to be mentioned here which in the long run certainly will be one of the main influencing factors for the development of the coefficients. If technological progress is considered to be autonomous, it will be introduced into the function only via the above mentioned trend ap-

proach. In addition, however, the induced technological progress should
also be taken into account in the explanatory approach. Technological progress might for instance be induced by increased research investments and
by higher capital input into places of work. Thus, induced technological
progress can be denoted as an increase of the capital intensity of the industries.

Besides the price relations and the indicators for autonomous and induced technological progress, a variable for the explanation of the cyclical fluctuations should be applied that can show the effect of fluctuations
of the production capacity utilization rate on the input structure. In
this connection it must be taken into account that the input coefficients
are influenced by the utilization of the capacity of the receiving sector.
If the utilization of the capacity increases, waste grows as a consequence
of the accelerated production speed and of increased overtime work, and
thus the factor consumption per product unit may increase.

Having outlined the main variables that influence the development of
the production coefficients, a few hints should be made regarding their
calculation.

In order to find out the rate of utilization in each industry, a calculation had, as a first step, to be made of the production capacity of
each industry. This was done, analogous to the method of the Sachverständigenrat (German Council of Economic Advisors)[3], by estimating the trends
of the capital productivity by individual industries. By connecting the
trend values of capital productivities with the values of the actual production, the production capacities are obtained for the individual industries. Their confrontation with values of realized production leads to the
amount of capacity utilization by industries.

As already in the calculation of the production capacity, the estimation of capital intensity by industries contains the capital stocks by industries in addition to the labour volume.

The labour volumes have been calculated by multiplication of labour
hours and labour force by industries. Subsequently, the quotient from capital stock and labour volume could be calculated and incorporated into the
estimation function of the input coefficient as the indicator for induced
technological progress.

In addition to the trend variable as indicator for autonomous technological progress, the input-output price relation had to be calculated according to equation (3), in order to make apparent, in the attitude functions, substitution processes in consequence of price shifts. The price
relation has been formed by confronting the price of intermediate demand of
the supplying industry with the price of the production value of the acquiring industry. Totally, the estimation approach to the input-output coefficients is as follows:

$$a_{ij} = a_{ij} (p_{ij}, k_j, y_j, t) \tag{4}$$

---

[3] Sachverständigenrat zur Begutachtung der gesamtwirtschaftlichen Ent-
wicklung, Ein Schritt voraus. Jahresgutachten 1983/84, Stuttgart und
Mainz 1983, p. 261.

with a_{ij} = real input coefficient,

$\quad$ p_{ij} = input-output price relation,

$\quad$ k_j = capital intensity,

$\quad$ y_j = rate of capacity utilization,

$\quad$ t $\quad$ = trend variable,

$\quad$ i $\quad$ = supplying industry,

$\quad$ j $\quad$ = acquiring industry.

TABLE 6 Distribution of significant elasticities
from a multiple regression analysis[a]

Ser. No.	Energy sectors	Price relation	Capital intensity	Time trend	Capacity rate	Total no. of sectors
2	Electricity	31 (60.8)	30 (58.8)	16 (31.4)	0 (0.0)	51
3	Gas distribution	17 (34.7)	37 (75.5)	38 (73.6)	0 (0.0)	49
5	Coal mining	34 (69.4)	7 (14.3)	45 (91.8)	0 (0.0)	49
7	Oil production	2 (50.0)	4 (100.0)	1 (25.0)	2 (50.0)	4
9	Min. oil refining	49 (96.1)	47 (92.2)	1 (2.0)	2 (3.9)	51

[a] in brackets appear the percentage shares in relation to the
total number of sectors.

In order to show elasticities by industries, all the variables have
been logarithmized. The following table 6 shows the results for the
input coefficients of five different energy sources. In a comparison of
the number of the significant elasticities, the varying importance of influence of the alternative explanatory factors becomes clearly evident.
Whilst the specific coal input in almost all cases can be explained by the
development of prices and by a trend variable as indicator for autonomous
technological progress, the specific input of mineral oil in the industries
almost exclusively can be explained by the price sensitivity and capital
intensity as indicator for induced technological progress. On the other
hand, the specific input of gas does not seem to depend thus much on the
development of prices, for the indicators of technological progress in this
case show comparatively higher explanatory values. The electricity input

by industries on the other hand can be determinded to approximately equal
parts by the development of the price relation as well as by an increasing
capital intensification. For the consumption of oil, too, capital intensification contributes a great deal of explanation.

The variable of capacity utilization does not seem to play an important role in all the tested attitude functions in respect of the specific
energy coefficients. This gives reason to assume that cyclical fluctuations rather can be covered by variables such as price relation and capital
intensity. Moreover, in connection with a trend variable, they seem to
make quite a good explanatory contribution for the development of the production coefficients in the long run.

Especially the variables of price relations play a dominant role in
the development of the input coefficients. In table 7, the significant
own-price elasticities by industries have been combined to an unweighted
average value. This table shows that the industries do not respond so
sensitively to price changes of oil input as for instance in respect of the
specific coal consumption. Whilst the average own-price elasticity of
-1,72 with the coal input coefficients ranges relatively high, the own-
price elasticities of the other four energy sources are between -0,51 (oil)
and -,84 (electricity) and, therefore, are lower than One.

TABLE 7   Average own-price elasticities of the energy coefficients
          by industries 1960-1981

Ser. No.	Energy Sectors	Own-Price Elasticity	Number of Branches	Number of Signifi-cant Elasticities	Standard Deviation
2	Electricity[a]	-0,84	51	30	0,71
3	Gas distribution	-0,71	49	17	0,67
5	Coal mining	-1,72	49	34	0,90
7	Oil production	-0,51	4	2	0,41
9	Min. oil refining	-0,60	51	49	0,70

[a]without sector 2.

After the analysis of the own-price elasticity, an examination could
also be made of the cross-price elasticities of energy coefficients - or
rather of the input coefficients in general. This, however, should be re-
served to a later analysis which in details would have to examine possible
substitution processes between the input factors resulting from different
price developments. In this analysis, an attempt was made only to to answer the question of stability or variability of input coefficients in input-output models. As shown by the empirical results, there exists a clear
instability of the production coefficients in the course of time which can
be explained by means of economic factors such as price relations and capital intensification.

TABLE 8   Sector titles

```
 1 LANDWIRT       Agriculture
 2 ELEKTRIZ       Electricity
 3 GASVERTLG      Gas distribution
 4 WASSERVER      Water supply
 5 KOHLENBGB      Coal mining
 6 SONST.BGB      Other mining
 7 ERDOELGEW      Oil production
 8 CHEMIE         Chemistry
 9 MIN.OEL        Mineral oil refining
10 KUNSTST        Plastics
11 GUMMI, ASB     Rubber
12 STEINE         Stone and clay
13 FEINKERAM      Fine ceramics
14 GLAS           Glass
15 STAHLPROD      Iron and Steel
16 NE-METALL      Non-Ferrous Metals
17 GIESSEREI      Foundries
18 STAHLBAU       Steel construction
19 FAHRZ.BAU      Ships, planes
20 MASCH.BAU      Machinery construction
21 KRAFTWAGEN     Vehicle construction
22 ADV-WAREN      Office mach., computers
23 ELEKTROT       Electrical goods
24 FEINM.,OPT     Precision engineering
25 EBM-WAREN      Hardware
26 HOLZ           Saw mills, timber man.
27 PAPIERERZ      Woodship
28 PAPIERVER      Paper man.
29 LEDER          Leather
30 TEXTIL         Textile
31 BEKLEIDUNG     Clothing
32 NAHRUNGSM      Food
33 MILCHPROD      Milk
34 FLEISCH        Meal
35 GETRAENKE      Beverages
36 TABAKWAREN     Tobacco
37 BAU            Construction
38 GROSSHAND      Wholesale trade
39 EINZELHAND     Retail trade
40 EISENBAHN      Railway
41 SCHIFFAHRT     Shipping
42 UEBR.VERK      Other transport
43 NACHRICHT      Communication
44 BANKEN+BG      Banking
45 VERSICHRG      Insurance
46 GASTSTAETT     Catering
47 VERLAGSW       Publishers
48 GESUNDHEIT     Health Service
49 WOHN.VERM      Renting
50 S.DIENSTL      Other Services
51 PRIV.HH        Private organization
52 STAAT          Governmental unit
```

ESTIMATION OF INPUT—OUTPUT COEFFICIENTS USING NEOCLASSICAL PRODUCTION THEORY

Christian Lager and Wolfgang Schöpp

International Institute for Applied Systems Analysis,
Laxenburg, Austria

1. INTRODUCTION

Over the years there has been much research and investigation into the question of change in input—output (IO) coefficients, which lie at the heart of any IO model. This research has taken many productive directions. Besides technical progress, two main reasons for changes in IO coefficients have been identified:

- Input factor substitution (including substitution of domestic products by imported commodities) caused by changes in the input price system (price effects), and
- Changing output structures of the industries concerned (product-mix effects).

An extensive literature exists on price effects: Tilanus (1966) concluded that the classical assumption of IO analysis, namely that value coefficients are constants, is less workable than the hypothesis that value coefficients (cost shares) are stable. Klein (1952) proved that this hypothesis requires a multiproduct Cobb—Douglas function. Using recent production theory, much more flexible assumptions were used by Frenger (1978), Bonnici (1983), Nakamura (1984), and Andersson *et al.* (1984), by applying Diewert (generalized Leontief) production or cost functions to IO data. Frenger (1978) analyzed the price-responsiveness of IO coefficients for textiles, construction, and metals and concluded that "there would seem to be little doubt that the Leontief assumption would have to be rejected ... relative prices have a significant effect on the viability of IO coefficients". Bonnici (1983) estimated a complete set of price-dependent IO coefficients derived from corresponding Diewert cost functions for all 17 sectors covered by a time series of annual IO tables. A comparison of the traditional method (forecasting on the basis of the coefficients from the most recent year available) with the generalized Leontief model showed that "... the forecasts of the generalized Leontief model outperform those of the (common) IO model in two out of every three cases". Contrary to Tilanus, Bonnici concluded that, whenever a time series of IO tables is available, there is considerable scope for relaxing the somewhat rigid assumption of fixed IO coefficients.

Another body of literature is devoted to product-mix effects. Here, the idea is that changes in the input coefficients of aggregate industries are attributable to changes in the industries' internal output profiles rather than to shifts caused by changes in the production processes.

Sevaldson (1960) wrote in the introduction to the 1954 Norwegian IO tables: "Lack of sector homogeneity makes product mix the dominant source of changes in the coefficients". A cross-sectional analysis on an establishment level by Forssell (1969), for six fairly homogeneous industry groups, showed that two-thirds of the explained dispersion of input coefficients among establishments could be attributed to heterogeneity in commodity mix while just one-third was found to be due to replacement of particular inputs by other commodities. Lager (1983) analyzed the changes in the energy coefficients of five of the most energy-intensive sectors in Austria and found that explicit consideration of product-mix effects produced a significant decline in the price elasticities. This result might encourage the assumption that changes in the input price system lead not only to changes in the (micro)technologies involved but also to remarkable effects on the output structure, and therefore that they contribute in two ways to changes in the technical coefficients of industry groups. However, it is generally agreed that changes in technology as well as shifts in production structure have explanatory power for estimating changes in the input coefficients. Consequently, emphasis on product-mix effects leads to rather large IO tables and disaggregated, but simple, models. On the other hand, the introduction of factor substitution implies flexible production functions and more or less aggregated, but complicated, modeling.

2. GENERAL CONSIDERATIONS

The aim of this study is to contribute to this "trade off" in such a way that both product-mix effects and factor substitution caused by changes in prices can play a role in explaining shifts in IO coefficients. This approach has been supported and stimulated by recent developments in the availability and structure of IO statistics: more and more IO tables are now compiled according to the concepts of the System of National Accounts (SNA) 1968 (UN 1968). Industrial interactions are described by two matrices: the *make matrix* shows the production of commodities by industries while the *use matrix* shows the demand of industries by commodities. The demand of an industry for a certain commodity (x_i) can be specified as

$$x_i = \sum_k a_{ik} \cdot Q_k$$

where Q_k is the volume (value at constant prices) of commodity k produced in that industry and a_{ik} is the input coefficient, which specifies the requirement of input i for output k.

If we assume that the input coefficients a_{ik} are functions of the input price indices $p = (p_1, p_2, \ldots, p_n)$, we can relate the changes in the industrial input requirements to changes in the price system *and* to changes in the production structure:

$$x_i = \sum_k a_{ik}(p) \cdot Q_k$$

If we choose a flexible functional form for the input coefficients $Q_{ik}(p)$ that allows for changes in the substitution elasticities, we would soon have problems associated with the estimation of too many parameters. A typical problem with the estimation of a sophisticated production function is that the observations are frequently not well distributed over the complete possibility set, but are grouped in clumps close together. This makes it very difficult to distinguish between different functional forms. Statistically speaking, one must also be very careful with the number of degrees of freedom assigned to a given problem, and it should be remembered that it is hard to separate very similar effects by using statistical analysis.

Therefore, following recent production theory, we will define a multi-input/multi-output technology for a whole industry and then try to derive micro demand functions for single commodities.

Suppose that an industry faces a series of competitive input markets with given input prices $[p = (p_1, p_2, \ldots, p_n)]$. Suppose further that there exists a technologically determined input requirement set that determines inputs for each exogenously determined (e.g. by demand, capacity) set of producible outputs $[Q = (Q_1, Q_2, \ldots, Q_m)]$. The cost function[1] for the industry is then defined by

---

[1]Instead of using cost functions we could also use a profit function that relates profits to input as well as output prices.

$$C = C(p,Q)$$

and specifies the least cost of producing the output bundle Q at given input prices p. (For the sake of simplicity, technical progress is ignored here.)

Further, we assume that the technology used for a single product is in no sense related to the production processes for other commodities produced in the same industry. For example, the input requirements for steel products do not depend on the quantity of aluminum produced in the same industry. Therefore, for any individual output Q_k, a separable, non-joint, single-output cost function can be specified:

$$C_k = C_k (p,Q_k)$$

The total cost of production is then simply

$$C = \sum_k C_k (p,Q_k)$$

In addition, we assume *linear homogeneity* for all commodity cost functions and therefore

$$C = \sum_k g_k (p) \cdot Q_k$$

Using Shephard's Lemma, $x_i = \partial C / \partial p_i$, we obtain again

$$x_i = \sum_k a_{ik} (p) \cdot Q_k$$

where

$$a_{ik} (p) = \frac{\partial g_k (p)}{\partial p_i} .$$

Therefore, the input coefficients for a multi-product technology can be derived from a linear-homogeneous, non-joint cost function:

$$a_{ik} (p) = \frac{\partial^2 C(p,Q)}{\partial q_k \, \partial p_i} .$$

3. THE TRANSLOG COST FUNCTION WITH LINEAR HOMOGENEITY IN THE INPUT PRICES AND CONSTANT RETURNS TO SCALE

To test the restrictions described in Section 2 we start with a more general approach. Thus, we define a production possibility frontier that does not imply non-jointness or constant returns to scale *a priori*, but that does enable us to apply statistical tests to these restrictions. For this purpose we choose the translog function introduced by Christenson *et al.* (1973), which is a second-order approximation of any function.

We approximate the cost function at $p_i = 1$, $Q_k = 1$ by:

$$\ln (C) = a_0 + \sum_{i=1}^{i=n} \alpha_i \ln(p_i) + \sum_{k=1}^{k=m} \beta_k \ln(Q_k) + \frac{1}{2}\sum_{i=1}^{i=n}\sum_{j=1}^{j=n} \gamma_{ij}\ln(p_i)\ln(p_j)$$

$$+ \frac{1}{2}\sum_{k=1}^{k=m}\sum_{l=1}^{l=m} \vartheta_k \ln(Q_k)\ln(Q_l) + \sum_{i=1}^{i=n}\sum_{k=1}^{k=m} \delta_{ik} \ln(p_i)\ln(Q_k)$$

The parameters of the translog function equal the first- and second-order derivatives at the point of expansion:

$$a_0 = \ln C_0 \ , \quad \alpha_i = \frac{\partial \ln C}{\partial \ln p_i} \ , \quad \beta_k = \frac{\partial \ln C}{\partial \ln Q_k}$$

$$\gamma_{ij} = \frac{\partial^2 \ln C}{\partial \ln p_i \, \partial \ln p_j} \ , \quad \vartheta_{kl} = \frac{\partial^2 \ln C}{\partial \ln Q_k \, \partial \ln Q_l} \ , \quad \delta_{ik} = \frac{\partial^2 \ln C}{\partial \ln p_i \, \partial \ln Q_k}$$

Symmetry of the second-order derivatives requires that $\gamma_{ij} = \gamma_{ji}$ and $\vartheta_{kl} = \vartheta_{lk}$.

One usual condition for a cost function is linear homogeneity in input prices. It is easy to prove that this requires that

$$\sum_{i=1}^{i=n} \alpha_i = 1, \quad \sum_{i=1}^{i=n} \gamma_{ij} = 0, \quad \sum_{k=1}^{k=m} \delta_{ik} = 0.$$

Constant returns to scale requires linear homogeneity in the outputs. Thus, taking the symmetry restriction and linear homogeneity into account, we obtain an additional set of restrictions:

$$\sum_{k=1}^{k=m} \beta_k = 1, \quad \sum_{k=1}^{k=m} \vartheta_{kl} = 0, \quad \sum_{i=1}^{i=n} \delta_{ik} = 0,$$

and

$$\sum_{j=1}^{j=n} \gamma_{ij} = 0, \quad \sum_{l=1}^{l=m} \vartheta_{kl} = 0.$$

4. NON-JOINTNESS RESTRICTION ON THE TRANSLOG COST FUNCTION

As described in Section 2, non-joint production requires a cost function of the type:

$$C = \sum_k C_k (p, Q_k).$$

Consider the first- and second-order derivatives of this general non-joint cost function:

$$\frac{\partial \ln C}{\partial \ln Q_k} = \frac{1}{C} \frac{\partial C_k}{\partial \ln Q_k} \ , \quad k = 1, 2, \dots, m,$$

$$\frac{\partial^2 \ln C}{\partial \ln Q_k \cdot \partial \ln Q_l} = - \frac{1}{C^2} \frac{\partial C_k}{\partial \ln Q_k} \frac{\partial C_l}{\partial \ln Q_l} \ , \quad k \neq l, \ k, l = 1, 2, \dots, m.$$

The first- and second-order derivatives of $\ln C$ equal the parameters β_k and ϑ_{kl} at the point of expansion. Consequently, non-jointness requires

$$\vartheta_{kl} = -\beta_k \cdot \beta_i \quad \text{for all } k, l, \ k \neq l.$$

As described above, the translog function is a second-order approximation of the cost function at a point of expansion. Consequently, this restriction defines non-jointness only around that point of expansion.

5. HOW TO ESTIMATE THE TRANSLOG COST FUNCTION

Using Shephard's Lemma we obtain a system of n cost-share equations

$$s_i = \frac{\partial \ln C}{\partial \ln p_i} = a_i + \sum_{j=1}^{j=n} \gamma_{ij} \ln(p_j) + \sum_{k=1}^{k=m} \delta_{ik} \ln(Q_k)$$

where

$$s_i = P_i \frac{X_i}{C}$$

The use of the share equations makes it possible to justify the parameter restrictions that arise from the imposition of linear homogeneity. Since the sum of all the shares must be one, and the linear homogeneity and symmetry constraints are used, only $n-1$ equations remain to be estimated. The last equation depends on the others, and must be calculated from them.

The share equations described above do not permit the estimation of the complete cost function. In order to estimate the parameters ϑ_{kl} and β_k, we need to define additional equations. The cost function itself can be used to get the missing parameters. The other way out is to specify an output price rule.

If we assume that the manufacture of each product breaks even, we can relate total costs to total outputs, $C_k = p_k Q_k$. Therefore the nominal product-mix coefficient is defined as $v_k = C_k / C$.

Non-jointness requires that

$$\frac{\partial \ln C}{\partial \ln Q_k} = \frac{1}{C} \frac{\partial C_k}{\partial \ln Q_k} = \frac{C_k}{C} \frac{\partial \ln C_k}{\partial \ln Q_k}$$

Constant returns to scale in the micro cost function C_k yields

$$\frac{\partial \ln C_k}{\partial \ln Q_k} = 1$$

Consequently,

$$\frac{\partial \ln C}{\partial \ln Q_k} = \frac{C_k}{C} \equiv v_k$$

This enables us to define an additional, estimatable set of m nominal product-mix equations, which now include the parameters ϑ_{kl} and β_k :

$$v_k \equiv \frac{C_k}{C} = \beta_k + \sum_{l=1}^{l=m} \vartheta_{kl} \ln q_l + \sum_{i=1}^{i=n} \delta_{ik} \ln p_i$$

From the nominal product-mix equations v_k we obtain micro cost functions C_k. Applying Shephard's Lemma, we can devise demand equations for each single output k:

$$x_{ik} = \frac{C}{p_i} \left[\delta_{ik} + v_k \cdot s_i \right] \quad .$$

Dividing x_{ik} by Q_k, we can obtain commodity-by-commodity IO coefficients.

6. PRICE AND SUBSTITUTION ELASTICITIES

Here we begin by defining the price elasticity of input demand as the percentage change in input x_i when the input price p_j changes by one percent

$$\varepsilon_{ij} = \frac{\partial \ln(x_i)}{\partial \ln(p_j)},$$

$Q = \text{constant}, \ p_i = \text{constant, for } i \neq j.$

Next, the Allen elasticities of substitution are defined as follows:

$$\sigma_{ij}^A = \frac{C \cdot C_{ij}}{C_i \cdot C_j}, \quad C_i = \frac{\partial C}{\partial p_i}, \quad C_{ij} = \frac{\partial^2 C}{\partial p_i \partial p_j}$$

The Allen elasticities are symmetric, $\sigma_{ij}^A = \sigma_{ji}^A$.

Using Shephard's Lemma, a relation can be obtained between the Allen elasticities and the price elasticities:

$$s_i \cdot \sigma_{ij}^A = s_i \cdot \frac{C(\partial x_i / \partial p_j)}{x_i x_j} = \frac{(\partial x_i / \partial p_j)}{(x_i / p_j)} = \varepsilon_{ij}$$

One of the major advantages of the translog function is that the elasticities ε_{ij} and σ_{ij} are not, *a priori*, constant but depend on the cost shares. To obtain the explicit derivation, it is best to compute the Allen elasticities first. The use of the translog cost function yields:

$$\sigma_{ij}^A = \begin{cases} \dfrac{\gamma_{ij} + s_i s_j}{s_i s_j} & \text{for } i \neq j \\[2ex] \dfrac{\gamma_{ii} + s_i^2 - s_i}{s_i^2} & \text{for } i = j \end{cases}$$

Having computed the Allen elasticities, the fundamental relation shown above can be used to obtain the price and substitution elasticities:

$$\varepsilon_{ij} = s_i \sigma_{ij}^A = \begin{cases} \dfrac{\gamma_{ij} + s_i s_j}{s_j} & \text{for } i \neq j \\[2ex] \dfrac{\gamma_{ii} + s_i^2 - s_i}{s_i} & \text{for } i = j \end{cases}$$

Assuming a multi-product industry sector, we can also explain the effects of a change in the product mix. For this purpose we define an input/output elasticity Θ_{ik}, which tells us what happens to the input x_i if the output Q_k changes:

$$\Theta_{ik} = \frac{\partial \ln x_i}{\partial \ln Q_k}$$

$p = \text{constant}, Q_l = \text{constant, for } l \neq k.$

We will calculate the input/output elasticities Θ_{ik} from the ith cost share:

$$s_i = \alpha_i + \sum_{j=1}^{j=n} \gamma_{ij} \ln p_j + \sum_{k=1}^{k=m} \delta_{ik} \ln Q_k$$

Use of the cost shares then yields:

$$\frac{\partial x_i}{\partial \ln Q_k} = \frac{\delta_{ik}}{s_i} + \frac{\partial \ln C}{\partial \ln Q_k} = \frac{\delta_{ik}}{s_i} + \beta_k + \sum_{j=1}^{j=n} \delta_{jk} \ln p_j + \sum_{l=1}^{l=m} \vartheta_{lk} \ln Q_l \ .$$

7. APPLICATION TO A REAL DATA SET: PRELIMINARY RESULTS

The approach described in the preceding sections has been applied to a series of make and use tables for the Canadian economy covering the period 1961–1978. The data are expressed in terms of both actual and constant 1971 dollar producer prices and were supplied by Statistics Canada. We utilized the M (medium) aggregation level, in which these rectangular tables are classified into 43 industries and 92 commodities. The approach described below was applied to the "primary metal" industry. The outputs were aggregated into three commodities, as shown in Table 1, while the six inputs shown in Table 2 were distinguished.

TABLE 1. Outputs of the Canadian basic metal industries in 1971.

Output	10^6 Dollars	% of total
Iron and steel	2019.4	39.5
Nonferrous metals	2587.7	50.5
Other	512.0	10.0
Total	5119.1	100.0

TABLE 2. Inputs into the Canadian basic metal industries in 1971.

Input	10^6 Dollars	% of total
Iron ores and concentrates	151.1	3.0
Other metal ores and concentrates	1284.5	25.1
Energy	265.9	5.2
Basic metal products	879.2	17.2
Other inputs (including margins, indirect taxes)	918.2	17.9
GDP at factor costs	1620.2	31.6
Total	5119.1	100.0

For each of these six inputs a producer price index[2] was calculated.

The results of the analysis presented in this section are rather preliminary in nature: the significance of the elasticities has not yet been tested and therefore caution should be exercized with any interpretation of the results.

Table 3 presents a second-order approximation of the commodity-by-commodity IO coefficients for the base year (1971).

We restricted nonferrous ore input to basic ferrous products and ferrous ore input to basic nonferrous products. The input coefficients for "other inputs" are calculated as a residual. With relatively few exceptions, the estimates for the commodity-by-commodity coefficients seem to be reasonable: all negative coefficients are insignificant, and steel production requires much more energy per

---

[2] For this preliminary report no attempt was made to calculate margins or indirect taxes on the commodity inputs so that purchasers' price indexes could be derived.

TABLE 3.   Approximation of commodity-by-commodity IO coefficients for the Canadian basic metal industries in 1971 (t-values in parentheses).

Input	Output		
	Iron and steel products	Nonferrous metal products	Other products
Iron ores	0.056	0	0.067
	(7.6)		(2.6)
Nonferrous ores	0	0.540	-0.179
		(13.9)	(1.0)
Energy	0.126	0.023	-0.029
	(6.2)	(1.1)	(0.4)
Metal products	0.274	-0.058	0.541
	(7.1)	(1.6)	(5.1)
GDP at factor costs	0.315	0.343	0.103
	(14.1)	(13.0)	(1.0)
Other inputs	0.231	0.153	0.497

unit of output (value) than does the production of nonferrous metals. Statistics
Canada (1978) reported that, in Canada in 1971, 209 GJ was required per 1000 $
worth of output of the iron and steel industries, while for the aluminum or copper
industries the corresponding values were 163 GJ and 8 GJ, respectively.

As nonferrous ores are much more expensive than iron ores, the high non-
ferrous-ore input coefficient and the correspondingly small iron-ore coefficients
seem reasonable. On the other hand, it is not reasonable that the production of
"other products" should require more ferrous ores than does basic ferrous metal
production. No attempt has been made to estimate a time series of commodity-by-
commodity IO coefficients.

The influence of prices and changing output structures on the input requirements of the basic metal industries is demonstrated by a set of the relevant elasticities. To begin with, the symmetric Allen elasticities of substitution are presented in
Table 4.

TABLE 4.   Allen elasticities of substitution for the Canadian basic metal industries
in 1977.

	Nonferrous ores	Energy	Metal products	Other inputs	Value added
Iron ores	0.042	0.009	-0.003	-0.078	0.226
Nonferrous ores		0.001	-0.170	-0.104	-0.044
Energy			0.002	-0.012	0.138
Metal products					0.051
Other inputs					0.087

No large elasticities of substitution were found, thus indicating that relative
prices have only a small impact on input relations. GDP is found to be a partial sub-
stitute for ores and for energy. As might be expected, metal products are not substitutes for energy or ores, but are complementary to nonferrous ores. It seems reasonable that all inputs (trade and transport margins, taxes, overheads) are complementary to most of the inputs.

Own-price elasticities were calculated for all of the inputs. For energy, GDP, ferrous ores, and other inputs, negative elasticities were found. Table 5 presents a time series of own-price elasticities and Allen elasticities of substitution for energy and GDP expressed in terms of value added.

TABLE 5. Own-price elasticities ($\varepsilon_E, \varepsilon_{VA}$) and Allen elasticities of substitution ($\sigma^A_{E, VA}$) for energy and GDP (VA) for the Canadian basic metal industries, 1961–1977.

Year	ε_E	ε_{VA}	$\sigma^A_{E, VA}$
1961	-0.326	-0.730	0.154
1962	-0.271	-0.726	0.161
1963	-0.273	-0.723	0.164
1964	-0.212	-0.725	0.168
1965	-0.190	-0.714	0.178
1966	-0.185	-0.718	0.175
1967	-0.167	-0.740	0.161
1968	-0.156	-0.743	0.160
1969	-0.124	-0.736	0.168
1970	-0.212	-0.759	0.144
1971	-0.273	-0.732	0.157
1972	-0.300	-0.733	0.154
1973	-0.260	-0.749	0.147
1974	-0.378	-0.776	0.119
1975	-0.475	-0.760	0.120
1976	-0.480	-0.775	0.111
1977	-0.468	-0.733	0.138

A relatively large and constant own-price elasticity, varying smoothly in the region of -0.75, was found for GDP, indicating that there has been a significant and constant impetus to increase the productivity of primary inputs.

Comparatively smaller own-price elasticities were found for energy, and these varied over time with a characteristic pattern. In the course of the sixties, when real energy prices went down, elasticities moved from -0.32% to -0.12%. In the seventies, when energy became more expensive, the sensitivity of energy use to price grew again noticeably. This is reflected in the growth of the own-price elasticity, which jumped from -0.26 in 1973 to -0.48 in 1975.

The Allen elasticities of substitution for GDP and energy are rather small. The most surprising result is that, especially from 1971 to 1976, substitution elasticities fell. In 1977 the Allen elasticities started to increase again. To summarize: price-sensitive changes in the own-price elasticities for energy indicate that rising energy prices are likely to improve energy efficiency, while the relatively small and price-insensitive elasticities of substitution show us that rising energy prices do not stimulate substitution between energy and value added in the short term. The increase in the Allen elasticity noted for 1977 may indicate that there exists a time lag of about three years between a change in energy price and a response in terms of substitution behavior.

Finally, the changes in the inputs resulting from changes in the outputs were analyzed using the IO elasticities shown in Table 6.

Output elasticities for nonferrous ores varied around 1, indicating that the corresponding IO coefficients are rather stable, while the elasticities for iron ores

TABLE 6. Selected IO elasticities for the Canadian basic metal sector in 1965, 1970, and 1975.

Outputs				Inputs		
	Year	Iron ores	NF ores	Energy	Metals	GDP
Ferrous	1965	0.767	0	0.965	0.781	0.412
metal	1970	0.758	0	0.919	0.772	0.387
	1975	0.756	0	0.766	0.788	0.452
Non-	1965	0	1.105	0.153	-0.206	0.566
ferrous	1970	0	1.055	0.187	-0.219	0.597
metals	1975	0	1.109	0.245	-0.204	0.517

were somewhat lower at around 0.75, showing that the iron ores coefficients are not only affected by the output of ferrous metal but also by other factors.

Both the energy and the metal elasticities are different for the two groups of output. Therefore it seems that shifts in product mix influence both the energy and the metal input coefficients for the industry as a whole. The energy elasticities of around 0.9 noted in the sixties and early seventies indicated that the energy/output ratio for ferrous metal was relatively constant, while the declining elasticities since 1975 show again that there have been some attempts to save energy since the first oil shock. The negative elasticities calculated for metals transformed into nonferrous metals output are not significant.

REFERENCES

Andersson, A., R. Brännlund, and G. Kornai (1984). *The Demand for Forest Sector Products*. Working Paper WP-84-87. International Institute for Applied Systems Analysis, Laxenburg, Austria.

Bonnici, J. (1983). The relevance of input substitution in the interindustry model. *European Economic Review*, 22.

Christenson, L.R., D.W. Jorgenson, and L.J. Lau (1973). Transcendal logarithmic production frontiers. *Review of Economics and Statistics*, 55(1).

Forssell, O. (1969). Statistical unit, classification and aggregation in Finnish input-output study. In *International Comparison of Interindustry Data*. Industrial Planning and Programming Series, No. 2. United Nations, New York.

Frenger, P. (1978). Factor substitution in the interindustry model and the use of inconsistent aggregation. In M. Fuss and D. McFaddon (Eds.), *Production Economics: Approach to Theory and Applications*. Vol. 2. North-Holland, Amsterdam.

Klein, L.R. (1952). On the interrelation of Professor Leontief's system. *Review of Economic Studies*, 20(2).

Lager, C. (1983). Analysis of energy coefficients in Austria, 1964–1980. In A. Smyshlyaev (Ed.), *Proceedings of the Fourth IIASA Task Force Meeting on Input–Output Modeling*. CP-83-S5. International Institute for Applied Systems Analysis, Laxenburg, Austria.

Nakamura, S. (1984). An interindustry translog model of prices and technical change for the West German economy. *Lecture Notes in Economics and Mathematical Systems*, No. 221.

Sevaldson, P. (1960). Cited in Frenger (1978).

Statistics Canada (1978). *Energy Availability, Detailed Disposition and Industrial Demand Coefficients for Canada, 1971.*

Tilanus, C.B. (1966). *Input—Output Experiments, The Netherlands 1948—1960.* Rotterdam University Press, Rotterdam.

UN (1968). *A System of National Accounts.* United Nations, New York.

ON THE ENDOGENOUS DETERMINATION
OF IMPORT COEFFICIENTS IN AN INPUT—OUTPUT MODEL:
THEORETICAL AND PRACTICAL PROBLEMS

Laura Grassini

Faculty of Law, University of Florence, Florence, Italy

1. INTRODUCTION

The role of imports is of crucial importance in a country like Italy where they largely contribute to the amount of disposable resources. As described in Grassini (1983) the ratio of sectoral imports to sectoral domestic demand has been increasing during the last years for a large number of input—output sectors. From that derives the need of a careful analysis of imports by sectors in order to evaluate the effects of foreign prices on domestic prices and domestic demand. This can be done using input—output (i/o) models.

Here we present an application of the i/o framework in the computation of imports coefficients. This work is a part of a project for building a modern i/o model of the Italian economy: the Intimo (Interindustry Italian Model) model.

In the Intimo model the econometric specification of the sectoral imports is one of the dominant components of the model. In such a case we need an endogenous determination of imports coefficients in order to make the estimates of sectoral imports compatible with the imports implied by total output, derived from the solution of the Leontief equation. This is accomplished by a model which is a part of the standard Inforum type model (Almon, 1979).

In this paper the analytical procedure of the adjustment criterion is described and the numerical technique is analyzed. Some problems concerning endogenous determination of imports coefficients in an economy where some sectoral imports are very high with respect to domestic demand and the simultaneous treatment of total and imports coefficients are discussed.

(*) This research has been supported by a CNR grant, contratto n. 83.02360.53.

2. THE MODEL

Given $V = \{v_{ij}\}$ the intermediate consumption matrix and final demand components from an i/o table, we have (Fig. 1):

$$V = V' + V'' \tag{1}$$

with $V' = \{v'_{ij}\}$ is intermediate and final consumption covered with domestic production and $V'' = \{v''_{ij}\}$ the amount covered with imports (i=1,..,n; j=1,...,r; n is the number of i/o sectors and r-n the number of the final demand components). We can define the import share matrix $M = \{m_{ij}\}$ where

$$m_{ij} = v''_{ij} / v_{ij} \tag{2}$$

represents the import share of each flow.

Then, by definition:

$$u_0 = (M_0 \odot V_0)\, h \tag{3}$$

is the amount of imports by sectors at base year (time 0) where h is the column sum vector and $\odot$ denotes the element by element product.

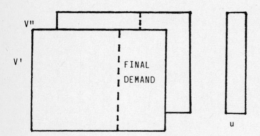

V''

V'

FINAL
DEMAND

u

FIGURE 1   Representation of V matrix and u vector

Moving from the base year at each time t (t=1,2,..) we have estimates $\hat{u}_t$ and $\hat{V}_t$ of sectoral imports u_t and matrix V_t : the former ones from econometric equations, the latter ones from the model for changes in technical coefficients (Nyhus,1983) and from the solution of the Leontief equation for the part of intermediate consumption; from econometric equations and exogenous informations for the part of final demand. Using matrix M we have the imports vector derived from an account identity:

$$\hat{u}_t = (M_0 \odot \hat{V}_t)\, h \tag{4}$$

where, generally, $\hat{u}_t \neq \hat{\hat{u}}_t$. The discrepancies are assumed due to modifications in matrix M.

Let us suppose that m_{ijt} is a function of m_{ij0} (where m_{ij0} and m_{ijt} are respectively the elements of matrix M at time 0 and t) as follows:

$$m_{ijt} = \begin{cases} 0 & \text{if } m_{ij0} = 0 \\ \dfrac{m_{ij0}}{m_{ij0} + k_{it}(1-m_{ij0})} & \text{if } 0 < m_{ij0} < 1 \end{cases} \qquad (5)$$

where $k_{it} \geq 0$ and $0 < m_{ijt} \leq 1$ (Fig. 2).

Furthermore we notice that

$$m_{ijt} \gtreqless m_{ij0} \qquad \text{for} \qquad k_{it} \lessgtr 1$$

with the implicit assumption that if the "content" of imports is increasing, low imports shares are growing faster and high imports shares are growing slower and viceversa.

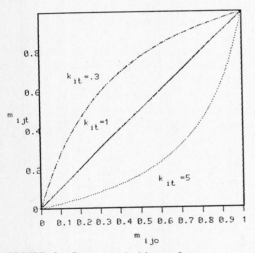

FIGURE 2 Representation of m_{ijt} vs. m_{ij0}

3. THE NUMERICAL PROCEDURE

Independently from the structural changes of i/o coefficients which take place along the time according to the model described in Nyhus (1983), matrix M is allowed to vary in order to match the estimated imports at time t and the imports implied by the imports share matrix. Using (5) we are faced with equations of the type:

$$F(k_{it}) = \sum_{j=1}^{r} m_{ijt} \, \hat{v}_{ijt} - \hat{u}_{it} = 0 \tag{6}$$

which are non linear in k_{it} and where $\hat{u}_{it}$ represents the i-th element of vector $\hat{u}_t$. The computation of k_{it} can be done resorting to the Newton method; the value k_{it}^{s} (the value of k_{it} at the s-th iteration is given by

$$k_{it}^{s} = k_{it}^{s-1} - F(k_{it}^{s-1})/F'(k_{it}^{s-1}) \tag{7}$$

where $F'(k_{it}^{s-1})$ is the first derivative of (7) with respect to k_{it} with $k_{it} = k_{it}^{s-1}$.

Once we have made clear what we expect from (5) on solving (6), we must be aware about the convergence of the procedure. It is possible to state a set of sufficient conditions which guarantee the convergence of the Newton procedure (Fontanella, Pasquali, 1978).

Let be $g(x) = 0$ the equation to be verified for $x = \bar{x} \in [a,b]$, where $g(x)$ is a continuous and derivable (at least up to the second derivative) function in $[a,b]$. In such cases the Newton method converges if

1. $g(a) \cdot g(b) < 0$
2. $sign(g'(x))$ is constant for each $x \in [a,b]$
3. $sign(g''(x))$ is constant for each $x \in [a,b]$
4. $g(x^{0}) \cdot g''(x^{0}) > 0$

where x^{0} is the starting value for x, $g'(x)$ and $g''(x)$ are, respectively, the first and the second derivatives of $g(x)$ with respect to x.

Let us consider the single element m_{ijt} as a function of k_{it} according to (5); then we have:

$$\lim_{k_{it} \to 0} m_{ijt} = 1 \qquad \lim_{k_{it} \to \infty} m_{ijt} = 0$$

$$\partial m_{ijt} / \partial k_{it} < 0 \tag{8}$$

$$\partial^2 m_{ijt} / \partial k_{it}^2 > 0.$$

Since the derivative of a sum of (derivable) functions is equal to the sum of the corresponding derivatives and at least one $\hat{v}_{ijt} > 0$, we have, for $F(k_{it})$, the following analytical properties:

$$\lim_{k_{it} \to 0} F(k_{it}) = \sum_{j=1}^{r} \hat{v}_{ijt} - \hat{u}_{it} > 0 \qquad \lim_{k_{it} \to \infty} F(k_{it}) = 0$$

$$\partial F(k_{it}) / \partial k_{it} = \sum_{j=1}^{r} \partial m_{ijt} / \partial k_{it} \; \hat{v}_{ijt} < 0 \tag{9}$$

$$\partial^2 F(k_{it}) / \partial k_{it}^2 = \sum_{j=1}^{r} \partial m_{ijt} / \partial k_{it} \; \hat{v}_{ijt} > 0.$$

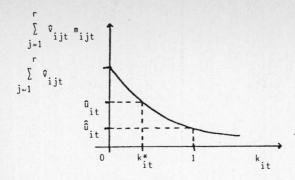

FIGURE 3   Representation of expression (6)

As it results from expressions in (9) and Fig. 3, the sufficient conditions 1,2,3 are verified in an interval $0 \leqslant k_{it} \leqslant k_2 < \infty$ where k_2 is any positive value of k_{it} such that $F(k_2) < 0$. Furthermore since $k_{it} = 0$ always satisfies the 4.th condition – apart from the case when $k_{it} = 0$ is just the solution – the iterative procedure converges for $k_{it}^0 = 0$ where k_{it}^0 is the starting value of k_{it}.

4. PRACTICAL PROBLEMS IN THE APPLICATION OF THE MODEL

Some questions may arise in the application of the model. The first one regards the value of $\hat{v}_{ijt}$ which may be also negative (Inventory changes). However we can retain that, in practice, such negative values are not so high, with respect to the intermediate and the other final flows, as to prevent the convergence of the iterative procedure.

Other questions arise when some m_{ij0} is equal to 1. It is not surprising with data referring to a small open economy where the availability of some products is strictly dependent on foreign production. In such a case the unity values are put equal to .999... according to the computer precision level, in order to allow the application of the model.

When each non-zero value of m_{ij0} is close to 1 problems may be more relevant. It means that almost the total amount of the i-th product derives from imports and the domestic production of sector i is close to zero. This situation may produce some troubles even in the solution of the Leontief equation performed by the Gauss-Seidel procedure. In such cases the adjustment of output's values, which should be close to zero, may produce significative non-zero (also negative) values due to interaction between output and inventories which are endogenously determined. A way to maintain data consistency is to introduce fixed values on output. Following this approach the Leontief equation should be recomputed at least for that sector i with fixed output:

$$\hat{q}_{it} = \text{fixed.} \tag{10}$$

For this aim one could recalculate, (apart imports if they are endogenous) final demand components or change only one of them, for example inventories. However, when imports and final demand components are given, then a fixed output implies a forced readjustment of technical coefficients.

In a more general context this problem can be formalized as follows. Let us consider the relation

$$\hat{v}_{i.t} = \sum_{j=1}^{r} \hat{v}_{ijt} \neq \hat{q}_{it} + \hat{u}_{it} \tag{11}$$

where $\hat{u}_{it}$ are imports treated as exogenous of sector i at time t and $\hat{v}_{ijt}$ is the i-th, j-th flow as described in section 2.

When (11) occurs and final demand components are given, then we can reconduce to the part

$$_n\hat{q}_{it} + _n\hat{u}_{it} \tag{12}$$

referred to intermediate flows. The new flow $\hat{v}^o_{ijt}$ for j=1,2,...,n summing up to (12) can be calculated as follows:

$$\hat{v}^o_{ijt} = \hat{v}_{ijt} + [(_n\hat{q}_{it} + _n\hat{u}_{it}) - _n\hat{v}_{i.t}] \cdot \hat{v}_{ijt} / _n\hat{v}_{i.t} \tag{13}$$

where

$$_n\hat{v}_{i.t} = \sum_{j=1}^{n} \hat{v}_{ijt} .$$

The use of such a "spreader" keeps the distribution of intermediate consumption among user sectors unchanged, that is: $\hat{v}^o_{ijt}/_n\hat{v}^o_{i.t} = \hat{v}_{ijt}/_n\hat{v}_{i.t}$ where $_n\hat{v}^o_{i.t} = _n\hat{q}_{it} + _n\hat{u}_{it}$ .The new technical coefficient will be:

$$\hat{a}^o_{ijt} = \hat{v}^o_{ijt} / \hat{q}_{jt} \tag{14}$$

where $\hat{q}_{jt}$ is output derived from the Leontief equation if $j \neq i$, from exogenous informations if j=i. Then the model for the endogenous determination of imports coefficients may be applied.

5. THE DATA

The data used for the application, which covers the period 1975-1983, are derived from different sources.

From the data set of the Intimo model are drawn data on the i/o matrix and i/o imports coefficients at base year (1975).

A time series on technical coefficients is produced by the model for i/o coefficients changes, based on logistic curves, as described in Nyhus (1983).

From the econometric side of the model data on sectoral imports and exports (Barnabani, 1983) and data on final demand components (Ciaschini, 1982; Grassini, 1983a) are derived.

Finally, by the i/o structure of the model (real side) and from exogenous informations data on sectoral output are obtained.

6. RESULTS AND COMMENTS

In the application of the model for the endogeneous determination of imports coefficients to Italian data, the 6-th sector Nuclear Fuel represents the specific case described in section 4. The availability of that product depends totally on foreign production then output is fixed equal to zero. In such a situation expressions (11) and (12) coincide, respectively, with $\hat{u}_{it}$ and $_n\hat{u}_{it}$, then (13) reduces to a redistribution of imports among user sectors.

Table 1 shows the values of technical coefficients of the row-sector Nuclear fuel of the Italian economy, referred to the base year (a_{6j0}), to each year t (t=1,2,...,8) as it results from the model for changes in technical coefficients ($\hat{a}_{6jt}$) and from the new flows ($\hat{a}^{\circ}_{6jt}$) as computed in expression (14).

As it results from Table 1, expression (11) sometimes occurs: in general $\hat{v}_{6.t} < \hat{u}_{6t} + \hat{q}_{6t}$, where $\hat{q}_{6t} = 0$. In some cases (years 1978 and 1979) significative changes in technical coefficients are introduced.

Since the adjustment procedure described in section 5 is applied to only one sector and there is not a high interdependence between Nuclear fuel and the other i/o sectors, we believe that no serious consequences for the coherence of the model may be produced.

Some results of the application are presented in Table 2: it shows a time series of imports for intermediate use for the 25 Italian sectors producing goods.

The application of the model for the endogenous determination of imports coefficients has shown as, in some situations, the use of fixed output can be considered. From the other hand the introduction of fixes on production is a delicate operation which requires a valid adjustment criterion in order to maintain data consistency between the real and the price sides of the model.

This methodological exercise represents just an extreme situation where the changes of technical coefficients do not produce a relevant contrast between the real and the price sides. However, in this context, the choice of changing technical coefficients seems to be the most riskful operation.

Apart from the practical considerations of section 4, we can assume that situations may occur, in which the level of output is known or must be fixed. Then the question about the use of fixes for output should be carefully analyzed in a more general way: with respect to the economic meaning of the operation and the adjustment criterion and with respect to the numerical procedure to be applied.

170

TABLE 1   Technical coefficients of the 6-th row sector Nuclear Fuel
----

| YEARS | | COLUMN | SECTORS | |
	j = 5	31	38	42
1975 a_{6j0}	.00151	.00003	.00006	.00023
1976 $\hat{a}_{6j1}$	.00161	.00003	.00007	.00025
1977 $\hat{a}_{6j2}$	.00181	.00003	.00007	.00028
$\hat{a}°_{6j2}$	.00541	.00009	.00022	.00083
1978 $\hat{a}_{6j3}$	.00197	.00003	.00008	.00030
$\hat{a}°_{6j3}$	.00435	.00008	.00017	.00066
1979 $\hat{a}_{6j4}$	.00213	.00004	.00008	.00033
$\hat{a}°_{6j4}$	.01356	.00023	.00054	.00207
1980 $\hat{a}_{6j5}$	.00229	.00004	.00009	.00035
1981 $\hat{a}_{6j6}$	.00244	.00004	.00010	.00037
$\hat{a}°_{6j6}$	.00306	.00005	.00012	.00047
1982 $\hat{a}_{6j7}$	.00259	.00004	.00010	.00040
$\hat{a}°_{6j7}$	.00333	.00006	.00013	.00030
1983 $\hat{a}_{6j8}$	.00273	.00005	.00011	.00042
$\hat{a}°_{6j8}$	.00352	.00006	.00014	.00054

5 : Electricity, water   31 : Inland transports
38 : Private education services 42 : Public education services
----

TABLE 2 Time series of imports for intermediate use at constant prices

SECTOR	75	76	77	78	79	80	81	82	83
Agriculture	2900	3276	3118	3442	3679	3632	3801	3890	3910
Coal	477	459	482	464	473	619	448	440	421
Coke	10	10	11	9	12	7	7	6	6
Oil	6157	6559	6514	7060	7230	6728	6861	6861	6696
Electricity	233	292	391	313	346	344	398	407	410
Nuclear feul	9	9	39	35	119	15	30	33	35
Fe/non Fe	2205	2909	2849	2841	3473	4027	3682	3701	3653
Non metals	401	477	503	490	614	745	745	691	660
Chemical p.	1886	2443	2414	2714	3178	3241	2974	2932	2888
Metal p.	188	215	178	204	244	324	298	313	341
Machinery	506	535	527	552	576	674	627	561	507
Precis. inst.	76	68	53	87	95	124	125	122	121
Elect. goods	696	880	959	897	1050	1237	1240	1215	1181
Motor vehic.	318	421	457	527	574	721	669	652	606
Other trans.	152	179	186	197	205	211	184	177	176
Meat	594	606	622	660	694	715	732	753	766
Milk, diary	280	306	320	321	348	372	341	340	336
Other foods	509	556	579	565	707	728	663	671	667
Beverages	65	72	72	80	94	99	103	111	107
Textiles	480	651	609	841	1072	1099	803	684	574
Leather	126	194	182	210	299	277	227	195	165
Wood, forn.	328	452	433	449	563	635	637	653	655
Paper	481	651	631	793	961	1073	930	1065	947
Rubber	218	334	342	365	457	513	526	529	530
Other manif.	29	36	40	52	61	72	71	71	71

REFERENCES

Almon, C. (1979). The Inforum-IIASA International System of Input-Output Models. WP-79-22. International Institute for Applied System Analysis, Laxenburg, Austria.

Barnabani, M. (1983). Un'analisi del commercio italiano con l'estero disaggregato per branca produttiva. Tesi di Laurea in Economia e Commercio. Università di Firenze. Anno Accademico 1982-83.

Ciaschini, M. (1982). Modern Input-Output Models as Simulation Tools for Policy Making. In M. Grassini and A. Smyshlyaev (Eds.), Input-Output Modeling. CP-83-S2. International Institute for Applied System Analysis, Laxenburg, Austria.

Fontanella, F., A. Pasquali (1978). Calcolo numerico. Metodi ed algoritmi. Vol. 1. Pitagora Editrice, Bologna.

Grassini, M. (1983). Structural Changes in Italian Foreign Trade. In A. Smyshlyaev (Eds.), Proceedings of the Fourth IIASA Task Force Meeting on Input-Output Modeling (1983). CP-83-S5. International Institute for Applied System Analysis, Laxenburg, Austria.

Grassini, M. (1983a). A System of Demand Equations for Medium-to-long term Forecasting with Input-Output Econometric Models. In Economic Notes, n. 2, 1983.

Nyhus, D. (1983). Observing Structural Changes in the Japanese Economy: an Input-Output Approach. In A. Smyshlyaev (Ed.), Proceedings of the Fourth IIASA Task Force Meeting on Input-Output Modeling (1983). CP-83-S5. International Institute for Applied System Analysis. Laxenburg, Austria.

INPUT—OUTPUT TECHNIQUES
IN THE JAPANESE ECONOMETRIC MODEL

Ryoichi Nishimiya

International Institute for Applied Systems Analysis,
Laxenburg, Austria

1. INTRODUCTION

The energy problem is one of the most serious problems facing Japan. The greater part of Japan's energy consumption depends on oil, but its domestic production of oil is practically zero. It is well known that before the oil crisis in 1973 Japan enjoyed a high rate of economic growth; the average growth rate of GNP during the 1960s was about 10 percent per year. After the oil crisis the growth rate of GNP has strikingly slowed down to an average of about four percent. In addition, the Japanese inflation rate was relatively moderate before the oil crisis; the average rate of change of the wholesale price index was about one percent per year. Since the oil crisis this has risen to about six percent per year.

The main purpose of this study is to make a quantitative analysis of the energy problems of the Japanese economy by constructing an appropriate econometric model.

2. THE DISAGGREGATION OF FINAL DEMAND

The model is an annual aggregative model of the Keynesian type, whose sample period is 1961—1979. In general, the method of estimation used is ordinary least squares. Some of the equations are estimated using the Cochrane—Orcutt iterative method.

It should be noted that the number of observations for the annual model is usually small; it is 19 in our model. This often leads to multicolinearity in the estimation of parameters. In addition, the explanatory variables of the equations of the energy model will include energy variables as well as ordinary economic ones, and therefore the number of the explanatory variables in each equation will increase. This means that the multicolinearity problem is likely to be more serious in the energy model than in the ordinary economic one. Therefore, in estimating some of the equations, we tried to utilize outside information such as estimates from cross-sectional studies and input—output coefficients. This procedure has enabled us to obtain a model that describes the economic aspects of the Japanese energy problem in some detail, in spite of the fact that time series data were available only for a limited number of years.

As regards the specification of the model, we constructed it with three characteristics in order to deal with the energy problem, as will be explained in this and the two following sections. The first characteristic of the model is the disaggregation of final demand. In connection with energy demand, we disaggregated consumption C into four categories and commodity imports MC into two categories.

Total consumption consists of consumption for foods CF, for auto and auto fuel CEA, for heating fuel CEH, and for other purposes CO.

Total consumption is explained in terms of disposable income, holdings of financial assets at the beginning of each year, lagged consumption, and the Gini coefficient. Each variable, except for the last of these, is expressed in both real and per capita terms.

CF, CEH, and CEA are explained in terms of total consumption and relative prices.

Commodity imports consist of imports of energy (oil and coal)ME, and others MO. MO is explained in terms of GNP and the price variable $PMO \cdot RATE / PVM$, where PMO is the deflator for MO(dollar base), $RATE$ is the index of the exchange rate, and PVM is the deflator for gross domestic supply.

3. INPUT—OUTPUT TECHNIQUES

The second main characteristic of our model is the application of the input—output technique to price equations in order to trace out the influence of the oil price rise on the price configuration of the whole economy. In the model prices are disaggregated into six industry prices:

P_1: Price for primary industry, excluding crude oil,

P_2: Price of crude oil,

P_3: Price for manufacturing, excluding petroleum and coal products,

P_4: Price of petroleum and coal products,

P_5: Price for tertiary industry,

P_6: Price of electric power and gas.

Within the input—output analysis, the price for industry i is given by:

$$P_i = \sum_{j=1}^{6} A(j,i) \cdot P_j + WNV_i \cdot W + D(i) \cdot PIF + S(i) \cdot P_i + T(i) \cdot P_i, \qquad (A.1)$$

or

$$P_i = (\sum_{\substack{j=1 \\ j \neq i}}^{6} A(j,i) \cdot P_j + WNV_i \cdot W + D(i) \cdot PIF / (1 - A(i,i) - T(i) - S(i)). \qquad (A.2)$$

Here $A(j,i)$, WNV_i, $D(i)$, $S(i)$, and $T(i)$ are input coefficients, labor input coefficients, depreciation ratio, surplus ratio, and indirect tax ratio, respectively. These coefficients, which represent the technical and institutional structure of each industry, were adopted from the input—output tables in 1975 prices. Input—output tables in constant prices are directly available for the base years, i.e. 1960, 1965, 1970, 1975, and for other years we have estimated by linear interpolation between successive pairs of base years. W and PIF are the wage rate and the deflator for fixed investment, respectively.

In years for which the input—output table is available, the observed prices and technical coefficients satisfy the above equations exactly. But in other years this is not the case, in general. Therefore we defined a constructed variable $P_i IO$ as in eqn. (4.1), and regressed the actual price of each industry on the corresponding $P_i IO$. This implies that prices are determined mainly by their cost structures. In the price equations for industries 1, 3, and 5, the index of capacity utilization was also introduced in order to allow for the influence of the demand and supply relation on price formation. Equations (4.2) to (4.10) present the estimated results of such price equations. P_1 and P_6 are further disaggregated into domestic and import prices (eqns. (4.3) and (4.10)); the former is given by the above scheme (eqns. (4.2) and (4.8)) and the latter is assumed to be exogenous. The oil price in yen, P_8, is defined as the product of the oil price in dollars and the exchange rate, where the former is treated as exogenous.

4. REPRESENTATION OF THE SUPPLY SIDE

The third characteristic of the model is that the supply side of the economy is represented by a neoclassical production function of the two-level CES type:

$$\ln X_i = \ln G(i) - \frac{1}{\rho(i)} \ln\left[\left(\sum_{j=1}^{6} \delta(j,i)\cdot X_{ji}^{-\rho(i)} + \varphi(i)\cdot V_i^{-\rho(i)}\right)\right] \qquad (A.3)$$

$$\ln V_i = \ln H(i) - \frac{1}{\vartheta(i)} \ln\left[\lambda(i)\cdot L_i^{-\vartheta(i)} + \kappa(i)\cdot K_i^{-\vartheta(i)}\right], \quad i=1,2,...,6. \qquad (A.4)$$

Here,

X_i = output of industry i,

X_{ji} = output j used in industry i,

L_i = labor input to industry i,

K_i = capital stock of industry i,

$G(i), \rho(i), \delta(j,i), \varphi(i), H(i), \vartheta(i), \lambda(i), \kappa(i)$ = parameters.

The elasticity of substitution between material inputs $\sigma(i)$ and that between labor and capital inputs $\mu(i)$ are respectively represented by:

$\sigma(i) = 1/(1 + \rho(i))$,

$\mu(i) = 1/(1 + \vartheta(i))$.

Cost per unit of output X_i is defined as:

$$C_i = \sum_{j=1}^{6} A(j,i)P_j + WNV_i\cdot W_i + CA_i\cdot PK, \qquad (A.5)$$

where

$A(j,i)$ = material input j per unit of output i,

WVN_i = labor input per unit of output i,

CA_i = capital input per unit of output i.

Minimizing C_i, subject to eqns. (A.3) and (A.4) and $X_i = 1$, will yield:

$$\ln A(j,i) = (\sigma(i)-1)\ln G(i) + \sigma(i)\ln\delta(j,i) + \sigma(i)\ln(C_i/P_j),$$

$$j,i=1,2,...,6; \qquad (A.6)$$

$$\ln VA(i) = (\sigma(i)-1)\ln G(i) + \sigma(i)\ln\varphi(i) + \sigma(i)\ln(C_i/PV_i)$$

$$i=1,2,...,6; \qquad (A.7)$$

where

$$VA(i) = V_i / X_i,$$

PV_i = deflator for value added of industry i;

and

$$\ln WNV_i = (\mu(i)-1)\ln H(i) + \mu(i)\ln\lambda(i) + \mu(i)\ln(PV_i / W_i),$$

$$\ln CA_i = (\mu(i) - 1)\ln H(i) + \mu(i)\ln\kappa(i) + \mu(i)\ln(PV_i / PK),$$

$$i = 1,2,\ldots,6. \tag{A.8}$$

In estimating eqns. (A.6) and (A.7) we assume that C_i is equal to P_i. For industry i, observation of $A(j,i)$ $(j=1,2,\ldots,6)$, $VA(i)$, P_i / P_j $(j=1,2,\ldots,6)$, and P_i / PV_i will enable us to estimate $\sigma(i)$, $(\sigma(i)-1)\ln G(i)$ and $\sigma(i)\ln\delta(j,i)$ $(j=1,2,\ldots 6)$. By pooling input coefficients for the three base years $A(j,i)_t$ and $VA(i)_t$, and the price variables corresponding to each base year,

$$\frac{1}{2}\left\{(P_i / P_j)_{t-1} + (P_i / P_j)_{t-2}\right\} \text{ and } \frac{1}{2}\left\{(P_i / PV_i)_{t-1} + (P_i / PV_i)_{t-2}\right\}$$

we estimated eqns. (5.1) to (5.5). $DA(j,i)$ is defined to be unity when the explained variable is $A(j,i)$ and zero otherwise. Thus the constant term (e.g., -2.148 in eqn. (5.1)) is an estimate of $(\sigma(i)-1)\ln G(i) + \sigma(i)\delta(i,i)$, while the coefficient of $DA(j,i)$ is an estimate of the difference between $\sigma(i)\delta(j,i)$ and $\sigma(i)\delta(i,i)$. Similarly, the coefficient of $DV(i)$, which is unity when the explained variable is $VA(i)$ and zero otherwise, is an estimate of the difference between $\sigma(i)\varphi(i)$ and $\sigma(i)\delta(i,i)$. The results show that the elasticity of substitution $\sigma(i)$ is close to unity for industries 1(1.161), 4(0.900), and 6(1.094), while it is 1.346 and 0.627 for industries 3 and 5, respectively. In the estimation the deflator for gross national supply, PVM, was used in place of the deflator for the value added of each individual industry, PV_i, since the latter is not available. Also, for industries 4 and 6, substantial changes in input coefficients after the oil crisis are taken into account by the introduction of the dummy variable $D7579$ or $TIM6$.

Disaggregation of value added, labor input, and capital input into the six individual industries would have made the model too complicated. Therefore, at the value added level, we estimated an aggregative version of eqn. (A.8) rather than the equations for the individual industries.

Analogously to eqn. (A.4), an aggregative production function at the value added level may be given by:

$$\ln VM = \ln B - \frac{1}{\vartheta}\ln\left\{\varepsilon_1(T\cdot NH)^{-\vartheta} + \varepsilon_2 KIF_{-1}^{-\vartheta} + \varepsilon_3 IE^{-\vartheta} + \varepsilon_4 MO^{-\vartheta}\right\} \qquad (A.9)$$

where

VM	$= V + M$:	gross national supply or GNP plus imports,
NH	=	persons engaged in terms of man-hours,
KIF_{-1}	=	capital stock at the end of the previous year,
IE	=	demand for crude oil,
MO	=	imports other than crude oil,
$B, \vartheta, \varepsilon_i$	=	parameters.

Technical progress of the labor-augmenting type is allowed for by the term T; i.e.

$$T_t = \frac{\sum_{j=0}^{9} e^{\lambda(t-i)} IF_{t-i}}{\sum_{i=0}^{9} IF_{t-i}} \qquad (A.10)$$

where IF_t = gross fixed investment. If the levels of IF are kept unchanged, T will grow at the rate of λ percent per year. But if the levels of IF in recent years are higher than those in past years, the rate of change of T will be accelerated, implying that the newer vintage of capital stock has raised the average level of technology.

Cost minimization will yield the following:

$$\ln\frac{NH\cdot T}{VM} = (\mu - 1)\ln B + \mu\ln\varepsilon_1 + \mu\ln(PVM/(W_1/H)),$$

$$\ln\frac{KIF_{-1}}{VM} = (\mu - 1)\ln B + \mu\ln\varepsilon_2 + \mu\ln(PVM/PK),$$

$$\ln\frac{IE}{VM} = (\mu-1)\ln B + \mu\ln\varepsilon_3 + \mu\ln(PVM/P_2),$$

$$\ln\frac{MO}{VM} = (\mu-1)\ln B + \mu\ln\varepsilon_4 + \mu\ln(PVM/(PMO/RATE)), \qquad (A.11)$$

where

W_1 = index of wage earnings per person,

$RATE$ = index of the exchange rate,

H = index of hours worked per person,

PK = price index for capital service, defined by eqn. (4.35).

5. THE FINAL TEST

The explanatory effectiveness of the model was assessed by a final test for two subperiods: (1) 1963–73 and (2) 1975–79. Columns (1) and (2) of Table 1 present the average absolute percentage error of the selected variables in this test. The values for $V(GNP)$ and PC (consumption deflator) for 1963–73, 3.87 percent and 3.27 percent respectively, seem to be tolerable, and those for 1975–79, namely 3.57 percent and 2.00 percent, respectively, are close to those before the oil crisis.

6. THE IMPACT AND DYNAMIC EFFECTS OF THE OIL PRICE CHANGE ON THE ECONOMY AS A WHOLE

The impact of oil price changes was calculated by making a simulation starting in 1963, in which a hypothetical price rise of 10 percent was added to the observed value of the oil price in 1963, while the subsequent rate of change in oil price was set at the same rate as the observed one, other exogenous variables being kept at the same level as in the final test. The results of the simulation for 1963–69 are shown in Table 2. In the first year, 1963, a 10 percent rise in oil price led to a significant rise in P_4 (5.20%) and P_6 (1.18%), while it resulted in a milder rise in P_1 (0.17%), P_3 (0.34%) and P_5 (0.24%). The price rises in PC (0.18%) and PWH (0.64%) were also moderate. GNP, consumption, and fixed investment were all found to decrease slightly. It can also be seen from the table that the effects of a once-for-all rise in oil price tended to dwindle in the years after 1963.

Table 3 presents the results of a simulation in which a hypothetical price rise in each period was set at the level of the observed rate of oil price change (%) plus 10%. It was found that, by and large, this sustained increase in the rate of change of oil prices tended to prolong the effects of the once-for-all increase.

TABLE 1   The average absolute percentage error in the final test.

Variable		(1) 1963—73	(2) 1975—79
V	: GNP	3.88	3.58
C	: private consumption	4.29	0.93
IF	: private fixed investment	11.19	12.99
X	: exports (yen, real)	5.87	6.91
M	: imports (yen, real)	3.58	2.82
P	: GNP deflator	3.34	2.15
PC	: consumption deflator	3.27	2.00
PWH	: wholesale price	3.61	4.21
P_1	: price, primary industry	6.46	4.57
P_2	: price, crude oil	3.03*	12.94
P_3	: price, secondary industry	4.26	4.41
P_4	: price, oil and coal products	5.53	6.12
P_5	: price, tertiary industry	6.51	3.62
P_6	: price, electricity and gas	5.66	9.90
N	: total persons engaged	0.98	1.28
NW	: employees	1.21	1.10
W	: wage rate	1.68	1.19

*The average of 1971—73. Average absolute percentage error

$$=(\sum_{t=1}^{T} |(\hat{x}_t)-x_t)/ x_t | / T)\times 100,$$

where

$\hat{x}_t$ = the calculated value of a variable in period t.

x_t = the actual value of a variable in period t.

T = number of periods.

REFERENCES

(1) M. Saito and T. Oono, "An Energy Model of the Japanese Economy, 1961—1979".

(2) M. Saito and R. Nishimiya, "The Causes of the High Economic Growth of Japan" (IIASA Working Paper, in preparation).

TABLE 2   The effect of a once-for-all increase of 10% in oil price, 1963-1969.

	1963	1964	1965	1966	1967	1968	1969
V (billions of 1975 yen)	-69	-94	-110	-114	-102	-74	-32
$V(\%)$	-0.125	-0.156	-0.156	-0.147	-0.121	-0.079	-0.032
$C(\%)$	-0.169	-0.252	-0.293	-0.320	-0.328	-0.323	-0.319
$IF(\%)$	-0.154	-0.301	-0.323	-0.285	-0.229	-0.162	-0.107
$X(\%)$	-0.176	-0.339	-0.427	-0.348	-0.247	-0.136	-0.020
$M(\%)$	-0.257	-0.886	-1.354	-1.404	-1.456	-1.500	-1.549
$P(\%)$	0.073	0.057	0.027	-0.024	-0.092	-0.175	-0.265
$PC(\%)$	0.179	0.230	0.220	0.183	0.128	0.062	-0.005
$PWH(\%)$	0.638	0.623	0.544	0.470	0.373	0.272	0.171
$P_1(\%)$	0.168	0.249	0.291	0.275	0.251	0.206	0.169
$P_2(\%)$	10.000	10.000	10.000	10.000	10.000	10.000	10.000
$P_3(\%)$	0.340	0.319	0.242	0.165	0.077	-0.018	-0.107
$P_4(\%)$	5.202	5.037	4.793	4.589	4.373	4.171	4.007
$P_5(\%)$	0.235	0.239	0.201	0.162	0.106	0.040	-0.028
$P_6(\%)$	1.184	1.092	0.937	0.852	0.753	0.666	0.578
$N(\%)$	-0.035	-0.125	-0.183	-0.180	-0.172	-0.157	-0.147
$NW(\%)$	-0.019	-0.082	-0.158	-0.211	-0.244	-0.261	-0.267
$W(\%)$	-0.001	0.032	0.023	-0.011	-0.061	-0.118	-0.181

TABLE 3   The effect of a sustained increase of 10% in oil price, 1963—1969.

	1963	1964	1965	1966	1967	1968	1969
V (billions of 1975 yen)	-69	-173	-345	-493	-624	-730	-775
$V(\%)$	-0.125	-0.289	-0.489	-0.636	-0.738	-0.775	-0.771
$C(\%)$	-0.169	-0.432	-0.732	-1.069	-1.410	-1.737	-2.091
$IF(\%)$	-0.154	-0.486	-0.867	-1.217	-1.470	-1.646	-1.852
$X(\%)$	-0.176	-0.516	-0.949	-1.305	-1.555	-1.677	-1.673
$M(\%)$	-0.257	-1.210	-2.402	-3.904	-5.526	-7.189	-8.946
$P(\%)$	0.073	0.112	0.163	0.103	-0.037	-0.304	-0.679
$PC(\%)$	0.179	0.415	0.646	0.838	0.967	1.015	1.005
$PWH(\%)$	0.638	1.308	1.901	2.468	2.903	3.218	3.410
$P_1(\%)$	0.168	0.424	0.699	0.969	1.237	1.436	1.655
$P_2(\%)$	10.000	21.050	33.630	47.340	62.780	78.930	97.530
$P_3(\%)$	0.340	0.674	0.915	1.087	1.159	1.109	0.985
$P_4(\%)$	5.202	10.680	16.310	22.040	27.800	33.400	39.140
$P_5(\%)$	0.235	0.486	0.692	0.865	0.973	1.000	0.965
$P_6(\%)$	1.184	2.376	3.502	4.663	5.747	6.799	7.779
$N(\%)$	-0.035	-0.163	-0.346	-0.533	-0.710	-0.853	-1.017
$NW(\%)$	-0.019	-0.103	-0.262	-0.477	-0.728	-0.985	-1.258
$W(\%)$	-0.001	0.031	0.055	0.043	-0.020	-0.142	-0.331

ENDOGENISING INPUT—OUTPUT COEFFICIENTS BY MEANS OF INDUSTRIAL SUBMODELS

Swami Amrit Terry (T.S. Barker)

University of Cambridge, Cambridge, UK

1. INTRODUCTION

Large scale multisectoral dynamic models of national economies, such as the Cambridge Multisectoral Dynamic Model (MDM) for the UK (Barker et al., 1980), the INSEE DMS for France (Fouquet et al., 1976) or the GALILEO model for Mexico (Brailovsky, 1984) usually adopt an aggregation much less detailed than that of the input—output tables available. This is done mainly so that the model can include the stochastic determination of real flows and can be extended to cover institutional and financial aspects of economic behaviour and still remain feasible in terms of data and resources required for estimation and solution.

The method developed below uses the detailed data in the available input—output tables together with the projections of the aggregated model in order to revise the aggregate input—output coefficients. The method is that of building submodels for groups of closely-related industries. Although they can be at different levels of complexity, the submodels developed here are elementary ones of quantity flows which allow for the influence of changes in product mix on the aggregated input—output coefficients.

The use of submodels is well developed for energy demands (e.g. Wigley, 1968 and applications in Smyshlyaev, 1983), although the purpose of them is the use of demand systems and quantity measurements rather than more disaggregation. They have also been developed for the analysis of special problems, such as profitability of ethanol in gasoline production (Robison, 1983). However, not many submodels have surfaced in the literature, although they have been discussed over a number of years for example in the working papers of the Cambridge Growth Project (Brown, 1963; Wigley, 1964; Hooker, 1965; Barker, 1978).

Section 2. below considers in more detail the submodel approach in projecting changes in input—output coefficients; Section 3. sets out the accounting framework, the notation, the basic equations and the method of solution of the elementary submodel; Section 4. presents an application to the British economy using the Cambridge MDM; and Section 5. gives a few conclusions.

---

*
The author is a member of the Cambridge Growth Project: the financial support of the UK Economic and Social Research Council for the project and the research reported here is gratefully acknowledged. The use of Cambridge Econometrics Forecast 84/3 is also gratefully acknowledged.

2. THE SUBMODEL APPROACH AND INPUT-OUTPUT COEFFICIENTS

There is now quite an accumulation of evidence to suggest that the sub-model approach to the projection of input-output coefficients is likely to be a useful one. The main advantages of the approach can be discussed one by one.

2.1. The Size of the Economy-wide Model

The most persuasive reason for building submodels is to avoid increasing the size of the main model, yet to allow for a detailed treatment of groups of industries for which more data is available. Submodels can be constructed within an accounting framework which is consistent with that of the main model. The detailed data on a group of industries can be organised in a standard set of tables and used to estimate the submodel which in turn can be integrated with the main model. The accounting framework helps to keep the definitions, the data and the results of the submodel and the main model consistent, yet allows the submodel to be developed independently of the main model.

2.2. Product Mix and Technological Change

Submodels allow formally for the effects of changes in product mix at the level of detail of the full input-output tables available. The effects on the aggregate input-output coefficient can be measured and the coefficient changed accordingly. This is the justification for this paper and the effects are demonstrated for a submodel of the Cambridge MDM in a later section. There is evidence that changes in product mix can be important in explaining differences in input coefficients between establishments: Forssell (1969) finds that two-thirds of the dispersion of coefficients for establishments in Finnish industries were accounted for by differences in product mix. The effects on changes over time seem to be less strong (a finding confirmed below): Forssell (1972) analyses input coefficients for 21 Finnish manufacturing industries 1954-65 and finds that, although they had noticeable effects, changes in product mix were less important than general technological changes or the effects of price movements.

However submodels are also very valuable in assessing technological change. This is often highly specific to particular inputs and as much detail as possible is needed to forecast the effects of the change on the input structure of different industries.

2.3. The Selective Approach

Submodels can be constructed selectively for groups of industries whose input-output coefficients are particularly important. The alternative approach is to project all the input-output coefficients at the more detailed level then aggregate them to find the coefficients of the main model. (This is done for the INFORUM system of models for the USA (Almon, 1983) where the more detailed model DOM has 425 sectors, but the dynamic model LIFT has 78 sectors.) The selective approach allows the model builder more flexibility in the procedure and is less centralised. There is evidence that a few identifiable coefficients are more important than others (Skolka, 1982; Tomaszewicz, 1983): submodels explaining these coefficients can be estimated first.

Furthermore, industrial experts are often expert only for a group of related industries: the method allows them to concentrate on the projections of a particular submodel. The submodel can also easily be extended to include quantity data in the units of measurement appropriate to each industry group, making the results easier to understand by industrial experts.

3. AN ACCOUNTING FRAMEWORK FOR SUBMODELS

This section develops the notation and accounting framework for the submodel, starting from that of the UN System of National Accounts (SNA) (UN, 1968) assumed to be adopted in the main model.

3.1. Notation in a System of National Accounts

Figure 1 shows the commodity and industry rows and columns in a symbolic SNA.

	Commodities Q	Industries Y	Final Demands consumers C	
Commodities Q		QY (absorption matrix)	QC	
Industries Y	YQ (make matrix)			
Imports M	(QM)'			

FIGURE 1   Part of a Symbolic SNA

YQ is the make matrix showing the make of commodities (columns) by industries (rows).   QY is the absorption matrix showing the absorption of commodities (rows) by industries (columns).   (QM)' shows the imports classified by commodity where ' denotes transposition of the matrix.   QC is an example of a final demand matrix showing absorption of commodities (rows) by consumer expenditure categories (columns).   Total commodity and industry outputs (Q and Y respectively) can be defined as

$$Q = (YQ)'.i \qquad\qquad (1)$$

$$Y = YQ.i \qquad\qquad (2)$$

where i is the unit vector and . denotes vector or matrix multiplication.

3.2. The Submodel Make and Mix Matrices

Suppose the submodel covers several industries and distinguishes a total of NSY subindustries and a total of NSQ subcommodities. Then three submodel make matrices can be defined:

YQ1 showing the make of commodities by each subindustry, with the make of own commodities shown as zero;

YQ2 showing the make of subcommodities by each industry, with the make by own industries shown as zero; and

YQ3 showing the make of subcommodities by subindustries.

These three matrices cover the whole production of the submodel and the sum of their elements is the sum of the outputs of the industries grouped into the submodel. Totals of subcommodity and subindustry outputs can be defined as

$$SQ = (YQ1)'.i + (YQ3)'.i \tag{3}$$

$$SY = YQ2.i + YQ3.i \tag{4}$$

From the definitions of the submodel make matrices and equations (1) and (3), three mix matrices can be formed:

$$YQ1C = YQ1.\hat{Q}^{-1} \tag{5}$$

$$YQ2C = YQ2.\hat{SQ}^{-1} \tag{6}$$

$$YQ3C = YQ3.\hat{SQ}^{-1} \tag{7}$$

where ^ denotes that a vector is transformed into a diagonal matrix and $^{-1}$ denotes inversion. The mix matrices show the proportions in which each (sub)industry makes each (sub)commodity. Given (sub)commodity outputs they can be used to calculate (sub)industry outputs assuming an 'industry technology'.

3.3. The Submodel Absorption Matrix

Again three matrices can be defined:

QY1 showing the absorption of subcommodities by industries with own industry absorptions shown as zero;

QY2 showing the absorption of commodities by subindustries with own commodity absorptions shown as zero; and

QY3 showing the absorption of subcommodities by subindustries.

The sum of the elements of these three matrices come to the sum of the commodity absorptions by all the industries in the submodel.

From these definitions and equations (2) and (4) three input-output matrices can be calculated

$$QY1C = QY1.\hat{Y}^{-1} \tag{8}$$

$$QY2C = QY2.\hat{SY}^{-1} \tag{9}$$

$$QY3C = QY3.\hat{SY}^{-1} \tag{10}$$

These matrices show the (sub)commodity input requirements per unit of (sub)-industry output. Given the (sub)industry outputs they can be used to calculate intermediate demands.

The absorption matrices for final demand are similarly calculated as

$$QC1C = QC1.\hat{C}^{-1} \tag{11}$$

$$QG1C = QG1.\hat{G}^{-1} \tag{12}$$

$$QV1C = QV1.\hat{V}^{-1} \tag{13}$$

where C, G and V refer to all the final demand vectors for consumers' expenditure, government expenditure and fixed investment respectively. Each of these converter matrices shows the absorptions of subcommodities by final demand categories.

The remaining components of final demand are stockbuilding, which is treated as exogenous and exports which is discussed below.

3.4. Export and Import Ratio Matrices

This is a problem area because ideally exports and imports of the sub-commodities should respond (like those in the main model) to activity levels abroad and at home respectively and to relative prices. Since in the elementary submodel no relative prices are derived, this cannot be done and the trade flows are derived from ratios of exports and imports to output. The base ratios are

$$QX1C = QX1.\hat{SQ}^{-1} \tag{14}$$

$$QM1C = QM1.\hat{SQ}^{-1} \tag{15}$$

The ratios are used to calculate levels of trade in a projection year and then the levels are scaled to add to the totals given in the main model so as to pick up the effects of price changes and other factors at the aggregate level. This treatment works only if the scaling factors are 'small', otherwise the solution process does not converge.

3.5. The Solution

The submodel is solved by the usual Gauss-Siedel iterative procedure. The steps for the solution in year T (omitting the subscript T) are

Pre-iteration steps:

$$QC1 = QC1C.\hat{C} \tag{16}$$

$$QG1 = QGIC.\hat{G} \tag{17}$$

$$QV1 = QV1C.\hat{V} \tag{18}$$

$$FH1 = QC1.i + QG1.i + QV1.i + QS1 \tag{19}$$

(where FH1 is the vector of final home demand for the subcommodities including QS1 as exogenous stockbuilding and i is the unit vector)

$$QY1 = QY1C.\hat{Y} \tag{20}$$

$$YQ1 = YQ1C.\hat{Q} \tag{21}$$

Iteration loop for iteration I:

$$QX1(I) = QX1C.SQ(I-1) \tag{22}$$

$$QM1(I) = QM1C.SQ(I-1) \tag{23}$$

(QX1(I) and QM1(I) are then scaled to add to main model exports and imports
X and M)

$$QY3(I) = QY3C.\hat{SY}(I-1) \tag{24}$$

$$SQ(I) = QY1.i + FH1 + QY3(I).i + QX1(I) - QM1(I) \tag{25}$$

$$YQ3(I) = YQ3C.SQ(I) \tag{26}$$

$$SY(I) = YQ1.i + YQ3(I).i \tag{27}$$

Post-iteration steps:

$$YQ2 = YQ2C.\hat{SQ} \tag{28}$$

$$QY2 = QY2C.\hat{SY} \tag{29}$$

4. SUBMODEL IMPLEMENTATION WITH THE CAMBRIDGE MULTISECTORAL DYNAMIC MODEL OF THE BRITISH ECONOMY

The Cambridge MDM has 40 industrial sectors whilst the 1975 input-output
table for the British economy which is used as the source for the model's
coefficient matrices has 102 sectors. There is therefore a lot of structural information in the table which has not been used in the model. This
section discusses the implementation of submodels to use some of this information.

4.1. Sources of the Data

The data for the submodels come from three sources. First there is
the set of detailed input-output tables for 1975 which are in turn derived,
with the help of the UK Central Statistical Office, from the published tables
for 1974 (UK CSO, 1980). The coefficient matrices for the submodels (viz.
YQ1C, YQ3C, QY1C, QY3C, QC1C, QG1C, QV1C, QX1C and QM1C of section 3. above)
are all derived directly from these tables.

The second source is the set of coefficient matrices used in the
Cambridge MDM. These are at a more aggregated level and except for the
absorption coefficients their only use is a check on the submodel coefficients. However the MDM input-output coefficients change over time with the
projections incorporating the views of industrial experts and our own judge-

ment on technical change.   The changes in these coefficients are applied to
their components in the submodel matrix QY1C.
    The third source of data is the Cambridge Econometrics Forecast of June
1984 covering the period 1982-1993.   This provides a recent projection of
outputs, final domestic demands, imports and exports (viz. Q, Y, C, G, V, QS,
X and M of section 3. above), all at constant (1975) prices and consistent
with the input-output tables of the base year.

4.2. The Estimated Submodels

    Table 1 lists the 8 submodels which have been estimated.   The smallest
is for Other Transport which uses the information on the two components of
this industry in the detailed tables viz. Sea & Inland Water Transport and
Air Transport & Miscellaneous to calculate the projected input coefficients
for the industry allowing for changes in output mix.   The largest is that
for Engineering which contains 8 industries, 31 subindustries, 4 commodities
and 26 subcommodities.
    The industries and commodities in the submodels are chosen so as to use
the detailed data available and incorporate the main input-output connections,
yet to keep the size of the submodel as small as possible.   Thus the chemicals submodel includes the Other Manufacturing industry to allow for the flow
of the subcommodities Synthetic Resins and General Chemicals to the subindustry for Plastic Products.

TABLE 1   The estimated submodels for the model of the UK

Submodel	MDM industries (number of subindustries)	MDM commodities (number of subcommodities)
Food	Agriculture (2)	Agriculture (2)
	Food Processing (10)	Food Products (10)
Chemicals	Chemicals (9)	Chemicals (9)
	Other manufacturing (3)	
Metals	Iron & Steel (2)	Iron & Steel (2)
	Non-Ferrous Metals (2)	Non-Ferrous Metals (2)
	8 Engineering & Vehicle Industries (31)	
Engineering	8 Engineering & Vehicle Industries (31)	Mech. Engineering (10)
		Elect. Engineering (9)
		Motor Vehicles (2)
		Metal Goods (6)
Textiles	Textiles (8)	Chemicals (10)
	Leather, Clothing & Footwear (3)	Textiles (8)
		Leather, Clothing & Footwear (3)
Paper	Paper & Board (3)	Paper & Board (3)
	Printing & Publishing (1)	Printing & Publishing (1)
Construction	Building Materials (4)	Building Materials (4)
	Timber & Furniture (2)	Timber & Furniture (2)
	Construction (1)	
Other Transport	Other Transport (2)	Other Transport (2)

4.3. Projections of Input-Output Coefficients

Table 2 shows projections of some important coefficients. It should be noted that the MDM projections are intended to include the effects of changes in technology, prices and product mix on the input structure of the industries in the submodel whereas the ISM projections include the effects of changes in product mix on their own. Therefore any comparison of the MDM and ISM projections is an assessment of whether the explicit changes due to product mix and the implicit changes due to technology, prices etc. are plausible.

Most of the ISM projections show very little effect of product mix on the coefficients. These cast doubt on the MDM projections in those instances, e.g. Chemicals into Other Manufacturing, where some effect of product mix (increasing use of plastic products) has been taken into account. Otherwise the discrepancies are mainly due to technical change, e.g. the replacement of insulated electrical wire by glass fibre resulting in the falling coefficient of non-ferrous metals into electrical engineering.

TABLE 2   Some projections of input-output coefficients for the UK

input	output		commodity inputs per unit of industry output			
			1975	1982	1985	1990
10. Chemicals	21. Textiles	MDM	.0757	.0787	.0800	.0810
		ISM	.0757	.0714	.0724	.0716
10. Chemicals	27. Other Manufacturing	MDM	.1802	.1868	.1896	.1942
		ISM	.1802	.1803	.1803	.1804
11. Iron & Steel	13. Mechanical Engineering	MDM	.1204	.1191	.1185	.1185
		ISM	.1204	.1205	.1204	.1203
11. Iron & Steel	20. Metal Goods n.e.s.	MDM	.1796	.1753	.1736	.1707
		ISM	.1796	.1796	.1797	.1797
12. Non-ferrous Metals	15. Electrical Engineering	MDM	.0578	.0511	.0481	.0432
		ISM	.0578	.0574	.0576	.0576
21. Textiles	22. Leather, Clothing & Footwear	MDM	.2451	.2386	.2359	.2315
		ISM	.2451	.2473	.2485	.2490

Note: MDM   Cambridge Multisectoral Dynamic Model, Version 6.
ISM   Industrial Submodel as described in the text.

There are, however, two coefficients, chemicals into textiles and textiles into clothing, where changes in product mix have affected the projections more significantly. It appears that the chemical-intensive subindustries in textiles, viz. man-made fibres, textile finishing and carpets, have been declining in relation to the other textile industries so that chemical inputs have been falling, contrary to the general industrial trend. In the case of textiles into leather, clothing and footwear, the product mix has moved in favour of textiles as clothing has increased relative to leather and footwear.

4.4. Further Research

This research remains at a preliminary stage. Some of the directions for further work are as follows.

Technical change. This can be introduced into the submodel projections using the views of industrial experts where available.

Feedback to the main model. The new coefficients calculated by the submodels can be incorporated into the main model. It may be enough just to revise the aggregated input-output coefficients, but experiments in which there was full interaction between MDM and a submodel might be tried.

More complex submodels with time-series data. Perhaps the first extension of the submodel should be to incorporate time series information available on the subindustries' production and the subcommodities' exports and imports. This immediately raises the problems of how to reconcile the data for years other than the base year of the input-output tables. Some kind of adjustment procedure, similar to that used for the model database (see Barker, van der Ploeg and Weale, 1984), will need to be used to provide more recent input-output coefficients for the projections.

More complex submodels with prices. The submodels can readily be extended to include prices of principal products of subindustries, derived from costs and prices of exports and imports of subcommodities. Relative prices will be needed if the crude determination of trade flows is to be replaced by econometric equations allowing for price substitution.

5. CONCLUSIONS

An elementary quantity submodel has been developed to utilise the detailed structural information available in input-output tables but not necessarily used in the more aggregated multisectoral model. This method is particularly useful if the following conditions are all met.

(1) There are substantial inter-industry flows and the detailed tables disaggregate the input sectors more than main model.

(2) There are substantial changes in the product structure of the sub-model industries.

(3) The changes in product structure arise from changes in the mix of final demand or intermediate demand sectors distinguished in the main model.

(4) The input structure substantially differs between subindustries.

These conditions are fairly restrictive so that it is not surprising that the submodels produced rather small changes in most input-output coefficients. However they do provide the framework for introducing industrial expertise and judgement at a more detailed level than before and a means of updating the coefficients for years when partial but detailed information is available on input-output flows.

6. REFERENCES

Almon, C. (1983). 1983 INFORUM modeling experience: division of labor among models, long-run stability and the analysis of protectionism, pp. 9-16 in A. Smyshlyaev (ed.) Proceedings of the Fourth IIASA Task Force Meeting on Input-Output Modeling, IIASA, Laxenburg, Austria.

Barker, T. (1978). Industrial submodels in MDM. Cambridge Growth Project Paper 455, Department of Applied Economics, University of Cambridge, UK.

Barker, Terry, Vani Borooah, Rick van der Ploeg and Alan Winters (1980). The Cambridge Multisectoral Dynamic Model: an instrument for national economic policy analysis. Journal of Policy Modeling, Vol. 2, No. 3, pp. 319-344.

Barker, T., van der Ploeg, F. and Weale, M. (forthcoming). A balanced system of national accounts for the United Kingdom. Review of Income and Wealth, forthcoming.

Brailovsky, V. (1984). Analytical bases for the construction of GALILEO, a multisectoral dynamic model of the Mexican economy. Economía Applicada S.C., Mexico City.

Brown, A. (1963). Decentralised simulation models. Cambridge Growth Project Paper 157, Department of Applied Economics, University of Cambridge, UK.

Forssell, O. (1969). Statistical Units, Classification and Aggregation in a Finnish Input-Output Study, Industrial Planning and Programming Series No. 2, Interindustrial Comparisons of Interindustry Data, United Nations, New York.

Forssell, O. (1972). Explaining changes in input-output coefficients for Finland. In A. Brody and A.P. Carter (eds) Input-Output Techniques, North Holland.

Forssell, O. (1983). Experiences of studying changes in input-output coefficients in Finland. pp. 219-226 in A. Smyshlyaev (ed.) Proceedings of the Fourth IIASA Task Force Meeting on Input-Output Modeling, IIASA, Laxenburg, Austria.

Fouquet, D., Charpin, J.-M., Guillaume, H., Muet, P.-A. and Vallet, D. (1976). DMS, modèle de prévision à moyen terme. d'Economie et Statistique No. 79, revue mensuelle de l'INSEE, Paris.

Hooker, O. (1965). A submodel of the iron castings industry. Cambridge Growth Project Paper 202, Department of Applied Economics, University of Cambridge, UK.

Robison, H.D. (1983). The long-run profitability of ethanol in high-octane gasoline: an application of input-output analysis. pp. 297-306 in A. Smyshlyaev (ed.) Proceedings of the Fourth IIASA Task Force Meeting on Input-Output Modeling, IIASA, Laxenburg, Austria.

Skolka, J. (1982). Important input coefficients in Austrian input-output tables for 1964 and 1976. pp. 409-436 in M. Grassini and A. Smyshlyaev (eds) Input-Output Modeling, IIASA, Laxenburg, Austria.

Smyshlyaev, A. (editor) (1983). Proceedings of the Fourth IIASA Task Force Meeting on Input-Output Modeling. IIASA, Laxenburg, Austria.

Tomaszewicz, L. (1983). Variations in input-output coefficients: the application of estimation and forecasting techniques for the case of Poland. pp. 207-218 in A. Smyshlyaev (ed.) Proceedings of the Fourth IIASA Task Force Meeting on Input-Output Modeling, IIASA, Laxenburg, Austria.

UK CSO (1980). Input-Output Tables for the United Kingdom, 1974. Central Statistical Office, HMSO, London.

UN (1968). System of National Accounts. United Nations, New York.

Wigley, K.J. (1964). Some problems arising in submodel construction. Cambridge Growth Project Paper 179, Department of Applied Economics, University of Cambridge, UK.

Wigley, K.J. (1968). The Demand for Fuel 1948-1975. A Submodel for the British Fuel Economy. Vol. 8 in Richard Stone (ed.) A Programme for Growth, Chapman and Hall, London.

STRUCTURAL CHANGE IN THE BELGIAN ECONOMY

Hilda Tahon[1] *and Dirk Vanwynsberghe*[2]

[1]Krediet Bank NV, Brussels, Belgium; [2]Economic Research International, Herent, Belgium

1. INTRODUCTION

Input—output tables tend to be rather out of date in a number of countries and particularly in Belgium. A quick estimate of a recent table using all available data is therefore a very necessary as well as helpful step in modeling industrial development. Such an updated input—output table can be vastly improved by studying the major input coefficients in the table. The research reported here represents a part of this update process.

2. THE BASIC DATA

This study covered major coefficient changes between the years 1965, 1970, and 1975.

The official tables for each of the three years are available in terms of current producer prices and had to be reworked slightly for the year 1965 (mainly a question of aggregation). The tables distinguish between inputs from national sources and those of foreign origin at the level of intermediate flows and final demand components.

The three comparable tables eventually had 50 sectors on product base definitions with:

- 1 agriculture section.
- 5 energy sectors.
- 1 construction sector.
- 26 manufacturing sectors.
- 17 service types.

3. THE METHOD

Given the fact that input data for the service sectors are usually less reliable, we limited ourselves to the nonservice sectors in the table. In this sense, only 33 sectors are studied with regard to their coefficient changes, including service inputs for these sectors. In total 1650 (33 x 50) coefficients were theoretically possible candidates for analysis.

Three types of adaptation had to be made to the published tables:

- aggregation of the subsectors reported in the 1965 table,
- minor product group changes in the 1965 table,
- constant price adaptations.

The constant price calculations were performed in producer prices (base 1970) as 1970 was chosen as the base year.

Different methods are available for selecting the most important coefficients within input—output tables. We used a rather pragmatic approach, based on the principles that the *most important* flows in absolute terms, i.e.

output shares, and the *biggest input coefficients* had to be studied. An analysis of the base-year table for 1970 showed that these conditions were satisfied if we examined the five major input coefficients for each of the 33 industries studied.

For the periods 1965—70 and 1970—75, we calculated the rates of growth of the total coefficients, as well as those for imports and for domestic production, in both current and constant prices.

4. DOMINANT INPUT SECTORS

The method described above led to the result that only a very limited number of input sectors needed to be considered. Indeed, some ten sectors out of the total of fifty defined the major input coefficients in the 33 industries considered. In a few cases very specific inputs (like coke in steelmaking) had to be added to the list and these needed to be studied separately.

The dominant sectors in the base year changed their relative order of importance in the 1965 and 1975 tables but remained the same for all three years studied. The most important sector "Services to enterprises" was the dominant input sector in 20 of the 33 industries and maintained that position over the whole period. "Metal products" started in second place in 1965 but ended up behind both "Chemicals" and "Trade" in 1975. Also, "Electricity" increased in importance and was one of the dominant inputs in one-third of the cases by 1975. The most pronounced decreases in importance were for "Iron and steel" (four places), "Metal products" (three places), and "Agriculture" (two places). A loss of one place in the list of dominant inputs was noticed for "Paper and printing", "Machinery", and "Oil products". Table 1 gives an overview for the period 1970—75.

TABLE 1   Dominant inputs in Belgian industries, 1970—75.

Sector	Number of dominant input coefficients	
	1970	1975
Services to enterprises	20	20
Metal products	15	12
Trade	11	18
Chemicals	11	15
Agriculture	11	9
Iron and steel	10	6
Electricity	8	11
Paper & printing	8	7
Machinery	7	6
Oil products	6	5

5. DISTRIBUTION OF COEFFICIENT CHANGES

Having reduced the number of coefficients to be studied more carefully to some 165 out of the 1650 possible candidates, by concentrating on the dominant ones, we begin by analyzing the general distribution of the changes in each period.

As a great number of coefficient changes were calculated using current table prices, one may expect rather different results for constant price comparisons. Table 2 outlines the distribution of coefficient changes, concerning which a number of remarks can be made.

TABLE 2   Coefficient change distribution.

Change (%)	1970 − 1965		1975 − 1970	
	Current	Constant	Current	Constant
0− 5	53	52	64	63
5−10	20	21	18	19.5
10−15	12	18	9	7
15−20	6	4.5	3	4
20−25	3	2.5	1	1.5
More than 25	6	7	5	5

First, since the distribution is very similar in terms of both constant and current prices, we can concentrate further on the current price changes. Second, the changes considerably decreased in the more recent period. The 1965−70 period was one of strong and stable economic growth compared to the less favorable developments in the later period.

More than half of the coefficients, and as many as 64% in 1975−70, fall in the zero to 5 percent range. Examining this at a more detailed level, one sees that 17 percent of the changes were less than 1% in the first period, about 10 percent were between 1 and 2%, and a similar proportion were between 2 and 3%. The 4% and 5% ranges each account for about 5 percent of the changes. The tendency to smaller variations in the second period is also clearly reflected at the more detailed level. The zero to 1% range loses a few percentages, but all the other ranges increase considerably.

The period 1965−1970 was characterized by a considerable opening of the Belgian economy. A comparison of Tables 2 and 3 shows that both domestic and imported coefficients taken separately changed considerably more than the total ones and that they did not exhibit the decrease in variation in the second period. It is fairly clear that offsetting movements are responsible for the lower variability of the total coefficients (as compared to the domestic and imported ones).

TABLE 3   Imported versus domestic coefficient changes.

Change (%)	1970 − 1965		1975 − 1970	
	Domestic	Imported	Domestic	Imported
0− 5	38.5	31.5	41.5	33.5
5−10	29.5	25.0	29.5	31.5
10−15	15.0	14.8	9.5	17.5
15−20	7.0	9.0	8.5	8.0
20−25	2.0	5.0	2.0	4.5
More than 25	7.5	14.8	8.5	5.0

6. MAJOR CHANGING COEFFICIENTS

Of the ten dominant input sectors only three were mainly responsible for the major variations in the coefficients: Oil products, Machinery, and Paper & printing. All three are ranked at the bottom of the list of dominant sectors (see Table 1). Electro equipment and Warehousing were two other sectors that showed major variations during the first period. In the second period all the sectors mentioned, with the exception of Warehousing, behaved in a much more stable way.

The machinery input increased in general during the first period and was responsible for extreme coefficient increases in Mining (47%), Metal products (24%), Transportation means other than cars (19%), and Office equipment (14%). This trend was reversed in the second period.

The strong increase in electro equipment input in the first period was totally dominated by the imported contribution (the domestic coefficients decreased). When, in the second period, imports stopped penetrating the market, total coefficients became almost stable.

Paper & printing showed a similar result. The strong import penetration in the first period was mainly responsible for the instability of the total coefficients. The imports lost considerable market shares in the later period and the total coefficients became normal.

7. CONCLUSIONS

Studying a limited number of input coefficients in detail can help one to achieve a better understanding of overall coefficient change. The coefficients concerned are associated either with specific technological processes or with dominant input sectors. In total some 10 percent of the total number of coefficients have to be considered.

The overall results do not differ substantially, regardless of whether constant or current price tables are used.

A rather stable and strong growth period does not automatically guarantee less variation in the major coefficients. Periods with growth problems may be characterized by more stable coefficients.

The use of domestic and imported coefficients results, in general, in more variation in the system, but this distinction makes it possible to explain a number of the more extreme variations. Import penetration not only offsets domestic inputs, but also affects the coefficients quite considerably.

AN ECONOMETRIC MODEL OF THE SOVIET IRON AND STEEL INDUSTRY

Anatoli Smyshlyaev

International Institute for Applied Systems Analysis,
Laxenburg, Austria

1. INTRODUCTION

This paper summarizes numerous econometric studies of the structure of the iron and steel industry in the Soviet Union, which have examined the demand for steel products, technological transformations within the industry, and the demand for raw materials and energy. Since there are relatively few links between this and other industries, within an input—output framework an econometric model of the steel industry can be considered as an industrial submodel that gives a comprehensive description of the structures of production and inputs. The impact of the industry on the economy as a whole is, however, very significant; its demand for energy amounts to 8% of total national energy consumption and its high capital intensity results in a share of between 7% and 10% of gross fixed capital formation.

The Soviet iron and steel industry is one of the biggest in the world. It produces annually up to 150 million tons of crude steel and up to 120 million tons of rolled products. Its growth was generally rather stable over the period 1960—1980, although a slowdown in the production figures can be observed for 1979—1982, after crude steel production had reached a peak of 151.5 million tons in 1978. A new peak of 153 million tons was later reached in 1983.

The structure of this paper is as follows. Section 2 briefly reviews the well-known technological processes involved in this industry and outlines the structure of the model used. Section 3 presents a somewhat longer analysis of the industry's performance; Section 4, which reports some econometric results, ignoring relative prices and expressing the shares of technologies as time trends, does not go into too much detail. Finally, the conclusions indicate some important questions and show the applicability of the model.

2. OVERVIEW OF THE MODEL

The task of the modeler is essentially the reverse of that depicted in the flow-chart of the main technological processes in the iron and steel industry (Figure 1); the object is to derive, step by step, the requirements for raw materials and energy from the given demand for finished steel products.

There are two distinct but complementary ways to model transactions within the industry. One is based on "technological" parameters, for example units of pig iron per unit of steel, expressing the behavior of the industry in terms of technological progress, returns to scale, etc. The second approach is to estimate log-linear equations where a clear distinction is made between "technological" progress and increases in production; for example, pig iron used is a function of steel production.

Both approaches will possibly give the same quantitative results and both can be used in forecasting. However, in the first case one gets a clear picture of the changes in input coefficients, whether their dynamics are steady or not. Most of the ratios considered below can be interpreted as technological parameters, for example energy intensities, raw material inputs per unit of pig iron produced, while others are really shares of related products or export—import quotas. To deal with ratios is advantageous when engineering data for either the past or the future are

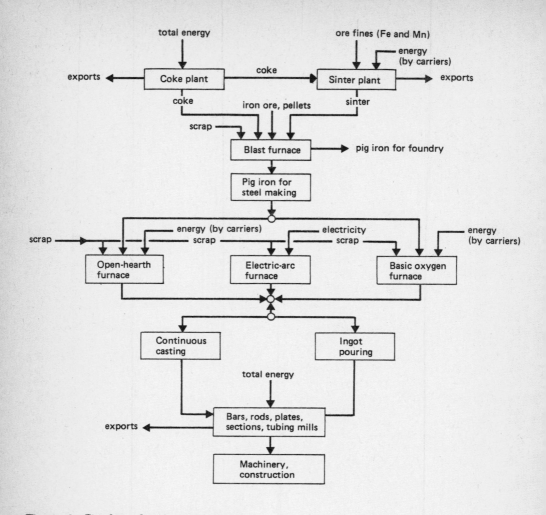

Figure 1. Steel production processes.

involved; it is easy to replace (or to adjust) an equation by using these technological data. In contrast, when using log-linear equations, one gets a set of elasticities and, in a reduced form of a model, a clear picture of the differences in rates of growth for different products (both inputs and outputs) with respect to the growth of demand for end-use rolled products.

A simplified flow-chart of the model looks as follows:

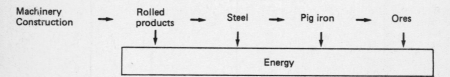

One of the most important questions related to this model is the estimation of energy demand, which is rising more rapidly than any of the production figures expressed in physical units. Table 1 presents some details. The energy used by the iron and steel industry in 1982 is estimated to have been approximately 6370 GJ, or about 7.1% of total energy demand, as compared to 8.6% in 1970 and 8.1% in 1975.

TABLE 1 Energy consumption (GJ) in the Soviet iron and steel industry, 1963—1980.

	1963	1970	1975	1980
Iron and steel industry	2240	3507	4378	4785
Percentage per ton of:				
Rolled products	42.2	43.6	46.6	46.4
Crude steel	28.4	30.3	31.1	32.1
Pig iron	39.0	41.0	42.8	44.5

The structure of energy inputs (Table 2) is changing in favor of natural gas and electricity, while the share of coal dropped from 52% in 1970 to 43.5% in 1980. Thus, the various developments in energy conservation related to each process (ECE, 1983) overshadowed the other effects, namely the required increase in the quality of end products and/or product-mix effects.

TABLE 2 The structure (percentage shares) of net energy consumption in the Soviet Union, 1970—1980.

Energy carrier	1970	1975	1980
Coal	51.7	47.2	43.5
Oil	5.0	5.5	5.1
Natural gas	31.5	34.3	36.1
Electricity	11.8	13.1	15.3

Within the Soviet iron and steel industry, the bulk of the energy requirement (about 45%) goes into pig-iron production; 13% is used in agglomeration processes and coke production, while the last stage, rolling, accounts for between 10% and 12%.

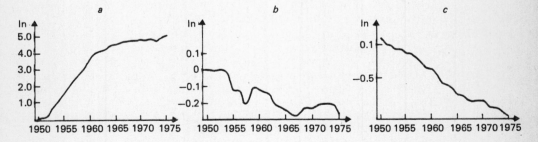

Figure 2. Changes in the inputs of various energy carriers per unit output of the Soviet iron and steel industry, 1950—1975: *a*, natural gas; *b*, oil; *c*, coal.

It is not immediately obvious whether the breakdown of iron and steel production figures into distinct processes, followed by a stage-by-stage analysis, is any more valuable than a macroeconomic consideration of the input and output structures of the industry as a whole. For example, why not relate energy consumption

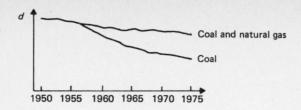

Figure 3. Share of various energy carriers in the energy consumption of the Soviet iron and steel industry, 1950–1975.

to the volume of finished steel products? Raw material inputs are relatively trivial, so that such a breakdown still would not link an industry model effectively with other branches of the economy.

The "common sense" argument in favor of the stage-by-stage approach is that the information obtained is valuable in itself, since it helps to identify possible structural shifts in the industry's development. In other words, technological parameters for the industry as a whole may reflect to a marked extent the impacts of product- (or technology-) mix effects, which cannot be studied at the macro level.

One example is the demand for coal. Analysis of the stage-by-stage utilization of coal by the iron and steel industry gives us a fairly clear picture of the expected demand for the bulk of coal deliveries, because this bears rather fixed proportions to the production of pig iron, coke, and sinter. But it also implies knowledge of the distribution of coke between different processes and outside consumers. An attempt to explain coke demand in terms of pig iron production assumes a regular relationship between total pig iron production and the proportion used for steel-making, while this ratio is actually constantly changing. Just replacing the unknown aggregate demand by an unknown structure does not take us much further.

We could relate coal demand to end products but the mixture of technologies involved might lead to instability in the "technical" parameters. The incorporation of too many secondary effects would transform the technological relations into a rather weak econometric model. This approach would also imply a fixed proportion of steel produced from scrap, while the share of the electric-arc process in fact varies over time.

The demand for different energy carriers has developed irregularly over the period studied, as shown in Figure 2. Substitution effects have also varied widely within the iron and steel industry as a whole, since different processes have different energy intensities and very different energy-input structures.

Note that here we include in the iron and steel industry a number of specialized plants, as well as the category known as "minor metallurgy," which consists of specialized parts of machinery plants. Including pig iron for foundries and steel castings is more questionable, because the bulk of pig iron for foundries is produced outside the specialized plants, largely from scrap from pig iron deliveries. The remainder of the pig iron produced within the industry is used for tubes and the basic installations needed to produce steel and rolled products, and in this case it is accounted as having been used by the industry itself after amortization.

The share of steel for castings produced by the industry is relatively small.

With one exception, the intermediate products of the iron and steel industry are used within the industry itself or else are exported; the exception is coke, which is also delivered to other branches of the economy.

3. DATA SOURCES AND OBSERVED TRENDS

Three main sources ("Narkhoz," "CMEA," and "UN") were used for the period 1960–1982. These are complementary in many respects. For example, data on the total production of crude steel are available in Narkhoz and CMEA, whereas these sources only report the steel produced by different processes (oxygen, Martin process, electric arc) in the case of steel produced in specialized plants. In contrast, UN gives crude steel production by type of process for steel production as a whole. CMEA adds to the data in Narkhoz some information on pig iron production for steel making, while Narkhoz provides additional information on the qualities (i.e. metal content) of the iron and manganese ores used.

All of these data originate from the USSR Statistical Board, so that there is very little risk of methodological discrepancies in utilizing and combining data from different publications. In addition to the three major sources, we have also used data from the ECE study "Strategy for Energy Use in the Iron and Steel Industry" (referred to as "ECE") and a number of papers published in recent years in Russian.

3.1. Mining and Preprocessing

This stage covers coke production, iron and manganese ore mining, and the production of sinter and pellets. The requirements here are mostly on the capital side, but energy inputs (specifically, coal for coke, electricity, and coke breeze for agglomerates) are also considered.

The production of iron ore is represented by three variables: iron ore mined (*fercr*), i.e. the weight of crude ore, iron ore shipped (*ferore*), and the shipped content of iron ore expressed as the percentage metal content (*fer%*); Table 3 shows the development of these variables over the period 1960–1980.

TABLE 3 Soviet iron ore production, 1960–1980.

	1960	1970	1975	1980
fercr (million tons)	141.55	355.36	441.79	498.13
ferore (million tons)	105.86	195.49	232.80	244.76
fer%	54.08	106.46	127.94	132.89
ferore / fercr	0.75	0.55	0.53	0.49
fer%/ ferore	0.51	0.54	0.54	0.54
fer%/ fercr	0.38	0.30	0.29	0.27

Two of the ratios in Table 3 (*ferore/ fercr*, *fer%/ fercr*) show a further decline in the "quality" of iron ores since 1970; this was after the most significant changes between mined and shipped ores had taken place between 1960 and 1970. But the continuous decline in these ratios may also partially explain the supply rigidities and the possible increase in investment requirements. Another indicator is also of interest: the shares of iron ore shipped in the form of concentrates or as mined, respectively (see Table 4). The latter share decreased from 44.8% in 1966 to 30.9% in 1978 and to 25.9% by 1982. This reflects the fact that "high quality" iron ore, which can be shipped in the form in which it is mined, has decreased not only relatively but also in absolute terms from 85.7 million tons in 1976 to 63.2 million tons in 1982, after having earlier grown from a level of 72.7 million tons in 1966. The ratio between iron ore mined and iron ore shipped from the mines as concentrates increased by 20% from 1966 to 1982; i.e. in 1966, 2.1 tons of iron ore mined were transformed at source for every ton shipped as concentrates, while in 1982,

2.45 tons of crude iron ore were required for every ton of concentrates shipped.

TABLE 4 Iron ore and concentrates shipped in the Soviet Union, 1966–1982.

Category shipped	1966	1976	1980	1982
Total	160.3	241.2	244.8	244.4
As concentrates	88.6	155.5	176.6	181.2
As mined	71.7	85.7	68.2	63.2

The production of manganese ore did not increase as fast as that of iron ore; manganese ore shipments (*mnore*) took nearly 23 years to double, while the manganese metal content (*mn%*) did not decrease so much as the metal content of iron ore, although a decline was noted between 1975 (35%) and 1980 (31%). The greater part of total manganese ore production during the period went for export.

It is important to note that the metal content of both kinds of ores stabilized in 1970–1975 before dropping later.

Developments in the production of two kinds of agglomerates (sinter and pellets) differed significantly. The production of pellets was almost zero in the early 1960s and grew to 55 million tons by 1982, while sinter production grew steadily from 65 to 150 million tons over the same period, as shown in Table 5.

TABLE 5 Production of agglomerates in the Soviet iron and steel industry, 1960–1980.

	1960	1966	1970	1975	1980
Sinter	65.1	115.7	138.2	151.9	153.8
Pellets	−	1.6	10.6	27.2	50.9

The growth of coke production (*coke*) was steady, at about 2.5% per annum during the period studied. The share of exports (*excoke*) increased in the 1960s before stabilizing in the 1970s; imports of coke (*imcoke*) remained relatively constant.

Expressing the energy inputs needed for coke production in terms of tons of coal equivalent (tce), we find that they correspond to approximately 10% of the total production of coke. We examined the effects of changes in this percentage on the basis of Pavlenko and Tichomirov's (1983) assertion that a 1% change would be equivalent to 7 million tce in 1960 and 8 million tce in 1980. We have used the available figures for coke production and its consumption in pig iron production, together with "technological" parameters from ECE and from Pavlenko and Tichomirov (1983).

The demand for coke breeze in agglomeration is estimated to have been 3.3 million tons in 1960 and 6.5 million tons in 1980. It can also be observed that there has been a significant substitution of coke breeze by natural gas, whose share grew 1.5 times over the decade 1970–1980, while the total energy requirement per ton of agglomerate dropped by 10% over the same period.

3.2. Pig Iron Production

The domestic demand for iron ore, sinter, and pellets was derived with the help of "engineering" data, together with data (UN) on the consumption of iron ores (*feroc*), agglomerates (*sinoc*, *peloc*), and total ores (*oreoc*). Trends in the consumption of these raw materials are shown in Table 6.

Due to the internal changes in the structure of agglomerate, we obtain an unstable "technological" parameter (*oreoc/pig*), which is 1.775 for 1965 and 1975 and 1.8 for 1970 and 1980. It is clear that every component of this parameter was

TABLE 6 Raw material inputs (million tons) in pig iron production in the Soviet Union, 1960—1980.

	1960	1966	1970	1975	1980
pig	46.76	70.26	85.93	102.97	107.28
oreoc	87.49	128.9	154.94	182.79	194.41
of which:					
feroc	23.66	17.44	11.43	12.57	8.90
sinoc	63.83	109.86	132.92	143.03	143.31
peloc	0.00	1.61	10.62	27.20	42.20
creoc / *pig*	1.871	1.775	1.803	1.775	1.812
feroc / *pig*	0.506	0.248	0.133	0.122	0.083
sinoc / *pig*	1.365	1.564	1.547	1.389	1.336
peloc / *pig*	0.000	0.023	0.124	0.264	0.393
(*sinoc* +*peloc*)/ *pig*	1.365	1.589	1.671	1.653	1.729

increasing or decreasing smoothly. When we take into account the fact that the "quality" of iron ore mined remained rather stable between 1970 and 1975, we can also explain the very slow process of iron ore "substitution" over the same period that its consumption increased from 11.43 to 12.57 million tons. The significant slowdown in 1975—1980 can be ascribed to the (possibly forced) substitution brought about by the lower quality of iron ore mined.

In the last ten years, the consumption of coke in blast furnaces (*cokeocp*) has decreased significantly in relative terms, mainly due to its substitution (directly and indirectly) by natural gas. The share of pig iron produced using natural gas increased from 79% in 1965 to 93% in 1980.*

TABLE 7 Energy inputs in pig iron production in the Soviet Union, 1960—1980.

	1960	1966	1970	1975	1980
pig	46.76	70.26	85.93	102.97	107.20
cokeocp	33.85	43.31	49.24	56.23	57.80
cokeocp / *pig*	0.724	0.616	0.573	0.546	0.540
cokeocp / *energyoc*	–	–	0.730	0.720	0.710

Demand for scrap is easy to estimate after we subdivide the pig iron production figures into their two major components — pig iron for steel making (*pigosm*) and pig iron for foundries (*pigof*) — whose growth behavior differs significantly. Since the scrap consumption per ton differs by a factor of ten for these two processes, "technological" parameters are best quoted separately for each: *scraposm* fell from 0.021 in 1966 to 0.015 in 1975, while *scrapof* rose from 0.108 to 0.125 over the same period. Pig iron for foundries reached a peak of 9 million tons in early 1970 and then dropped steadily over the years, while pig iron for steel making reached a peak of 102.5 million tons in 1978. Thus, the slowdown of total pig iron production in 1978—1982 must be divided into two parts — a continuous secular slowdown (which accelerated in the late 1970s) in pig iron for foundries and a more recent slowdown in pig iron for steel making. Other minor components included in total pig iron

*Observe that one cubic meter of natural gas substitutes 0.8—0.9 kg of coke in pig iron production. Thus, if the major part of the slowdown in coke input (from 0.72 tons per ton of pig iron in 1960 to 0.54 tons per ton in 1980) has been due to this substitution, then we can estimate natural gas consumption as being in the region of 10 billion cubic meters.

production, such as ferromanganese and "spiegel" pig iron, have also steadily decreased since 1970, so that by 1980, 93% of total pig iron production went into steel making.

3.3. Steel Making

Steel production figures on average bear a close relation to the growth of pig iron production; their rates of growth (3.8% per annum over the period 1961–1982) essentially do not differ. Crude steel production increased from 65.3 million tons in 1960 to a peak of 151.5 million tons in 1978, before dropping to 147.2 million tons in 1982. The relationship between the two time series can be seen in Table 8. Another ingredient for steel making is scrap, of which 55 million tons was consumed in 1966. In the manufacture of steel, 0.57 tons of scrap are used per ton of steel as compared with 0.62 tons of pig iron.

TABLE 8 Steel production (million tons) and its relation to pig iron production in the Soviet Union, 1960–1982.

	1960	1965	1970	1975	1980	1982
steel	65.3	91.0	115.9	141.3	147.9	147.2
steel / pig	1.40	1.38	1.35	1.37	1.38	1.38
steel / pigosm	1.70	1.62	1.53	1.51	1.48	1.48

No further analysis of the steel making process can be pursued without breaking down the steel production figures into three main processes, each of them very different in terms of raw material and energy demand. Between them, the oxygen converter (*oxy*), open-hearth (*martin*), and electric-arc (*elec*) processes account for over 97% of Soviet steel production, with the remainder being produced using the Bessemer process. The changing structure of steel production can be seen from Table 9. The share of *martin* steel went down steadily from 84% to 60% over the period studied, and it was replaced by *oxy* steel, whose share grew from 4% to 28% over the same period. But what is more important is that the share of *elec* steel remained relatively constant over time. This pattern is very different from that in other developed countries, where the electric-arc process generally has a much larger share.

TABLE 9 Structure of Soviet steel production, 1960–1979.

	1960	1965	1970	1975	1979
oxy	2.5	4.0	19.9	34.8	42.3
martin	55.1	75.9	84.1	91.5	91.1
elec	5.8	8.5	10.7	14.0	14.9
oxy / steel	0.04	0.04	0.17	0.25	0.28
martin / steel	0.84	0.83	0.73	0.65	0.60
elec / steel	0.09	0.10	0.09	0.09	0.10

The differences in the input structure for the different types of steel are summarized in Table 10.

Simple calculations show that about 80% of the decrease in energy input per ton of steel was due to structural shifts in technology mix, with the rest being due to increased energy efficiency within each technology. For example, natural gas requirements for the open-hearth process were 5 billion cubic meters in 1966 and increased by 20% to 6 billion cubic meters by 1980, due to a combination of efficiency increases and the slow growth of *martin* steel; the corresponding

TABLE 10 Structure of inputs per ton of steel produced by various processes in the Soviet Union, 1980.

Process	Input		Percentage share	
	Pig iron (tons)	Energy (GJ)	Electricity	Natural gas
oxy	0.880	0.84	33.3	66.7
martin	0.580	4.05	1.4	37.9
electric	0.033	6.97	87.2	10.6

technical parameters were 0.069 in 1966 and 0.066 in 1980. The share of natural gas in energy input increased over the same period from less than 50% to 60%.

To complete the picture it should be noted that some steel is also produced outside the iron and steel industry as defined here. The amounts involved are relatively small but there are large proportional variations from one process to another. Electric arc steel produced outside the industry increased threefold in amount from 1960 to 1980, while the outside contribution to martin steel production remained small and relatively constant.

Of particular interest is the continuous casting process, which is heavily reliant on technological advance; in the Soviet Union it accounts for only 10% of all steel produced, which is significantly lower than in other developed countries.

3.4. Finished Steel Products

At least 20 end products may be identified, but these are aggregated here into two main groups: *plates* (including tubes and ingots) and *sections*. The shares of sections and plates in total finished rolled products (*rolf*) have changed very smoothly over time, as shown in Table 11.

TABLE 11 Structure of rolled steel products produced in the Soviet Union, 1960–1980.

	1960	1965	1970	1975	1980
sections	29.02	38.09	49.51	58.55	59.4
plates	14.08	23.02	30.54	39.35	42.7
sections/rolf	0.66	0.62	0.61	0.59	0.58
plates/rolf	0.32	0.37	0.38	0.40	0.42

The absolute level of tube production did not decrease in the late 1970s and a peak of 18.2 million tons was reached in 1979; however, the rate of growth declined between 1977 and 1983, as shown in the 1983 level of 18.7 million tons.

Total energy requirements for rolling mills account for only 12% of total energy use in the iron and steel industry. Approximately half of the direct energy input is secondary energy derived from other processes in the industry. The bulk of the net energy consumption is supplied by natural gas and electricity (up to 15 billion kWh).

3.5. The Use of End Products

The bulk of the end products of the Soviet iron and steel industry are destined for the machinery and construction sectors, which themselves contribute significantly to investment. Among the machinery-sector industries, some use metal products intensively (e.g. metallurgical equipment, metal structures, transport equipment) while others do not rely so heavily on rolled steel products (e.g. electrical appliances). Average rates of growth in machinery have been considerably higher than that of iron and steel end- product production, with the slowest growth being recorded by those industries closely connected to investment formation. The elasticities of the growth of individual industries (given below in parentheses) with respect to that of the machinery sector as a whole over the period 1965—1980 reveal three main groups: *low* growth was observed for forging (0.44), bearings (0.45), metallurgical and boring equipment (0.50), railway equipment (0.52), energy equipment (0.58), transport equipment (0.59), food and lighting equipment (0.67); the *average* group included autos (1.0), tools (0.85), chemical equipment (0.78), building equipment (0.74), metal structures (0.74), repairs (0.72), and electrotechnology (0.70); the single *high* growth industry was electrical appliances and devices (2.3).

The share of equipment in gross fixed capital formation grew approximately fivefold in 20 years, from 11.2 billion roubles in 1960 to 50.2 billion roubles in 1980; over the same period the ratio between equipment investment and the production of finished rolled products (expressed in billion roubles per million tons) rose from 0.27 in 1960 to 0.49 in 1980.

To model the demand for end products we can use the 1972 Soviet input—output data as a system of weights and then relate the growth in end products to machinery and construction, assuming an average rate of technological progress (in terms of metal saved per rouble of output). Alternatively, we could use an aggregated index for machinery and construction, and rely on the trends reported by Yaremenko (1981) for the products of the iron and steel industry expressed in value terms.

4. ECONOMETRIC RESULTS

In general, two types of equations have been estimated, "technical" equations and time-trend equations. Time trends for technical coefficients have been estimated in both linear and exponential form. It has also been found valuable to estimate the relationships between different inputs, such as the substitution of coke in pig iron production by natural gas.

The fast and relatively steady growth of all economic indicators over the period 1960—1982 led to a high level of significance in the parameter estimates for the second set of equations; therefore we do not report here standard goodness-of-fit characteristics except for those equations in which the slope coefficients or the time-trend parameters are insignificant. Due to colinearity between the time variable and the explanatory variables we have sometimes chosen the simplest form, omitting time trends.

We also examined carefully the development of various technical parameters, some of which have exhibited strong and consistent time trends and others that appear to have made "U-turns" in recent years.

The flow-chart on the next page shows aggregate-level elasticities (ε) of the demands for semi-finished and raw material inputs, together with estimates r of the time trends or residual technological-progress and product-mix effects.

The next two subsections present details of the regression analysis. Note that for pig iron production there have been important substitutions not only between energy carriers but between materials: this is illustrated by the last three regressions in Section 4.2, and has caused significant changes elsewhere in the structure of the industry.

Finished rolled products $\xrightarrow[r = 0.2\%]{\epsilon = 0.91}$ Crude steel $\xrightarrow{\epsilon = 1.15}$ Pig iron for steel making

Pig iron for steel making $\xrightarrow[r = -0.4\%]{\epsilon = 0.95}$ Pig iron $\xrightarrow[r = -3.4\%]{\epsilon = 1.9}$ Demand for agglomerates

$\xrightarrow[r = 1.3\%]{\epsilon = 0.4}$ Demand for coke $\xrightarrow[r = 1.7\%]{\epsilon = 0.24}$ Coke production

Demand for agglomerates $\xrightarrow[r = 3.0\%]{\epsilon = 1.3}$ Agglomerates production $\xrightarrow[r = 1.6\%]{\epsilon = 0.62}$ Demand for iron ore mining

4.1. Technical Parameters and Shares

$steel / rolf = 1.49 - 0.0037\,t$

$pigosm / steel = 0.586 + 0.0050\,t$

$pig / pigosm = 1.234 - 0.0084\,t$

$sinteroc / pig = 1.4508 + 0.0172\,t$

$(sinter + pell) / sinoc = 1.054 - 0.0012\,t$

$ferore / (sinter + pell) = 1.4043 - 0.0079\,t$

4.2. Relationships Between Physical Indicators

The following regression equations are logarithmic and t-values are given in parentheses:

$$steel = 0.755 + \underset{(77.3)}{0.907}\ rolf + \underset{(4.0)}{0.002}\ t$$

$$pigosm = -1.14 + \underset{(54.1)}{1.144}\ steel + \underset{(1.6)}{0.0014}\ t$$

$$pigosm = -1.279 + \underset{(199.6)}{1.177}\ steel$$

$$pigom = -0.587 + \underset{(11.4)}{1.007}\ martin + \underset{(0.4)}{0.01}\ t$$

$$pigom = -0.697 + \underset{(36.0)}{-11.034}\ martin$$

$$scrapom = -0.100 + \underset{(7.9)}{0.843}\ martin + \underset{(3.9)}{0.006}\ t$$

$$pig = 0.411 + \underset{(58.0)}{0.946}\ pigosm - \underset{(5.6)}{0.004}\ t$$

$$cokeoc = 1.916 + 0.411 \; pig + 0.13 \quad t$$
$$\qquad\qquad (4.3) \qquad\qquad (2.7)$$

$$coke = 3.186 + 0.244 \; cokeoc + 0.272 \quad t$$
$$\qquad\qquad (0.9) \qquad\qquad (1.9)$$

$$coke = 1.442 + 0.742 \quad cokeoc$$
$$\qquad\qquad (23.5)$$

$$sinoc = -2.964 + 1.862 \quad pig - 0.033 \quad t$$
$$\qquad\qquad (15.1) \qquad\qquad (5.2)$$

$$sinter = -1.178 + 1.297 \quad sinoc - 0.030 \quad t$$
$$\qquad\qquad (17.4) \qquad\qquad (6.3)$$

$$ferore = 2.065 + 0.616 \quad sinter + 0.016 \quad t$$
$$\qquad\qquad (13.2) \qquad\qquad (8.9)$$

$$pig = 4.744 + 0.685 \; sinoc + 1.033 \; peloc - 1.83 \quad t$$
$$\qquad (1.0) \qquad (7.6) \qquad\qquad (4.3) \qquad\qquad (2.1)$$

$$pig = 0.771 \; sinoc + 1.232 \; peloc - 2.62 \quad t$$
$$\qquad (39.8) \qquad\qquad (9.3) \qquad\qquad (6.9)$$

$$sinoc / pig = 1.332 \quad - 2.51 \quad (peloc / pig) + 0.047 \quad t$$
$$\qquad\qquad (52.6) \qquad (9.6) \qquad\qquad (8.3)$$

5. CONCLUSIONS

Our study of the historical development of the Soviet iron and steel industry over the last twenty years has highlighted the need for a joint consideration of technical coefficients and the shares of different technologies and products. Very marked overall shifts in energy and raw-material requirements can arise from processes of substitution that are intrinsically relatively stable, and the growth in some products necessarily takes place at the expense of others.

A stage-by-stage analysis of the technological transformations and energy requirements of the industry showed that steel produced by the oxygen convertor process requires 2–2.5 times as much energy per ton as electric-arc steel. Using this and other weighting information, together with various time series of total energy use in the iron and steel industry, we developed an econometric model that takes into account product-mix effects and energy-saving processes at each stage of production. Detailed regressions were reported for a number of parameters of particular interest.

Technological progress, particularly that of an energy-saving nature, clearly plays a major role at all stages of production. Nevertheless, the growing demand for high-quality end products has been responsible for increases in the demand for primary inputs, both raw material and energy, which have to a certain extent cancelled out the energy savings achieved technically.

As pointed out by Gladyshevski *et al.* (1980), the slowdown in the growth of finished steel products has led to adaptation elsewhere in Soviet industry through three mechanisms: a slowdown in other metal-intensive industries; substitution of iron and steel products by other materials; and more rapid price increases (or price rises without any corresponding improvement in quality) for products like machinery with a high metal content.

Finally, Narkhoz has provided information on the utilization of capital stock within the iron and steel industry, in terms of tonnage of steel produced per cubic meter (blast furnace) or square meter (open hearth) of capacity, and in terms of the percentage of "idle time" for each process. Production per unit of capacity has climbed fairly steadily since 1960, although a slowdown in recent years and a slight decline in the rate of utilization indicates how closely the performance of this capital stock is related to that of industry as a whole.

REFERENCES

CMEA (various years) *Statisticheskij ejegodnick stran-chlenov SEV (Statistical Yearbook of the CMEA Economies)*. Finansy i Statistica, Moscow.

ECE (1983) *Strategy for Energy Use in the Iron and Steel Industry*. United Nations, New York.

Egorichev, A. (1984) Povyshenie effectivnosti ispolsovaniya energoresoursov v chernoi metallurgii (Efficiency of energy resources utilization in the iron and steel industry). *Promyshlennaje Energetika*, 07.

Foreign Trade (various years) *Vneshnaya Torgovlja SSSR (USSR Foreign Trade)*. Finansy i Statistica, Moscow.

Gladyshevski, A., Belous, G., and Lavrenov, N. (1980) Problemy modelirovanija i prognozirovanija osnovnyh potokov chernyh metallov (Modeling and forecasting of the demand for finished steel products). In: *Modelirovanie structury proizvodstva (Modeling of Production Structure)*. CEMI, Moscow (in Russian).

Kogan, Y. (1984) Elektroenergija v systeme proizvodstvennych resoursov (Electricity in the system of productive resources). *Voprosi Ekonomiki*, 4 (in Russian).

Ksenofontov, M. (1980) Modelirovanie formirovanija narodnokhozajstvennoj potrebnosti v toplivno-energeticheskich resoursach (Modeling of energy demand). In: *Modelirovanie structury proizvodstva (Modeling of Production Structure)*. CEMI, Moscow (in Russian).

Lavrenov, N. (1976) Ispolzovanie materialnyh balansov dlya postroenia dynamicki ukrupnennych pokazatelej meszltraslevyh svyazej chernoij metalurgii (Use of material balances for iron and steel industry modeling). In: *Model meszotraslevyh vzaineodejsbvij (Model of Interindustry Interactions)*. CEMI, Moscow (in Russian).

Narkhoz (various years) *Narodnoye Khozjastvo SSSR (Statistical Yearbook of the USSR Economy)*. Finansy i Statistica, Moscow.

Pavlenko, V. and Tichomirov, A. (1983) Modelirovanie dynamici toplivno-energopotrebleniya v chernoi metallurgii SSSR (Modeling of energy use in the USSR iron and steel industry). *EMM*, 19(4)(in Russian).

Smyshlyaev, A. (1982) *Model of Interindustry Interactions as a System of Simultaneous Equations*. Working Paper WP-82-28. International Institute for Applied Systems Analysis, Laxenburg, Austria.

Smyshlyaev, A. and Pavlenko, V. (1981) Prognozirovanie struktury proizvodstva v chernoi metallurgii SSSR (Forecasting of the USSR iron and steel industry production structure). *EMM*, 17(3) (in Russian).

UN (various years) *Quarterly Bulletin of Iron and Steel Production*. United Nations, New York.

Yaremenko, Y. (1981) *Structurnye izmenenija v socialisticheskoj ekonomike (Structural Changes in a Socialist Economy)*. Mysl., Moscow (in Russian).

THE EFFECTS OF STRUCTURAL CHANGES ON DANISH ENERGY CONSUMPTION

Ellen Pløger

Energy Systems Group, Risø National Laboratory, Denmark

1. INTRODUCTION

The aim of this paper is to present some preliminary results from a study of how changes in output-mix have influenced the energy consumption in the Danish manufacturing industries.

The study, which is supported by the Danish Ministry of Energy, strives for including the output-mix effects as an explicit factor in a total analysis of the changes in energy consumption.

2. DATA

The analysis will be based on 2 sets of data from the national accounts.

First of all the analysis will use the timeserie of input-output (IO) tables in constant (1975) prices. This timeserie, which is made public by the Danish Statistical Office, covers for the time being the period 1966-80 and is using a classification of 117 industries among which 82 are manufacturing industries.

In order to analyse the changes in energy consumption by using an IO-model, it is necessary to have energy data that are directly compatible with the IO-tables. Such data are also available from the Danish Statistical Office who has set up balances for approximately 20 energy products in both monetary and physical terms. To get an expression for the total energy consumption in each of the industries, but without making any double counting, the consumption in physical terms have been transferred to calorific values of primary energy.

The existence of annual IO-tables and supporting datamatrices for energy consumption makes it possible to carry out a mutual study of the development of energy consumption in different industries and of the development in the interaction of industries.

3. THE BASIC MODEL

The development of the energy consumption in the Danish manufacturing industries is shown in figur A.

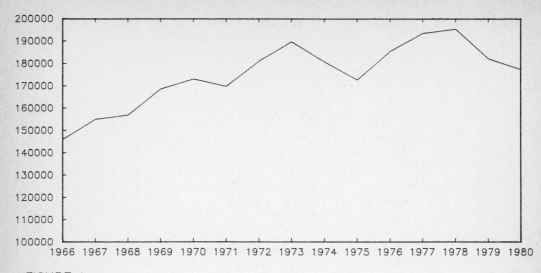

FIGURE A:

ENERGY CONSUMPTION IN THE DANISH MANUFACTURING INDUSTRIES 1966—1980 (TJ)

It can be seen that this consumption has been rather fluctuating – although a trend could be made out in the period 1966-78. The problem with such a historic development is that it is extremely difficult to use this kind of picture to predict the future development. Before trying to do any such kind of guesswork it is necessary to try to reveal the causes of the movements in the energy consumption.

Much information can be obtained by analysing the data by use of a static IO-model with endogeneous imports (i.e. the import matrix is seperated out)

$$x = (I-A)^{-1} \cdot D \cdot d \qquad\qquad (1)$$
where

x is a column vector for the output of industries
$(I-A)^{-1}$ is the inverse Leontief matrix
D is a matrix for the composition of final demand where
a column contains the proportions delivered from industries into each category of final demand.
d is a column vector for the absolute level of final demand
by category.

By multiplying both sides of eq. 1 by the energy consumption per unit of output calculated from the energy matrices, an expression for the total energy consumption in a single year is obtained.

$$e \star x = e \star \left[(I-A)^{-1} \cdot D \cdot d \right] \tag{2}$$

where $\star$ denotes element multiplication.

This relationsship can be established for any year and consequently the changes in energy consumption between the years t and t-1 can be written as:

$$e_t \star x_t - e_{t-1} \star x_{t-1} =$$

$$e_t \star ((I-A)_t^{-1} \cdot D_t \cdot d_t) - e_{t-1} \star ((I-A)_{t-1}^{-1} \cdot D_{t-1} \cdot d_{t-1}) \tag{3}$$

This equation[1] makes it possible to distinguish the changes in energy consumption caused by

1) changes in the interaction of industries
   (changes in the $(I-A)^{-1}$ matrices)
2) changes in the composition of final demand
   (changes in the D matrices)
3) changes in the level of final demand
   (changes in the d vectors)

and

4) changes in the energy coefficients
   (changes in the e vectors)

Such a decomposition of the changes in energy consumption into different technology and demand factors makes the model an adequate tool to explain a historic development like the one seen in figure A. Specially one would be interested in knowing whether the decreases in energy consumption from 1973 to 1975 and from 1978 to 1980 reflect the introduction of energy saving technology and other kinds of energy conservation or whether the decreases were merely caused by an economic recession.

However, if it shall be possible to interpret the factor for changes in energy coefficients either as changes derived from changes in the technology used for producing a specific good or as an explicit application of energy conservation, it is necessary to assume that the production in each of the industries is homogeneous over time. If this assumption is not fullfilled the changes in energy coefficient could just as well be explained by changes in the kinds of goods that is produced by the industry.

In the ideal situation where the basic assumption of IO-analysis is correct and each industry produces one and only one commodity by using one and only one input structure, the problem of changes in output-mix is non-exsistent. However, this assumption will not be met in real life, and an analysis of the effect of changes in output-mix can therefore also be seen as a kind of check of the homogeniety assumption.

The degree to which the assumption of homogenous production is realistic is related to both the applied classification of industries and to the length of the period to be analyzed.

It is obvious that the assumption of homogeneous production is most realistic when the analysis is based on a very disaggregated classification of industries because the definition of an industry then will be given by a single or a small basket of goods. This means that the results of an analysis of output-mix effects will depend on the classification used, so the results of one analysis can not be transferred to other analyses unless these are using the exact same classification.

---

1) A more detailed description of the model is given in Pløger (83)

The timeaspect of the analysis is due to the fact that the innovation of new products takes time and consequently the assumption of a homogeneous production will be more realistic if the analysis is dealing with a rather short period of time. This is important if an IO-model is used for forecasting or in a static, comparative analysis (as eq. 3), where the results are based on the assumption of unchanged IO-coefficients (energy coefficients). However, the changes in output-mix which can be observed from one year to another will mostly not be caused by the entering of new products but by shifts in the relative importance of the already known products and hereby changing the average technology used by the industry.

4. IO-MODELS AND CHANGES IN OUTPUT-MIX

The effects of changes in the output-mix on the basic IO-model can most simply be described by looking at the conditions in a single firm. If a firm decides to change the mix of its production (without changing the level of production) this will change the input structure of the firm as well as the distribution of its output. The input structure will be changed because the production of the "new" output will demand other inputs than the avarage "old" production and the distribution of its output will be changed as the different categories of demand (other industries and different categories of final demand) try to include this "new" product in their consumption and hereby affecting the composition of their demand.

This knowledge points at trying to trace the changes in output-mix either by a detailed analysis of the actual production of the different commodities or by studying the changes in the input-mix of the different industries/the composition of the different categories of final demand.

However, the detailed study of the commodities actually produced is not very easy to handle, when the IO-tables are established from a level of 1600 commodities [2]. Moreover will a study of the changes in the input-matrix and in the coefficient matrix of final demand be influenced by a lot of other factors such as technological changes, changes in relative prices, changes in the income distribution and in the terms of trade.

These considerations lead to the conclusion that the only feasible way of getting an impression of whether changes in output mix have influenced the energy consumption is to study the changes in output-distribution that has taken place during the period.

As the aim of the study is to try to isolate the effects of changes in output-mix in a complete analysis of the changes in energy consumption it will be natural to start by looking at the results of the basic analysis and to see if these results gives any sign of possible changes in the output-mix.

5. RESULTS OF THE BASIC ANALYSIS

The results of the model described in eq. (3) is given in table 1.

---

[2] The 1600 commodities (four-digit CCCN) is an aggregation of the basic 3000-4000 commodities.

TABLE 1 Changes in energy consumption in manufacturing industries 1966-80 (TJ).

| | DEMAND | | | TECHNOLOGY | | | TOTAL |
	Total	Compo-sition	Level	Total	IO-coef.	Energy-coef.	CHANGE
1966-70	29787	-734	30521	-2641	-1100	-1541	27144
1970-73	24304	1987	22319	-7683	1523	-9205	16622
1973-75	-17467	-11872	-5595	252	297	-40	-17215
1975-78	25162	3594	21568	-2243	-206	-2035	22918
1978-80	9943	6113	3830	-28239	-6970	-21268	-18294

The last column in the table shows that the energy consumption in the manufacturing industries increased by 27144 TJ from 1966 to 1970 [3] (equal to approximately 4.5% per year). This increase was mainly caused by the changes in final demand as the combined effects of changes in the level and composition of final demand increased the energy consumption by 29787 TJ. An opposite effect was seen in the changes in technology which caused a decrease in the energy consumption by 2641 TJ (calculated under the assumption that final demand had remained unchanged from 1966 to 1970).

Table 1 stresses the importance of changes in final demand and it should specially be noticed that the changes in the total energy consumption are developing almost parallel to the development in the energy consumption pulled by final demand in the period 1966-78. Secondly it should be noticed that the changes in energy consumption caused by changes in the energy coefficients have caused decreases in the total energy consumption in all of the 5 subperiods. Specially it is seen that the changes in energy coefficients from 1978 to 1980 have been able to offset the increase caused by the changes in final demand.

Table 1 includes 2 signs which can suggest that changes in output-mix might have taken place. The first sign is a part of the factors for changes in final demand. One of the categories of final demand is exports and the energy consumption necessary to this production has increased during the period from about 30% of the total energy consumption in 1966 to about 35% in 1980 but with a trough in the mid 1970'ies. It is very likely that this growth in exports has been associated with the development of new products or at least it might have pulled a change in the composition of production of the existing products in order to please the export markets.

The second sign of possible changes in output-mix is the factor for changes in IO-coefficients in the period 1978-80. It is seen that this factor suddenly becomes important although it has been almost neglectable in the previous periods. A detailed analysis reveals that most of these changes are related to non-metalic mineral products, because the input-distribution in certain industries has shifted away from the non-metallic mineral products. These shifts have specially been seen in construction enterprises where the decrease in new buildings has been replaced by a relative increase in the repair and maintenance of buildings and this activity has a quite different input-structure.

---

3) The subdivision of the period 1966-80 has been choosen because of the data sources, as the energy data are considered being of higher quality in the years for which a energy survey has been carried out (1966, 70, 73, 75, 78 and 80).

Such a shift, which heavily affects the manufacturing industry of non-metallic mineral products, could cause this industry to try to develop new products in order to survive.

These signs of possible changes in the output-mix along with the impression that a change-over of production takes place continuously underlines the importance of trying to trace the effects of changes in output-mix on the energy-coefficients.

6. ESTIMATION OF THE CHANGES IN ENERGY-COEFFICIENTS

The most common way of explaining the changes in energy coefficients is to let these be highly dependent of the changes in energy prices. This view, which rests on a cost-minimizing theory, will also be the basis of the relations put forward in this section.

Consequently the estimations will be based on the kind of relation given in eq. (4)

$$\Delta ce_j = f(\Delta pe_j) \tag{4}$$

where ce_j is the energy-coefficient in branch j and pe_j is the matching index for the energy price deflated by the price of labour.

However, in connection with this simple relation rises the problem of how to specify the dependence of energy prices. It can not be expected that it will be possible for the firms to adjust immediately to the new prices, so it is necessary to include some kind of lagstructure.

By looking at the results shown in table 1 it is possible to get an impression of how this lagstructure should be specified. Thus in section 5 it has already been mentioned that the changes in energy consumption from 1966 to 1978 almost completely reflected the changes in final demand, while the two developments seperated in the last subperiod. This result gives the interesting information that the decrease in energy consumption from 1973 to 1975 (cf. fig. A) was caused by a decrease in the production while the decrease in energy consumption in the period 1978-80 was caused by decreases in the energy coefficients. These changes in energy coefficients in the last subperiod must be interpreted as both a reaction to the 1973 price increase and a reinforced reaction caused by the 1979 price increase which stressed the importance of trying to reduce energy costs. Therefore the historic development suggests that some considerable lags can be seen and that the lenght of the lags can differ over time.

Based on these experiences it seems reasonable to assume a geometric lag structure, where the weights w_i are specified as

$$w_i = (1- \lambda) \lambda^i \quad 0< \lambda <1$$

which have greatest weight the first year followed by successively smaller weights.

Introducing this lagstructure gives the following basic relation

$$ce_t = a + b \sum_{i=0}^{\infty} (1- \lambda) \lambda^i pe_{t-i} \tag{5}$$

which can be transferred to a relation for the changes in energy coefficients

$$ce_t = a(1-\lambda) + b(1-\lambda)pe_t + \lambda ce_{t-1} \tag{6}$$

It is seen that in this relation the lag is now appearing on the dependent variable ce and not on the explanatory variable pe giving a relation, which is more easy to estimate. Eq. 6 will after a logerithmic transformation be estimated for each of the manufacturing industries.

By including the distribution of output, which is taken as an expression for the output mix, in the basic equation it is possible to check whether changes in output mix have had any significant influence on the energy coefficients.

The distribution of output is included in the equation by using the share of total production delivered to the different demand categories. The ideal situation would be to look at all of the individual 117 industries and 9 seperate categories of final demand, which are available in the Danish IO-tables, but this will not be possible to estimate and moreover can a shift between such disaggregated groups not necessarily be taken as a sign of changes in output-mix. Therefore in order to establish some groups, where shifts between these are likely to be a sign of changes in output-mix the following 3 have been choosen:

1. Input in industries
2. Deliveries to private consumption or investment
3. Deliveries to exports.

It has been found reasonable to let private consumption and investment be placed in the same group because the industries usually deliver either to private consumption or to investment.

As the sum of these shares is 1 the inclusion of all 3 groups will cause problems with multicollinearity in the regression. In order to avoid most of these problems only the groups 2 and 3, which both are of importance, but in most industries not the mayor part of production, have been included in the relation which now have the following form

$$ce_t = a(1-\lambda) + b(1-\lambda)pe_t + c(s2_t-\lambda s2_{t-1}) \\ + d(s3_t-\lambda s3_{t-1}) + \lambda ce_{t-1} \tag{7}$$

where s2 is the part of production delivered to private consumption and investment and s3 is the part of production delivered to exports.

Regarding the signs of the coefficients it has already been mentioned that λ should be possitive and less than one. Being the coefficient to the prices b should be negative but it is more difficult to have any a priori expectations of the signs of the coefficients c and d. These coefficients can be interpreted as the relative energy intensity of the products delivered either to private consumption and investments or to exports and can thus be both positive and negative.

7.   ESTIMATION RESULTS

As a first attempt to reveal the effect of changes in outputmix on the energy coefficients the equations 6 and 7 have been estimated for 20 industries producing food, beverages and tobacco and for 6 industries producing non-metallic mineral products. It has been considered useful to

TABLE 2. Estimation results of basic and extended relation.

Industries	basic relation				incl. export share				
	λ	a	b	R²	λ	a	b	d	R²
Slaughtering etc. of pigs and cattle	0.15*	-1.15	-0.64	0.49	-0.01*	-0.40	-0.60	1.04	0.72
Poultry killing, dressing, packing	0.94	-1.46	-6.12*	0.90	0.93	-1.24	-6.01*	0.12	0.91
Dairies	0.80	-0.34	-1.79*	0.69	0.75	-1.13	-0.99*	-0.77*	0.71
Processed cheese, condensed milk	0.53	0.49	-0.27*	0.32	0.48	0.22	-0.43	-0.71	0.73
Ice cream manufacturing	0.56	0.38	1.31	0.76	0.63	0.48	1.35	0.05*	0.76
Processing of fruit and vegetables	0.87	0.22	-0.95*	0.86	0.86	0.26	-0.97*	0.05*	0.86
Processing of fish	-0.01*	-0.69	-0.48	0.58	-0.09*	0.66	-0.48	0.05*	0.58
Oil mills	0.36	0.90	-0.18	0.24	0.48	0.08	-0.18	-0.76	0.69
Margarine manufacturing	0.24*	-0.17	0.01*	0.05	0.09*	0.12	-0.18*	0.12	0.26
Fish meal manufacturing	0.62	1.64	-1.13	0.62	0.62	1.62	-1.13	-0.08*	0.62
Grain mill products	0.56	-0.01	1.35	0.54	0.55	-0.08*	1.26*	-0.03*	0.54
Bread factories	0.65	0.54	0.23*	0.44	0.61	0.98	0.15*	0.13*	0.46
Cake factories	0.18	-0.51	-0.88	0.91	0.05*	-0.68	-0.71	-0.30	0.92
Sugar factories and refineries	-0.33	1.16	-0.05	0.12	0.37	0.96	-0.40*	-0.21	0.31
Chocolate and sugar confectionery	0.20*	-0.03	0.03*	0.06	-0.21*	0.43	-0.12*	0.35	0.32
Manufacture of food products n.e.c.	-0.02*	0.55	-0.22*	0.29	-0.01	0.62	-0.18	0.06*	0.31
Manuf. of prepared animal feeds	0.05*	1.50	-0.66	0.77	-0.18*	0.74	-0.48	-0.57	0.79
Distilling and blending spirits	1.07	1.45	7.58*	0.93	1.03	7.60	8.15*	1.58	0.97
Breweries	0.71	0.58	-0.18*	0.54	0.60	1.43	0.04*	0.52*	0.56
Tobacco manufactures	0.77	-0.40	-1.81*	0.55	0.88	0.45	-5.37*	0.44*	0.60
Manuf. of earthenware and pottery	0.56	0.88	-0.11*	0.42	0.56	0.08	0.36*	-0.96	0.53
Manuf. of glass and glass products	0.52	1.72	-0.93	0.98	0.51	1.41	-0.90	-0.22	0.99
Manuf. of structural clay products	0.60	2.56	-0.13*	0.42	0.61	2.49	-0.10*	-0.04*	0.43
Manuf. of cement, lime and plaster	0.29*	3.40	0.11*	0.14	-0.03*	2.66	0.35	-0.35	0.51
Concrete products and stone cutting	0.01*	0.12	-0.24	0.12	0.01*	0.38	-0.24	0.08*	0.14
Non-Metallic mineral products n.e.c.	0.56	1.84	-0.56	0.60	0.34	2.51	-0.76	0.58	0.71

* Unsignificant estimates

test the hypothesis on these 2 groups of industries, which are different in specially 2 ways. Firstly, energy is an important input in the production of non-metallic mineral products while it is a relative small cost in the production of food, beverage and tobacco.

Secondly, the distribution of output is different in the 2 groups, where the deliveries to private consumption and investment is a relatively small share in the second group, but important in the first. Concerning the export share this varies between industries in each of the groups.

The estimations showed great difficulties in getting significant estimates for the variable s2 and the inclusion of this variable caused in some cases unacceptable estimates of λ and b. For this reason the variable has been excluded from the estimations which are now reduced to a test of whether the introduction of the export share will improve the basic relation.

The estimation results is shown in table 2. The first section shows the results for the basic relation, while results for the relation including output-mix are shown in section 2.

Generally the results yielded from the basic relation are not quite satisfactory but it must be kept in mind that this relation is a quite simple ad hoc specification and not a sophisticated production function. However, the aim of the estimations is to try to include the output-mix effects as an explanatory variable rather than to analyse to possibilities of substitution between different kinds of input.

The evaluation of including production-mix effects can be done by looking at the R^2-values and the price elasticities. When the output-mix effects are included the results can be summerized in the following 4 points (taking into account only the relations giving significant estimates):

1. No estimations results are deteriorated by the inclusion.
2. Those estimation that have a very low value of R^2 will improve but without reaching an acceptable degree of explanation.
3. Many of the estimations that have a medium value of R^2 in the basic relation reached an acceptable level of R^2 by including the output-mix.
4. Those estimations with very high R^2 will of course only increase slightly.

Looking at the values of the estimated coefficients it can be seen that the industries producing food, beverage and tobacco tend to adjust more quickly to the price changes than the industries producing non-metallic mineral products. The more quickly reaction of the latter group of industries must be due to the fact that energy is a relatively more important input in the production of non -metallic mineral products than in the production of food, beverage and tobacco. Consequently, the introduction of energy conservation will tend to affect the production technology as such and the adjustment in this group can therefore be expected to take place along with the replacement of the capital equipment. However, the inclusion of a time variable representing technical progress has not been able to improve the estimation results.

The estimates of the long run price elasticities b are seen to decrease in the first group when output-mix effects are included with a maximum decrease of 30%. The picture in the second group is somewhat more confusing. Surprisingly the estimations show no significant difference between the size of the elasticities in the two groups and these elasticities vary greatly within the two groups.

Regarding the sign and the size of the relative energy intensity of exports (the coefficient d) this is seen to vary between the industries.

However, the general pattern is that in those industries, which have a high export share, an increase in exports will cause a decrease in energy coefficients while in industries, which have a low export share, an increase in exports will increase the energy coefficient. The only mayor exceptions from this pattern is "slaughtering and meatprocessing" and the beverage industries, which have both a high export share and a relative energy intensive export.

The reason for this general pattern of a energy extensive export could be that a maximum reduction in costs is necessary in order to compete on the international markets, that exportproducts are more manufactured than those sold on the home market and that if the export product is new this is likely to be produced using a new and more energy saving technology.

8.   CONCLUSION

Summerizing the preliminary results these seem to give 2 important conslusions:

1.   It seems possible to use the changes in production shares as an expression for changes in output-mix.
2.   It seems that the basic hypothesis of the importance of including output-mix effects in order to explain the development in the energy coefficients is confirmed.

However, further analyses must be carried out before the basis hypothesis is varified. First of all the specification must be estimated for other groups of manufacturing industries and other expressions for changes in output-mix should be tested.

Secondly the specification must be improved by testing other kinds of lagstructure and by introducing a more satisfactory deflation of the energy price in order to take into account other inputs than labour.

Finally the estimation results of the energy intensitivity for exports must be varified by studying the actual product-mix in selected industries.

REFERENCES

Foell, W.K. et al. (1979): Assessment of Alternative Energy/ Environment Futures for Austria: 1977-2015, IIASA, Laxenburg, Austria.

Lager, C. (1983): Analysis of Changing Energy Coefficients in Austria 1964-80, in A. Smyshlyaev (ed.). Proceedings of the Fourth IIASA Task Force Meeting on Input-Output Modeling, IIASA, Laxenburg, Austria.

Pløger, E. (1983): Input-Output Analysis of the Changes in Energy Consumption in Danish Industries 1966-79, in A. Smyshlyaev (ed.) Proceedings of the Forth IIASA Task Force Meeting on Input-Output Modeling, IIASA, Laxenburg, Austria.

Thage, B. (1982): Techniques in the Compilation of the Danish Input-Output tables: A new approach to the treatment of Imports, in Skolka, J. (ed.) Compilation of Input-Output tables, Berlin.

United Nations (1973): Input-Output Tables and Analysis, United Nations, New York.

THE ROLE OF ENERGY INTENSITY IN ECONOMIC DEVELOPMENT

Pal Erdösi

Institute for Industrial Economics, Budapest, Hungary

1. INTRODUCTION

This paper offers a short overview of three investigations dealing with the interactions between energy and the economy. At the center of these investigations — which relate to both the past and the future — lie questions concerning the energy intensity of the Hungarian economy.

As is the case in other countries, Hungary has a great interest in reducing the overall energy intensity of its economy, because of the heavy burden of providing the necessary supply of energy. Around half of Hungary's energy supply is provided by imported energy carriers. The increases in oil prices in the 1970s influenced very favorably Hungary's terms of trade and the share of imported energy in total imports has rapidly risen. At the same time about half of total industrial investment in Hungary is currently needed for energy-related development.

Therefore a governmental program exists for reducing the energy intensity of the economy by structural changes in production (at the levels of industrial sectors, commodities, and products), by saving energy and raw materials (particularly those of high energy intensity), and by rationalizing energy consumption in the production process; all of these measures are resulting in higher efficiency within the economy.

The resultant structural changes in the economy will fall into two groups: first, those that involve changing the ratio between energy-related and non-energy-related sectors, and second, those involving shifts between non-energy branches of differing energy intensity.

The three investigations outlined below build upon the analysis of past experiences in the Hungarian economy, and provide a basis for correct decision making and the assessment of possible future developments.

2. ENERGY INTENSITIES AND FACTORS THAT HAVE INFLUENCED THEM IN THE PAST

Several studies have examined this topic for different periods between 1950 and 1983; the most recent dealt with the years 1970—1983, with special emphasis on the period 1978—1983. The main results of the studies may be summarized as follows.

The average energy intensity of Hungarian mining and manufacturing industry has shown a continuous decrease over the period studied; today's intensity is only 40% of the corresponding value for 1950. Improvements in the energy intensity for the material sphere have been more modest (70%) and they have been smallest of all for the economy as a whole (75%); improvements in the two latter energy intensities began to be noticeable from 1960 and 1965, respectively, after some earlier increases.

The main reasons for the reductions in all three types of energy intensity during the period 1960—1975 have been the favorable changes in the overall supply structure in favor of oil and gas. The intensity of the use of electricity can be characterized similarly, but all three curves exceed the 1950 intensity values, except that for industry over the last few years.

Special conditions appear to have played a role in the most recent period, 1978—1983, with the stagnation of total national energy consumption, at the same time as a modest increase in both national income and the total output of the economy. However, the question is which factors affected this stagnation and to what extent. The "break" in the energy consumption curve in 1978 seems to have been caused in almost equal proportions by two main factors: the recession in production, and the improvement in the average energy intensity of the Hungarian economy, which again was itself affected by several factors.

It must be stressed that by far the larger part of the improvement in energy intensity, and the consequent reduction in energy consumption, has been attained by various structural changes in the economy (both in terms of branches and products), while only a much smaller part has been due to direct energy savings related to changes in technological processes.

It is clear that very useful and practical conclusions can be drawn from the results of these analyses for both the future development of the economy and for the general area of energy and material conservation.

3. AN INPUT-OUTPUT MODEL FOR ANALYZING DIRECT AND CUMULATIVE ENERGY INTENSITIES

A special model for analyzing energy-intensity relations has been prepared on the basis of a national input—output model for 1976 (with nearly 100 × 100 sectors). The special version has 42 sectors, 9 of which are energy-related, 25 are individual sectors of high energy intensity, and 8 are aggregated sectors of low energy intensity. The new model was converted to 1980 price levels; this was important first and foremost because of the intervening energy price increases. The investigation covered the following areas:

- Direct and cumulative energy-intensity factors for each sector in kcal/Ft; the Ft values used were the total output and the total production of each sector, respectively;

- Direct and cumulative energy-content factors for each sector, in Ft/Ft, again based on total output and total production;

- Direct and cumulative capital intensity for each sector, in Ft/Ft;

- Indirect, "hidden" energy imports and exports (the Hungarian economy is very open, with nearly half of the national income associated with foreign trade);

- Direct and cumulative effects of raw material savings on energy consumption and on the energy intensity of the economy.

Finally, the investigations were repeated with two alternative models of different energy intensities (higher and lower, respectively, than that of the original model). They were derived from the original one by changing the domestic production/import ratio within each of the two groups of sectors.

Some of the main results are as follows. There are big differences (multiple ratios) between the two groups of sectors, regarding both their direct and their cumulative energy-content factors (0.03–0.10 vs. 0.3–0.5 and 0.1–0.25 vs 0.4–0.6 Ft/Ft, approximate values). "Hidden" energy imports and exports turn out to be of similar magnitude to total direct energy imports. This situation could advantageously be altered by decreasing exports and increasing imports of materials of high energy intensity. Finally, production structures of higher energy intensity have capital intensities that are much higher and production efficiencies that are lower than structures with lower energy intensities.

All of these investigations will be repeated, utilizing a recently prepared input—output model for the year 1981.

4. AN INPUT—OUTPUT MODEL FOR ANALYZING THE EFFICIENCY OF ENERGY SUPPLY SYSTEMS

Any given total final energy demand (for producers and dwellings together) can be satisfied by a number of energy-supply systems of differing structures. These naturally result in different total energy requirements and energy intensities, as well as different demands on national resources (investment, manpower, imports); the losses and the efficiency of the supply system can thus, potentially, vary in a very wide range.

Using a special input—output model, numerical calculations were made for two specific cases: an *ex post* examination of total national energy consumption in 1975 and potential future developments for the next 15 years.

The model includes both primary energy production and conversion processes (primary and secondary energy carriers) in a 14 × 14 matrix; there are four rows and columns for primary energy production and eight for conversion processes. The 13th row and column contain energy consumed in the transportation of energy, while the 14th account for losses in storage and distribution (pipelines and wiring). Not only conversion losses but also final energy use and self-consumption in all the energy-related sectors are handled within the model.

Two fundamental types of matrices have been worked out: the first is the specific consumption matrix, with a_{ij} coefficients, and the second is the specific loss matrix, with v_{ij} coefficients. By utilizing the inverse matrices of both types, multifaceted analyses can be carried out, for example:

- Deciding on total energy requirements for meeting given (or planned) final energy needs;

- Comparing and ranking the energy-producing and conversion processes in terms of their cumulative characteristics (efficiency, losses) derived from the different inverse matrices;

- Identifying those process phases that are responsible for major inefficiencies in the process, with an eye to constructive intervention;

- Calculating the cumulative energy conservation in terms of final energy savings;

- Determining the total, cumulative requirements for national resources (such as investment) in meeting the final energy increment;

- Calculating the different effects arising from substitutability among the energy carriers (e.g., energy imports vs. domestic production and conversion), etc.

Concrete numerical examples have demonstrated that the model system is suitable for answering many of the most important current questions as well as those relating to the future development of the energy economy.

TRANSFORMATION MATRICES IN INPUT—OUTPUT COMPILATION

Carsten Stahmer

Federal Statistical Office, Wiesbaden, FRG

1. INTRODUCTION

Within the framework of the United Nations' "System of National Accounts" (SNA)[1] proposals are made for integrating input-output tables in national accounting. According to the SNA, input-output tables with uniform column and row classifications should not be calculated directly, but input-output compilation should start with computing two b a s i c t a - b l e s with different column and row classifications. One of these tables, the o u t p u t table, shows the output in a breakdown by industry (producers) and commodity group. The output table is also called the make matrix. The other table, the i n p u t table, shows the intermediate use of the commodities by industry (users) and commodity group (use matrix), the final uses by commodity group and the gross value added by industry. Under the aspect of data availability, these tables are the best presentation scheme for input-output figures. In a second step, the basic tables are transformed to input-output tables with uniform row and column classifications (commodity x commodity or industry x industry tables). These tables are used for input-output analysis.

In an annex to chapter III of the SNA several possible t r a n s - f o r m a t i o n p r o c e d u r e s are described. According to these transformation processes, the input data are transformed, using the data on outputs by industry and commodity. Normally, the input matrix is transformed as a whole, using certain technology assumptions. In my paper, some possible improvements of these transformation procedures are described, using special transformation matrices for certain rows and columns of the input table. Thus it is possible to influence the transformation procedure in a very specific way. These methods are already adopted in the Federal Republic of Germany for compiling the input-output tables of the Federal Statistical Office[2]. The special transformation matrix of 1980 compensation of employees is given as an example.

2. BASIC TABLES OF THE SNA

In the following scheme the relationship between the two basic tables of the SNA is shown:

---

* Federal Statistical Office, Wiesbaden.
[1] United Nations (1968).
[2] See Federal Statistical Office (1984). Cf. also Stahmer (1982) .

Input table

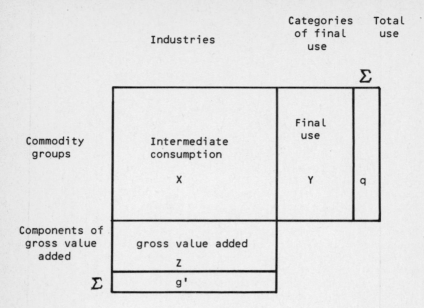

Output table

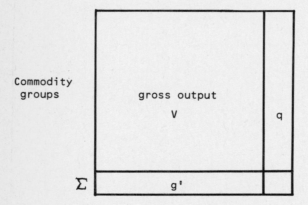

The first quadrant of the i n p u t table comprises the data of the intermediate consumption by commodity and industry, the second quadrant the final use by commodity and different categories, for example private consumption, capital formation and exports. The third quadrant shows the value added by industry and different components, for example depreciation and compensation of employees. The industry classification is extended to non-market production of government and private non-profit institutions. Using matrix notation, the input table is written as follows.

$$(1) \quad IOT_{SNA} = \begin{pmatrix} X & | & Y \\ ---&|&--- \\ Z & | & O \end{pmatrix}$$

where X, Y and Z represent matrices containing the data of the three quadrants. The column sums of X and Z are the gross output by industries (row vector g'), the row sums of X and Y are the total use of commodities by commodity groups (column vector q).

The o u t p u t table contains data on the domestic output by commodity group and industry. To facilitate the presentation of the transformation procedure, imports of goods and services are neglected. These data could be shown in an additional column in the output table. The row sums of the output table are the gross domestic output by commodity group (column vector q), equal to the total use in the input table. Besides the problems of foreign trade, the problems of differing price concepts of the input and output tables are neglected in this paper, too. Normally, the flows of the output table are valued at producers' prices, the flows of the input table at purchasers' prices. Therefore, in a complete system an additional column of the output table shows the transition from producers' prices to purchasers' prices.

3. COMPILATION OF COMMODITY X COMMODITY TABLES

Input-output tables with u n i f o r m column and row classifications are compiled by transforming the input table using the data of the output table. To get a commodity x commodity table it is necessary to transform the institutionally defined columns of the input table. To get an industry x industry table, you have to transform the commodity-defined rows of the input table. In this section, the transformation procedure of the commodity x commodity table is described. The procedure to compile an industry x industry table will be discussed in the next section.

The columns of the first and third quadrants of the input table show the input structure of the industries. To get the input structure of commodity-defined branches, it is necessary to estimate new input structures for each commodity group by taking the relevant inputs of all industries producing the commodities of the particular commodity group as main or secondary activity. Data on a commodity breakdown of the industries' production are given in the output table. Since the input structures of the commodity-defined branches are unknown, it is necessary to use certain assumptions for transforming the industries' input structures. Probably the most meaningful a s s u m p t i o n from an economic point of view is that the input structure for producing a certain commodity group is the same, independently of the industry in which commodities of this commodity group are produced (commodity technology)[3]. If this assumption is made, the unknown input structures of the branches can be determined by solving a set of mathematical equations. The transformation procedure is described in detail in an annex to chapter III of the SNA. In the context of this paper, the procedure is shown using special transformation matrices for each type of inputs. These matrices are modified in a second step, if further information on input structures of branches defined by commodity groups is available.

In the s p e c i a l t r a n s f o r m a t i o n m a t r i c e s a breakdown of the input data of using industries is given according to the commodities produced in the industries. An item in the table shows how many inputs of a particular type were used in an industry (columns) to produce a particular commodity group (rows). The column sums of the special transformation matrices show the input data of the industries to be transformed. These data correspond to a row of the first or third quadrant of the input table. The row sums are the results of the transformation procedure. They contain data on the inputs of a certain type used for the production of the different commodity groups. They correspond to a row of the first quadrant of a commodity x commodity table.

Using the commodity technology assumption, the special transformation table for a particular type of inputs can be presented as follows:

	Using industries				Σ
	$a_{k1} v_{11}$	.	.	$a_{k1} v_{1m}$	$a_{k1} q_1$
Commodity groups	.		.		.
	.		.		.
	.		.		.
	$a_{kn} v_{n1}$	.	.	$a_{kn} v_{nm}$	$a_{kn} q_n$
Σ	u_{k1}	.	.	u_{km}	

where $u_{k1}, \ldots, u_{km}$ represent the given input values of the k_{th} type of input (k_{th} row of the first and third quadrant of the input table) by m industries; $q_1, \ldots, q_n$ are the gross output by n commodity groups; $a_{k1}, \ldots, a_{kn}$ are the required input coefficients of the k_{th} row of the commodity x commodity table (compare formula 7); $v_{11}, \ldots, v_{nm}$ represent the n x m elements of the make matrix V. According to the commodity technology assumption, the input coefficients for producing a commodity group are the same in every industry where this group is produced. Therefore, the gross outputs in each row (a certain commodity group) are multiplied by the same input coefficients.

---

[3] Cf. SNA (1968), p. 39 ff.

In matrix algebra, the special (yet unmodified) transformation matrices can be defined as follows:

$$(2) \quad R_k = \hat{a}_k V$$

R_k represents the special transformation matrix of the k_{th} row of the first or third quadrant of the input table, $\hat{a}_k$ a diagonal matrix with the elements of the k_{th} row of the input coefficient matrix of the commodity x commodity table in the diagonal.

If the number of industries and commodity groups are equal and the rows (columns) of V are linearly independent, the unknown input coefficients can be determined as follows:

$$(3) \quad u_k = a_k V$$

$$(4) \quad a_k = u_k V^{-1}$$

where u_k represents the k_{th} row of the first and third quadrant of the input table and V^{-1} the inverse of the make matrix V. The transformation procedure for the first and third quadrant of the input table as a whole can be described as follows:

$$(5) \quad A = U V^{-1}$$

$$(6) \quad T = A \hat{q} = U V^{-1} \hat{q}$$

$$= U (\hat{q} D)^{-1} \hat{q}$$

$$= U (D^{-1} \hat{q}^{-1}) \hat{q}$$

$$= U D^{-1}$$

where T is the matrix of the absolute figures of the first and third quadrant of the commodity x commodity table, A the input coefficients of this matrix, U the first and third quadrant of the input table (matrices X and Z), $\hat{q}$ a diagonal matrix with the elements of q in the diagonal, $\hat{q}^{-1}$ the inverse of $\hat{q}$ and D the matrix of the row coefficients of V:

$$(7) \quad A = T \hat{q}^{-1}$$

$$(8) \quad D = \hat{q}^{-1} V$$

Using the inverse row coefficients of V ($= D^{-1}$), the absolute values of the commodity x commodity table can be obtained directly:

$$(9) \quad IOT_{cxc} = \left(T \ \begin{array}{|c} Y \\ \hline 0 \end{array} \right) = \left(U D^{-1} \ \begin{array}{|c} Y \\ \hline 0 \end{array} \right) = \left(\begin{array}{c|c} X D^{-1} & Y \\ \hline Z D^{-1} & 0 \end{array} \right)$$

Using D^{-1}, a row of the commodity x commodity table can be compiled as follows:

(10) $\quad t_k = u_k D^{-1}$

The experience gained in transforming the basic tables to commodity x commodity tables revealed that the exclusive use of the commodity technology assumption is not tenable. This is due mainly to the fact that in many cases the composition of commodities within a commodity group differs widely from one producing industry to another. Therefore the input structures for producing the commodity group could differ widely even if the commodity technology assumption can be applied for each individual type of commodity. D i f f i c u l t i e s also arise if an industry's input structure does not reflect for the most part the input structure of the corresponding main activity. The mathematical conversion model can only modify an industry's input structure to get the input structure of a branch.

If the model has to determine completely new structures it is possible to get implausible results. Furthermore, the use of the commodity technology assumption only can lead to negative items in the commodity x commodity table.

To avoid the disadvantages of the commodity technology assumption, the Federal Statistical Office m o d i f i e s the transformation procedure proposed in the SNA. For this purpose, the already mentioned special transformation matrices for converting certain rows of the input table are used in cases where the general assumption of commodity technology seems to be untenable. Using these matrices, it is possible to modify the assumptions of the transformation procedure according to available additional information. Basic data for the modification procedure are special transformation matrices compiled by using the commodity technology assumption.

These matrices are corrected in such a way that the column totals (the known data of the input table) remain unchanged. Corrections will in particular be necessary if the composition of the commodities of a table item deviates to a larger degree from the average structure of the respective commodity groups. Furthermore, the corrections take into account all available information on the input structures of branches defined by commodity groups.

Using modified special transformation tables, the relationship between data to be transformed and those transformed can be expressed as follows:

(11) $\quad u_k = t_k D_k$

where D_k are the row coefficients of the modified special transformation matrix for the k_{th} type of input. Multiplying (10) by the inverse row coefficients, you get:

(12) $\quad t_k = u_k D_k^{-1}$

Using special transformation matrices, the commodity x commodity table can be calculated in the following way:

$$(13) \quad IOT_{cxc} = \begin{pmatrix} \begin{array}{c} u_1\ D_1^{-1} \\ u_2\ D_2^{-1} \\ \cdot \\ \cdot \\ \cdot \\ u_r\ D_r^{-1} \end{array} & \begin{array}{c} Y \\ \hline \\ 0 \end{array} \end{pmatrix}$$

where u_1 , $\ldots$, u_r are the rows of the first and third quadrants of the input table and D_1 , $\ldots$, D_r the row coefficients of the special transformation matrices for the r types of inputs. Applying the general assumption of commodity technology, the left-hand part of matrix (13) becomes

$$(14) \quad IOT_{cxc} = \begin{pmatrix} \begin{array}{c} u_1\ D^{-1} \\ u_2\ D^{-1} \\ \cdot \\ \cdot \\ \cdot \\ u_r\ D^{-1} \end{array} & \begin{array}{c} Y \\ \hline \\ 0 \end{array} \end{pmatrix} = \begin{pmatrix} U\ D^{-1} & \begin{array}{c} Y \\ \hline \\ 0 \end{array} \end{pmatrix} =$$

$$= \begin{pmatrix} X\ D^{-1} & Y \\ \hline Z\ D^{-1} & 0 \end{pmatrix}$$

Of course, it is possible to use special transformation matrices for transforming only c e r t a i n types of input and apply the general assumption of commodity technology for the rest of the types of input. Compiling for example the 1980 commodity x commodity table for the Federal Republic of Germany, about fifteen types of input were transformed with special transformation matrices, the rest using the general assumption. In the table on the following page an example for a modified special transformation matrix is given. The table shows the transformation procedure for the 1980 compensation of employees.

4. COMPILATION OF INDUSTRY X INDUSTRY TABLES

In order to obtain industry x industry tables, the rows of the first and second quadrants of the input table (use of commodity groups by user sector and category of final use, respectively) must be transformed from a breakdown by commodity group to a breakdown by institutionally defined supplier sector. In the framework of SNA, user and supplier sectors are industries with establishments as statistical units. The third quadrant of the input table (gross value added by industry) remains unchanged.

Compensation of Employees 1980 by Commodity Group and Institutional Sector
Million Deutsche Marks

Ser. No.	Institutional Sector / Commodity Group	Agriculture, Forestry, Fishing	Electricity, Gas and Water, Mining	Manufacturing — Chemicals, Petroleum, Plastic and Non-Metallic Mineral Products, Quarrying	Basic Metals	Machinery except Electrical, Transport Equipment	Electrical Machinery, Fabricated Metal Products n.e.c.	Textiles, Leather, Wood, Paper and Products	Food, Beverages, Tobacco	Construction	Trade, Transport and Communication Services	Other Market Services	Non-Market Services	Institutional Sectors, Total
		1	2	3	4	5	6	7	8	9	10	11	12	13
1	Agricultural, Forestry and Fishing Products	6 457	-		-	-	-	-	41	-	-	-	-	6 498
2	Electricity, Gas, Water, Mining Products	-	23 819	502	585	69	1	91	19	-	97	-	-	25 183
3	Chemicals, Petroleum, Plastic and Non-Metallic Products ..	-	73	52 656	467	349	589	640	106	705	388	38	-	56 011
4	Basic Metals	-	93	410	26 391	2 141	761	7	-	-	99	-	-	29 902
5	Machinery except Electrical, Transport Equipment	32	62	328	1 013	93 679	2 447	112	-	86	3 236	8	-	101 003
6	Electrical Machinery, Fabricated Metal Products n.e.c.	4	280	804	1 060	1 524	58 259	272	7	78	1 475	-	-	63 763
7	Textiles, Leather, Wood, Paper and Products .	-	-	940	14	94	279	43 210	37	41	533	738	-	45 886
8	Food, Beverages, Tobacco	91	-	103	-	-	-	23	22 467	-	360	55	-	23 099
9	Construction	132	963	431	95	195	291	92	28	62 909	1 533	-	102	66 771
10	Trade, Transport and Communication Services	100	348	2 628	475	3 113	2 236	1 297	1 513	492	131 854	766	-	144 822
11	Other Market Services ..	64	362	278	110	2 016	187	166	112	119	825	86 345	-	90 584
12	Non Market Services ..	-	-										187 188	187 188
13	Commodity Groups, Total	6 880	26 000	59 080	30 210	103 180	65 050	45 910	24 330	64 430	140 400	87 950	187 290	840 710

The work of t r a n s f o r m i n g the input table to an industry x industry table involves, firstly, a breakdown of each of the rows of the input table by supplier sector and, secondly, the reaggregation of the extended table by supplier sector. Data on commodities delivered by the supplier sectors are contained in the output table. As mentioned already, the problems of treating imports of goods and services are not discussed in this paper.

Since statistical data on the use of commodities differentiated by supplier sector are available only exceptionally, a s s u m p t i o n s have to be made for the transformation procedure. The economically most meaningful assumption for transforming the rows seems to be that the use structure of a commodity group is the same, irrespectively of the sector supplying it. If this assumption is made, the transformation procedure is very simple. The totals of the commodities supplied by each sector and its breakdown by commodity group can be derived from the output table. The use structure of the commodities supplied by a particular sector can then be determined as a weighted average of the use structures of the various commodity groups supplied by that sector. Again, the transformation procedure is demonstrated by using special transformation matrices. These matrices can be modified in a second step if further information on use structures of industries is available.

Differing from the transformation procedure for computing commodity x commodity tables, s p e c i a l t r a n s f o r m a t i o n m a t r i c e s for compiling industry x industry tables refer not to rows but to columns of the first and second quadrant of the input table. The transformation process is shown for particular using sectors and categories of final use respectively. The row totals of the transformation matrix represent the inputs of a sector by commodity group, the column totals the inputs by delivering sector (industry). Therefore, contrary to the commodity x commodity transformation the data to be transformed are not the column but the row totals; the results of the transformation procedure are shown not in the row, but in the column totals. One item of the special transformation matrix shows − for a particular using sector − the value of a certain commodity group (row classification) delivered from a certain producer sector (column classification).

Assuming that the use structure of a commodity is independent of the delivering sector, you get for each using sector (category of final use) a special transformation table as follows:

	Delivering industries			
Commodity groups	$b_{1l} v_{11}$ · · · $b_{1l} v_{1m}$			$b_{1l} q_1$
	.	.		.
	.	.		.
	.	.		.
	$b_{nl} v_{n1}$ · · · $b_{nl} v_{nm}$			$b_{nl} q_n$
	s_{1l} · · · s_{nl}			

where $b_{1l} q_1, \ldots, b_{nl} q_n$ represent the data to be transformed, the elements
of the lth column of the first or second quadrant of the input table
$(l = 1, \ldots, s)$, b_{il} the elements of matrix B (row coefficients of the
input table, see formula 15), q_i the elements of the vector q of total supply, v_{ij} the elements of the matrix of total supply V and $s_{1l}, \ldots, s_{nl}$ the
result of the transformation procedure, the elements of the lth column of
the first and second quadrant of the industry x industry table. The matrix
B is defined as follows:

(15) $B = \hat{q}^{-1} (X \quad Y)$

In accordance with the assumption described, the same proportion of a
commodity group is used in a user sector, independently of the delivering
industry. Therefore, the coefficients b_{il} are the same in the rows of the
matrix.

In matrix algebra, the special (yet unmodified) transformation matrices
can be defined as follows:

(16) $c_k = \hat{b}_l V$

c_k represents the special transformation matrix of the kth column of
the first and second quadrants of the input table, $\hat{b}_l$ a diagonal matrix
with the elements of a column of matrix B in the diagonal.

Contrary to the commodity x commodity case, the coefficients B are not
unknown, but directly derivable from the data of the input matrix (see formula 15). Therefore, you get immediately the result of the transformation
procedure by multiplying the make matrix by a column of the matrix B:

(17) $s'_l = b'_l V$

where s'_l represents the transposed l^{th} column of the industry x industry
table. The transformation procedure for the first and second quadrant of
the input table as a whole can be described as follows:

(18) $S' = B' V$

Transposing S', you get:

(19) $S = V' B$

S is the matrix of the first and second quadrant of the industry x industry
table.

Using the row coefficients of V (= D), formula (19) could be transformed as follows:

$$(20) \quad S = V' \ B$$
$$= V' \ \hat{q}^{-1} \ (X \ Y)$$
$$= (\hat{q}^{-1} \ V)' \ (X \ Y)$$
$$= D' \ (X \ Y)$$

Using (19) and (20), the industry x industry table can be written as follows:

$$(21) \quad IOT_{ixi} = \left(\begin{array}{c|c} S & \\ \hline Z & 0 \end{array} \right) = \left(\begin{array}{c|c} V' \ B & \\ \hline Z & 0 \end{array} \right) = \left(\begin{array}{c|c} D' \ X & D' \ Y \\ \hline Z & 0 \end{array} \right)$$

Contrary to the transformation model used for compiling commodity x commodity tables, it is not necessary that the number of commodity groups and institutional sectors (industries) is the same. If more detailed information on the breakdown of inputs and outputs of the industries by commodities is available, the quality of the transformation procedure can be essentially improved. Such r e c t a n g u l a r input and output tables are compiled in Denmark with 117 industries and 1 600 commodities[4]. In a second step these data are used to compute an industry x industry table with 117 industries.

If statistical data are available on deliveries from one industry to another industry or to categories of final use, special transformation matrices can be established in which the transformation procedure with the assumptions described can be m o d i f i e d . Basic data for the modification procedure are the special transformation matrices compiled by using the assumption of same use structures independently of the delivering industry. These matrices are corrected in such a way that the row totals (the known data of the input table) remain unchanged.

Using modified special transformation matrices, the relationship between the data to be transformed (columns of the input table) and the results of the transformation procedure could be described as follows:

$$(22) \quad s'_l = w'_l \ D^*_l$$

w'_l is the transposed l^{th} column of the first or second quadrant of the input table ($l = 1, \ldots, s$), s'_l the transposed l^{th} column of the first or second quadrant of the industry x industry table and D^*_l the row coefficients of the modified special transformation matrix for the lth column.

Transposing (27), you get:

$$(23) \quad s_l = D^{*'}_l \ w_l$$

---

[4] See Thage (1982).

Using the modified special transformation matrices according to formula (23), the industry x industry table can be compiled as follows:

$$(24) \quad IOT_{ixi} = \left(\begin{array}{c|c} s_1 \; . \; . \; . \; s_s & \\ \hline z & 0 \end{array} \right) = \left(\begin{array}{c|c} D_1^{*'} w_1 \; . \; . \; . \; D_s^{*'} w_s & \\ \hline z & 0 \end{array} \right)$$

Applying the general assumption described, the upper part of matrix (24) becomes

$$(25) \quad IOT_{ixi} = \left(\begin{array}{c|c} D' w_1 \; . \; . \; . \; D' w_s & \\ \hline z & 0 \end{array} \right) = \left(\begin{array}{c|c} D' (X \; Y) & \\ \hline z & 0 \end{array} \right)$$

$$= \left(\begin{array}{c|c} D' X & D' Y \\ \hline z & 0 \end{array} \right)$$

This result has been derived already (compare formula 21).

Of course it is again possible to use special transformation matrices only for transforming certain columns, for example for the categories of final use. In the Federal Republic of Germany, the described compilation method of industry x industry tables has not been used up to now. The Federal Statistical Office and the German Institute of Economic Research plan to study the chances of realization within the scope of a common research project.

REFERENCES

Federal Statistical Office (1984). Subject-Matter Series 18: Volkswirtschaftliche Gesamtrechnungen (National Accounts). Series 2: Input-Output-Tabellen (Input-Output Tables) 1980. Mainz-Stuttgart 1984.

Stahmer, C. (1982). Connecting National Accounts and Input-Output Tables in the Federal Republic of Germany. In I. Skolka (ed.), Compilation of Input-Output Tables. Berlin-Heidelberg-New York 1982.

Thage, B. (1982). Techniques in the Compilation of Danish Input-Output Tables: A new Approach to the Treatment of Imports. In I. Skolka (ed.), Compilation of Input-Output Tables. Berlin-Heidelberg-New York 1982.

United Nations (1968). A System of National Accounts (SNA). Studies in Methods. Series F. No. 2. Rev. 3. New York 1968.

SETON'S EIGENPRICES: COMPARISONS BETWEEN POST-WAR HOLLAND AND HUNGARY

Erik Dietzenbacher and Albert E. Steenge

Faculty of Economics, University of Groningen,
Groningen, The Netherlands

1. INTRODUCTION[1]

Concise methods for the numerical implementation of general equilibrium models for technologically advanced countries were developed during the nineteen-thirties. In that period Leontief built the first input-output models for the United States. In the almost fifty years that have passed since, contributions to Leontief's system have been numerous; nowadays input-output analysis is widely used as a tool in economic theory and practice. However, despite the enormous progress that has been made, fundamental problems remain. This may partly be attributed to the fact that the "price-side" of the various Leontief models is still relatively underdeveloped. In theoretical work, prices are usually obtained as the solution to a dual problem, in empirical work they are typically standardized at unity. Another way of putting this is that connections between supply and demand as they exist in real markets are not incorporated in the present models (often linear ones). For example, most price models simply redistribute profits, focusing mainly on production costs. (See e.g. Fink (1981) for an extensive discussion of such models.)

We feel that a system recently proposed by Francis Seton (1981 and 1985, forthcoming) may fill an existing gap here. The method combines in one framework "cost-side" arguments, which impute all value to primary factors, and "use-side" arguments, which derive the prices of input factors from those of the final products. It thus becomes possible to determine product prices as well as factor prices endogenously. As we will see, prices in Seton's system are computed as the lefthand eigenvectors of certain matrices, and have been called "eigenprices".

In his original article, Seton discussed his methodology in the context of a comparative evaluation of structural characteristics and performance criteria across different socio-economic systems. The potential of the technique being given, an interesting point is the following: could it be that a particular type of economic organization is uniquely characterized by a particular pattern of eigenprices? In that case, to obtain a systematic classification of systems it will be necessary that (annual) fluctuations in the spectrum of eigenprices do not substantially distort the "normal" spectrum. Therefore it seems interesting to observe the pattern of eigenprices over a consecutive

---

[1] The authors are particularly indebted to Francis Seton of Nuffield College, Oxford, for extended discussions and comments. For the analysis and the interpretation of the Hungarian data, we like to thank Ferenc Bánhidi of the Hungarian Central Planning Office, György Szakolczai of the Econometric Laboratory of the Institute of Economics, and György Molnár, also of the Economic Institute of the Hungarian Academy of Sciences, all in Budapest.

period for a number of years. Because Seton's system essentially aims at revealing certain market imperfections, such a study might indicate how the observed economies have coped with emerging disequilibria.

Below we shall present two empirical studies. The first one considers a Western type of country, with a somewhat mixed economy, the Netherlands. Computations have been made for the postwar period 1948-1980, using data compiled by the Central Bureau of Statistics (Centraal Bureau voor de Statistiek). The second study concerns a socialist country with a strong emphasis on central planning, i.e. Hungary. Here the years 1970-1979 have been analyzed, i.e. the period of the the so-called "second wave of reforms", using tables prepared by the Central Statistical Office (Központi Statisztikai Hivatal). Both countries are medium-sized, have a tradition in agriculture and have known periods of rapid industrialization. Holland is a member of the EEC and OECD, while Hungary is a member of CMEA (and, since 1982, of the IMF), with extensive contacts with the West.

In the next section we shall start with a brief review of the basic mathematical framework. After this, we shall discuss both countries separately and present the results. We shall conclude with a number of observations on the method.

2. SUMMARY OF MAIN CONCEPTS AND DEFINITIONS[2]

In this section we shall present a brief summary of the main concepts and definitions involved. We shall start with the open Leontief system, considering n commodities and m primary factors. The basic equation is given by

$$\grave{z} = A\grave{z} + \grave{y} \qquad\qquad \grave{z}, \grave{y} \in \mathbb{R}^n, A \in \mathbb{R}^{n \times n} \qquad (1)$$

Here $A = (a_{ij})$ denotes the matrix of input coefficients, with a_{ij} the direct input of commodity i per unit of production of commodity j. Exogenous final demand is given by $\grave{y}$, and the required total output by $\grave{z}$. Demand for the primary factors $\grave{w}$ is given by

$$\grave{w} = B\grave{z} \qquad\qquad \grave{w} \in \mathbb{R}^m, B \in \mathbb{R}^{m \times n}. \qquad (2)$$

The matrix $B = (b_{ij})$ gives the direct input of factor i in production process j. Thus the system's matrix of integrated or total factor inputs, all per unit of output, can be written as

$$C \equiv B(I - A)^{-1} \qquad\qquad C \in \mathbb{R}^{m \times n}. \qquad (3)$$

Central in the analysis is the so-called "norm-matrix", denoted by N. This matrix gives the fraction of each production factor, to be imputed to the production of the final categories. Seton showed that the norm-matrix can be written as

$$N = \hat{y}C'\hat{w}^{-1} \qquad\qquad N \in \mathbb{R}^{n \times m}, \qquad (4)$$

where $\hat{y}$ is the n×n diagonal matrix of elements y_i, $\hat{w}$ the m×m diagonal matrix

---

[2] Following Seton, we use an "acute" accent to denote a row vector (e.g. $\acute{p}$), a "grave" accent to denote a column vector (e.g. $\grave{y}$), and a "circumflex" to denote a diagonal matrix (e.g. $\hat{w}$). With $\acute{1}_n$ (resp. $\grave{1}_n$), we denote the n-dimensional row (resp. column) vector with all elements equal to one.

of elements w_i, and C' the transpose of C.

Seton has shown that when goods do have "utility" on the market for final products (as measured by prices ṕ), a value can be assigned to the different primary factors according to their contribution to the production of the final demand categories. These values are denoted by ń, the so-called factor norms:

$$ń = ṕN \qquad\qquad ń \in \mathbb{R}^m, p \in \mathbb{R}^n. \qquad\qquad (5)$$

Given the factor-norms ń, we may calculate the (cost-)prices ć of the products, using matrix C, as

$$ć = ńC \qquad\qquad ć \in \mathbb{R}^n. \qquad\qquad (6)$$

We notice that when $ć = ṕ$, we have a situation in which i) market prices exactly reflect the costs in terms of the incorporated factors, and ii) the factor prices correspond exactly to the utility of the final demands. Such prices will be called "eigenprices". Substituting (5) in (6), given $ć = ṕ$, we find

$$ṕ = ṕNC \qquad\qquad NC \in \mathbb{R}^{n \times n}, \qquad\qquad (7)$$

and postmultiplying (6) by N, using $ć = ṕ$ together with (5), we have

$$ń = ńCN \qquad\qquad CN \in \mathbb{R}^{m \times m}. \qquad\qquad (8)$$

Thus the eigenprices for the products are obtained as the elements of the lefthand (Frobenius-)vector of the matrix NC, while those for the factors are linked to the matrix CN. Seton concludes that such an "ideal" price system as defined by (7) and (8) generally will not exist, but a close approximation can always be given. These approximations, replacing (7) and (8), respectively, are defined as follows[3]

$$\phi ń = ńCN \text{ and } ṕ = \frac{1}{\phi} ńC. \qquad\qquad (9)$$

If we wish to compare the eigenprices computed according to (9) with the actual prices, i.e. $í_n$ and $í_m$, it is necessary to standardize ṕ. Following Seton, we keep the value of industrial supply constant for both types of valuation. So we write

$$í_n \tilde{y} = ṕ \tilde{y}. \qquad\qquad (10)$$

In the above framework, commodities or factors having an eigenprice above unity are undervalued. Analogously, eigenprices below unity indicate overvaluations. If the eigenprices correspond to a Frobenius eigenvalue differing from unity, the system will reveal the existence of an "eigensurplus", positive or negative. This is measured by the "eigensurplus ratio", $\frac{1}{\phi} - 1$, to be interpreted as the surplus remaining after the factors of production have been paid, according to the new valuations.

---

[3] The same results follow from the alternative approach $\phi ṕ = ṕNC$ and $ń = ṕN$, which is computationally less favourable, however.

3. THE NETHERLANDS, 1948-1980

We shall start this section with a brief characterization of the Dutch
economy. After this the results will be presented, followed by a short discussion.

3.1. Brief characterization of the postwar Dutch economy

Four stages may roughly be distinguished in the development of the Dutch
economy after the second world war, see e.g. Fortuyn (1983). The first period,
1945-1950, was characterized by rebuilding. To overcome the most immediate
scarcities from the war, the government imposed severe controls on economic
life. This led to low cost prices and a favourable competitive position on
foreign markets. The growing national product, combined with a large propen-
sity to save, induced expanding investments, especially in the industrial sectors, which gained importance at the cost of agriculture.
The second stage, 1950-1963, may be described as a period of recovery and
expansion. The labour supply was increased considerably, which resulted in an
intensification of the industrialization, necessary to increase employment
opportunities. Because of the substantial dependence on exports, costs of production had to be kept low to guarantee a competitive position. As most production processes were labour-intensive, this in turn implied wage controls
by the government. The policy of industrialization combined with wage regula-
tions appears to have been very successful; according to the Dutch Central
Bank, the recovery period was over in 1953. A drawback, however, of this policy was that it failed to stimulate the introduction of technological innova-
tions and mechanizations in labour-intensive production sectors. Although investments increased substantially, they were "extensive" rather than "intensive". For certain key sectors, this led to great problems in the subsequent
period. Serious progress was made with social security legislation.
The third stage was a period of continued growth and restructuring, and
covered the years 1963-1973. At the end of the previous period, tensions on
the labour market had accumulated. In 1963, these became so serious that it
was no longer possible to continue the policy of wage controls. The implication was an explosive wage increase and consequently a decrease in profits
for some "weak" sectors (e.g. textiles and metals) as well as for labour-intensive firms, thus implying underinvestments and capacity losses. This in
turn initiated industrial restructuring, mergers, centralizations, and clo-
sing-downs. Thanks to the continued economic growth and the shortage of labour, this did not cause serious problems in the sixties. However, in the
longer term loss of employment in the industrial sectors was inevitable, and
insufficiently compensated for by employment in other sectors. As a consequence, unemployment began to appear at the beginning of the seventies. A
growing number of people had to fall back on social security, which led to a
sharp rise in public expenses.
The fourth period regards the years from 1973 onward, and may be characterized as a period of continued restructuring and stagnation. In the first
years, national income declined, while unemployment rose substantially. At
first an anti-cyclical stimulation program was started, causing (increasing)
budget deficits and a significant inflation rate. Unemployment, however, kept
growing, which led to a reverse in social-economic policy around 1976. Reduction of the budget deficits was emphasized, to be achieved by cutting down
public expenses. This indeed led to a fall in the rate of inflation, but also
to a further rise of unemployment; more people made use of social security
benefits than ever before, and budget deficits increased further. Partially
triggered off by the second oil-crisis, economic growth stagnated in the late

seventies and actually became negative during the eighties. Consequently it became necessary to reduce collective spending, which implied cut-downs on wages and salaries (especially in public services), as well as on social bene-fits.

During the entire postwar period, the public sector greatly expanded in size. Despite this, the private sector is still largely regulated by market forces. There have been no substantial nationalizations and no large price discriminations for major sectors of the economy.

3.2. Empirical results for the Netherlands

For our calculations we used yearly input-output tables, published by the Dutch Central Bureau of Statistics (CBS). The original tables were based on a classification in some 30-odd sectors, following standard international use. Because such a classification is probably too detailed for our analysis, sectors were aggregated into 12 larger ones, while the primary cost catego-ries were aggregated into 3 categories. For each sector the total of indirect taxes was left as a residual.

During the period of 1948-1980, several major changes in the construc-tion of Dutch input-output tables have taken place. Until 1969, Dutch tables were in market prices, which included indirect taxes; this implied that turn-over taxes were recorded, in the original tables, as a primary cost factor for the producing sectors. From 1969 onwards, value-added taxes were regis-tered as a direct payment from purchasers to the government, implying corres-ponding entries in the fourth quadrant. Also an interest margin was explicit-ly introduced in 1969, standing for the difference between interest-revenues and -payments. Furthermore, in 1969 some changes in the sectoral registration were introduced, most of which were of minor importance in the aggregation we used. However, the alterations of 1969 did imply a break in the time series of input-output tables. To overcome the problems caused by the changes, the CBS published two tables that year, indicated below by 1969^1 and 1969^2; 1969^2 standing for the new classification (including the interest margin). For 1971 no input-output table was published. The results of our calculations are shown in table 1.

Looking at the table, we see that sector 1 (mainly agriculture) is under-valued during the entire postwar period, while the processing sector 2 (food, etc.) is generally overvalued. The typical manufacturing sectors 3, 5, 6, and 7 show undervaluation, which may reflect the high degree of competitiveness and a lack of concerted action in these manufacturing activities. Sector 8, covering the supply of electricity and gas, is undervalued until the first oil-crisis. The price increases of 1973 induce a significant dip in the ei-genprices, which slowly return to their original level since 1977, however. The oil industry, which makes up a major part of sector 4, is known for cer-tain monopolistic forces, reflected in the Seton system by persistent overva-luation. Sector 12, incorporating medical and cultural services, is underva-lued, reflecting its strong dependence on subsidization. Around 1976, the need to decrease public expenses, including the cutting down of subsidies, causes a significant fall in the sector's eigenprices.

The influence of the changes of 1969 is seen to be relatively slight. Comparing 1968 with 1969^1, we observe that the deletion of indirect taxes as a primary cost factor for the producing sectors substantially diminishes the eigensurplus ratio. This apparently stems from the fact that value-added taxes, from 1969 onwards, are no longer part of the residual: each sector's surplus (in Seton's sense) decreases significantly. Because these tax-changes are not uniform, eigenprices for some sectors are seen to change, while for others they do not change at all. Looking at the results for 1969^1 and 1969^2

we see that the differences are very small, indicating that our aggregation was more or less successful in neutralizing the break in the time series. Only sector 11 (banking and insurances) changes from under- to overvaluation, which might have been expected in view of the introduction of the interest margin.

The picture given by the primary cost factors is less varied, though some conclusions can be drawn. For example, we observe a slight, decreasing under-valuation of wages. It is interesting to note that the restraint shown by la-bour as regards demands for wage increases in the recovery period (late 1940's and early 1950's) is not reflected in the data. The same is valid for the pe-riod up to the breakdown of the system of centralized wage policy (1963-1964). Also the wage increases of 1963 and later years are not translated in a signi-ficant dip in the eigenprices for labour. The data, to a certain extent, do seem to reflect the recessions 1958-59 and of 1972-73. Compared to the preceding years, the remunerations for capital became undervalued in 1958 and in 1974. This is consistent with a certain abundance of these factors; in a recession a degree of oversupply of the production factors may be expected as a result of a decrease in production. Imports became less undervalued in 1958 and 1974, which corresponds to the stable, relatively high demand for imports.

All in all, we may remark that deviations from unity are generally rather small for the eigenprices of the primary factors. This may illustrate that fi-nal consumption goods were not over- or underpriced in relation to the amounts of embodied labour. On the other hand, it may also reflect the fact that the data record rather pre-income than post-income tax wages and capital remunera-tions. We feel that this is definitely an area for additional research.

4. HUNGARY, 1970-1979

Like in section 3, we shall start with a brief characterization of the Hungarian economy, after which the results will be presented and discussed.

4.1. Brief characterization of postwar Hungary

By the constitution of 1949, Hungary is a people's republic in which al-most all industry is owned by the state. During the early postwar period the expansion of heavy industry was emphasized, like in all other socialist coun-tries of Eastern Europe. Industrial expansion moderated somewhat in the fif-ties, after which (in the early sixties) efforts were made to promote large-scale production by merging enterprises into a limited number of very large ones. This heavy concentration, particularly of export-related industry, how-ever, adversely affected the production of consumer goods, semi-finished pro-ducts and spare parts.

The period we have considered is the period of the New Economic Mechanism (NEM), also known as the "second wave of reforms", see e.g. Brus (1979). Be-fore the introduction of the NEM, prices mainly had an accounting function. They were centrally determined and generally did not reflect supply and demand for goods and factors. Characteristic for the price system was the separation of producer and consumer prices through a wide range of turnover taxes and subsidies. Consequently, international price movements had only little influ-ence on domestic price developments.

The NEM was introduced in order to respond to the needs of an increasing-ly complex economy, characterized by a considerable reliance on foreign trade. The new mechanism aimed at replacing plan-directives by a use of "regulators" (such as prices, taxes, subsidies and credits), while the enterprises were given greater freedom to set their prices in response to market forces. Fur-thermore, the degree of plan-fulfilment was no longer predominant in the determination of workers' premiums, but the profits of the firms they were employed by. To smooth over the transition from the previous system to the new one, a number of "brakes" were put into use at the time of the NEM's introduction.

After the reforms of 1968, consumer prices generally exceeded producer prices for industrial goods, and remained below those prices for foodstuffs, transportation, communication and a number of services. However, government intervention, in the form of price controls and many sorts of persistent taxes and subsidies, was still extensive, particularly during these transitional years. The intention, though, was to reduce such limitations gradually; but policy responses to external shocks (the 1972-73 inflationary world boom, the 1974-75 world recession, and the deterioration of Hungary's terms of trade after 1973) led to a reduced use of market mechanisms and to increased central directions. In order to respond to the rise in world market prices, a considerable number of price adjustments were made 1975-76.

A second major price reform (the "third wave of reforms") was undertaken in the years 1979-80. The basic aims were to restore the link between domestic and foreign prices and to improve the link between producer and consumer prices. For an extensive discussion of developments in postwar Hungary, we may refer to Hare et al. (1981), IMF (1982), and Kornai (1983).

4.2. Empirical results for Hungary

For the calculation of eigenprices for Hungary, we mainly made use of input-output tables published by the Central Statistical Office (Központi Statisztikai Hivatal). (Other statistical information was obtained from various sources, such as Statistical Yearbooks from the same publisher.) The input-output tables have been prepared in such a way as to best suit the interest of the users, taking into account the special characteristics of the Hungarian economy. On the one hand, aggregation may take place following the usual definitions of economic activity. This procedure is especially useful for economic systems characterized by a decentralized production mechanism, where prices are basically determined by the laws of supply and demand. On the other hand, we may aggregate the tables according to the "organizational principle". In the case of Hungary, each enterprise belongs to a specific organization. This organization plays a dominant role in preparing the production plan, in dealing with parallel organizations for other industries, in "bargaining" with the central authorities, etc. To serve potential users best, the Hungarian tables offer the possibility to choose between the two aforementioned ways of aggregation. Because of the great importance of the particular organization to which a certain enterprise belongs, aggregation according to the "organizational principle" is probably the most appropriate one for our purpose. The tables are in current producer prices, including final demand. Following the study for Holland, the tables were aggregated into 12 productive sectors and 3 primary factor categories.

Eigensurplus, as defined in this paper, is a "pre-tax" surplus, extracted from the factors. As such, numerical exercises aimed at obtaining a quantitative estimate of the eigensurplus are critically dependent on the quality of the data, supposedly representing the remuneration of the factors. For the remuneration of labour we adopted the yearly totals of wages and salaries, and "contributions after wages", paid by the employers. Representing the remuneration of the factor capital was more difficult, because various forms of "bargaining" play a dominant role in the determination of the financial position of this factor. As the representative variable, we took the sum of "profits" and "amortizations". For the totality of imports, we took the sum of imports in rubles and in "non-ruble" currencies. Thus, the residuals are composed of a number of headings, standing for corrections for internal use of produced commodities, and various subsidies and taxes related to imports and exports. Also included in the residuals were the additional corrections making up for differences between producer and consumer prices. The results of our computations are shown in table 2, below.

These results reveal substantial differences between the Netherlands and Hungary. In contrast to the case for Holland, price differences between the various commodities and commodity groups are generally quite large. The eigenprices for the sector mining (which includes the exploitation and processing of Hungarian oil and gas) have increased from 1970 to 1974, reflecting the slow adaptation of official CMEA prices for energy to world market prices. From 1976 onwards, its eigenprices indicate overvaluation, as may have been expected. The domestic adjustments of 1975 and 1976 in energy prices are also reflected by the significant price increases for electricity, as shown by the drop in its eigenprice. The time series for metals, machinery and building materials are also quite easily interpreted along such lines. Chemicals show a pattern of overvaluation for the entire period, with a sudden jump of eigenprices in 1974. This apparently reflects price increases on the world market; about half of this sector's imports stem from Western countries. The later decrease in eigenprices may be indicative of the adaptability of this sector.

Food and agricultural activities are undervalued during the entire period, which is consistent with observations from many other sources. Also undervalued are the public services, which continue to be financed through the state budget.

Regarding the production factors, we observe that the remuneration for labour and especially for capital are rather close to unity, indicating a correct valuation. Imports, on the other hand, are largely overvalued, thus reflecting the various devices which are operative in the import-export trade.

5. FINAL REMARKS

Seton's eigenprices concept provides us with measures indicating whether a product or primary factor is over- or undervalued. As such, eigenprices may be regarded as prices that would exist in a situation without market imperfections. In this study, we have seen that the methodology may be a useful tool i) in studying historical developments and structural changes for a specific country and ii) in making international comparisons between countries.

When comparing the Netherlands with Hungary, we observe that the two sets of eigenprices show quite different patterns. For Holland, deviations from unity are small for all product prices, while they are quite considerable for Hungary. This may reflect the fact that prices in the Netherlands, to a large extent, are determined "freely", i.e. by the forces of demand and supply. It is tempting to speculate that the pattern as observed for Holland will also be found for comparable Western countries. Here, however, additional research will surely be needed. In Hungary, the government still plays a dominant role in the process of price determinations, quite independently of market clearing considerations. This may be the cause of the relatively large deviations from unity of the eigenprices. Here additional research on other East-European countries seems asked for.

Finally, we would like to make two remarks concerning the concepts we have investigated. First, one has to be aware of the fact that the determination of absolute eigenpriecs may be open to some debate. The magnitude of the measured eigenprices depends essentially on the way in which the eigenprices are standardized (in this study we have followed Seton, leaving the total of final industrial supply invariant). A different standardization will lead to different absolute eigenprices, although the relative proportions will remain the same. Secondly, especially in the highly aggregated versions we have employed, eigenyield and eigenprices are critically dependent on what interpretation we give to terms such as "labour", "capital", "tax", and the like. (For example, how do we allocate social security payments, how are depreciation outlays recorded, etc.) The classification of primary input categories here contains a certain degree of arbitrariness, which may cause special problems in international comparisons. For instance, if the same breakdown of the primary inputs is not possible for two countries, conclusions should be drawn only with great care.[4]

6. REFERENCES

Brus, W. (1979). The Eastern European Reforms: what happened to them? Soviet Studies, 31(2): 257-267.

Centraal Bureau voor de Statistiek. Nationale Rekeningen, various volumes. Staatsuitgeverij, 's Gravenhage.

Fink, G. (1981). Preisverzerrungen und Unterschiede in der Produktionsstruktur zwischen Österreich und Ungarn, Studien über Wirtschafts- und Systemvergleiche. Springer Verlag, Wien, New York.

Fortuyn, W.S.P. (1983). Kerncijfers 1945-1983 van de sociaal-economische ontwikkeling in Nederland. Kluwer, Deventer.

Hare, P., Radice, H. and Swain, N., eds. (1981). Hungary: A Decade of Economic Reform. George Allen & Unwin, London.

International Monetary Fund (1982). Hungary: An Economic Survey. Occasional Paper 15. Washington, D.C.

Kornai, J. (1983). Comments on the Present State and the Prospects of the Hungarian Economic Reform. Journal of Comparative Economics, 7(3): 225-252.

Központi Statisztikai Hivatal (1981). Ágazati Kapcsolatok Mérlege 1970-1979. Budapest.

Seton, F. (1981). A Quasi-Competitive Price Basis for Intersystem Comparisons of Economic Structure and Performance. Journal of Comparative Economics, 5(4): 367-391.

Seton, F., with contributions from A.E. Steenge, (1985, forthcoming). Cost, Use and Value: The Evaluation of Performance, Structure and Prices across Time, Space and Economic Systems. Oxford University Press, Oxford.

---

[4] See also the Appendix, which contains Table 1 (Holland 1948-1980) and Table 2 (Hungary 1970-1979).

APPENDIX

TABLE 1. Eigenprices for the Netherlands; 1948-1980.

	1948	1949	1950	1951	1952	1953	1954	1955	1956	1957	1958
Production sectors											
1	1.143	1.135	1.047	1.044	1.044	1.037	1.043	1.048	1.050	1.081	1.117
2	1.028	0.965	1.002	0.999	0.961	0.967	0.978	0.974	0.976	0.984	0.977
3	1.013	1.030	1.040	1.030	1.023	1.025	1.026	1.025	1.044	1.048	1.044
4	0.966	0.988	0.984	0.978	0.981	0.996	1.006	0.998	0.998	0.983	0.972
5	1.022	1.039	1.042	1.041	1.044	1.041	1.039	1.025	1.017	1.017	1.016
6	0.997	1.016	1.018	1.014	1.021	1.025	1.020	1.014	1.010	1.007	1.007
7	1.009	1.024	1.022	1.017	1.024	1.022	1.020	1.012	1.007	1.008	1.007
8	1.089	1.120	1.068	1.061	1.067	1.042	1.044	1.034	1.037	1.028	1.024
9	0.820	0.857	0.848	0.858	0.895	0.886	0.862	0.901	0.899	0.888	0.899
10	1.040	1.057	1.059	1.061	1.064	1.063	1.062	1.056	1.050	1.047	1.044
11	1.044	1.063	1.061	1.065	1.069	1.067	1.064	1.058	1.051	1.053	1.051
12	0.999	1.012	1.020	1.019	1.028	1.029	1.038	1.033	1.034	1.032	1.032
Primary factors											
Wages	1.002	1.007	1.007	1.006	1.008	1.008	1.007	1.006	1.005	1.004	1.004
Capital	1.005	0.999	0.993	0.994	0.995	0.994	0.996	0.996	0.996	0.999	1.001
Imports	1.014	1.011	1.016	1.012	1.007	1.008	1.010	1.006	1.007	1.006	1.003
Eigensurplus ratio	0.076	0.094	0.094	0.096	0.097	0.095	0.092	0.085	0.079	0.069	0.066

	1959	1960	1961	1962	1963	1964	1965	1966	1967	1968	1969[1]
Production sectors											
1	1.075	1.083	1.095	1.076	1.076	1.078	1.063	1.043	1.045	1.037	1.002
2	0.968	0.969	0.966	0.959	0.963	0.969	0.959	0.961	0.973	0.978	0.978
3	1.042	1.044	1.050	1.051	1.054	1.055	1.058	1.060	1.047	1.049	1.031
4	0.971	0.975	0.977	0.973	0.971	0.955	0.973	0.959	0.983	0.968	0.951
5	1.022	1.025	1.029	1.034	1.035	1.037	1.039	1.041	1.041	1.040	1.043
6	1.012	1.012	1.016	1.017	1.018	1.019	1.025	1.029	1.025	1.026	1.024
7	1.015	1.015	1.020	1.021	1.021	1.022	1.025	1.027	1.025	1.024	1.026
8	1.027	1.028	1.032	1.035	1.034	1.031	1.032	1.030	1.035	1.032	1.011
9	0.910	0.892	0.886	0.900	0.900	0.892	0.889	0.884	0.866	0.865	0.954
10	1.045	1.046	1.046	1.047	1.047	1.046	1.046	1.047	1.048	1.054	1.012
11	1.050	1.049	1.047	1.049	1.043	1.043	1.046	1.054	1.063	1.066	1.003
12	1.038	1.041	1.038	1.038	1.037	1.039	1.040	1.043	1.044	1.045	1.005
Primary factors											
Wages	1.005	1.005	1.005	1.006	1.006	1.005	1.006	1.006	1.005	1.005	1.004
Capital	0.999	1.001	1.000	0.998	0.997	0.998	0.997	0.997	0.998	0.999	0.995
Imports	1.002	1.003	1.005	1.005	1.006	1.006	1.007	1.007	1.008	1.007	1.003
Eigensurplus ratio	0.073	0.072	0.076	0.078	0.078	0.078	0.082	0.086	0.089	0.094	0.035

1969[1]: old classification.

TABLE 1. Continued.

	1969[2]	1970	1972[a]	1973	1974	1975	1976	1977	1978	1979	1980
Production sectors											
1	1.001	1.002	1.003	1.005	1.009	1.000	1.004	1.007	1.006	1.012	1.003
2	0.978	0.993	0.987	1.008	1.003	0.991	1.000	1.013	1.016	1.030	1.015
3	1.029	1.028	1.027	1.022	1.018	1.022	1.019	1.024	1.023	1.020	1.020
4	0.947	0.952	0.942	0.947	0.969	0.969	0.978	0.973	0.967	0.980	0.985
5	1.042	1.034	1.030	1.025	1.022	1.022	1.019	1.024	1.025	1.021	1.023
6	1.024	1.022	1.023	1.017	1.014	1.015	1.012	1.018	1.019	1.015	1.015
7	1.026	1.021	1.021	1.015	1.012	1.013	1.010	1.016	1.016	1.013	1.012
8	1.024	1.007	1.004	0.995	0.990	0.986	0.988	0.997	0.998	1.000	1.001
9	0.955	0.950	0.957	0.953	0.957	0.951	0.939	0.943	0.950	0.947	0.951
10	1.022	1.026	1.040	1.044	1.047	1.060	1.076	1.080	1.087	1.077	1.076
11	0.982	0.977	0.952	0.942	0.938	0.938	0.930	0.917	0.913	0.905	0.908
12	1.007	1.010	1.017	1.014	1.015	1.023	1.021	1.004	0.999	0.996	0.998
Primary factors											
Wages	1.003	1.002	1.003	1.002	1.002	1.002	1.001	1.000	1.000	0.998	0.999
Capital	0.997	0.997	0.999	0.999	1.001	1.000	1.002	1.001	1.001	1.002	1.001
Imports	1.002	1.003	1.000	1.002	1.000	0.999	1.001	1.003	1.004	1.005	1.004
Eigensurplus ratio	0.035	0.034	0.037	0.031	0.027	0.027	0.022	0.027	0.027	0.022	0.021

1969^2: new classification.
a)   : 1971 not available

Production sectors

    1 - Agriculture, foresty and fishing
    2 - Food, beverages and tobacco
    3 - Textiles and footwear
    4 - Chemical industry (including refineries, mining and production of oil and gas)
    5 - Metal industry
    6 - Construction
    7 - Other manufacturing industries
    8 - Public utilities
    9 - Trade
  10 - Transport, storage and communication
  11 - Banking and insurances
  12 - Other service industries

Primary factors:

Wages   - Wages and salaries (including employers' contributions for social security)
Capital - Other incomes and depreciation
Imports - Imports of commodities and services (on a c.i.f. basis)

Eigensurplus ratio: $\frac{1}{\phi} - 1$

TABLE 2. Eigenprices for Hungary: 1970-1979.

	1970	1971	1972	1973	1974	1975	1976	1977	1978	1979
Production sectors										
1	1.127	1.127	1.103	1.112	1.129	1.105	1.100	1.108	1.116	1.115
2	1.076	1.022	1.012	0.967	1.031	1.036	1.057	1.109	1.077	1.082
3	0.917	1.089	1.108	1.130	1.163	1.004	0.861	0.850	0.879	0.895
4	0.898	0.943	0.947	0.938	0.908	0.929	0.863	0.877	0.833	0.866
5	0.863	0.876	0.881	0.895	0.983	0.894	0.811	0.821	0.839	0.848
6	0.852	0.863	0.876	0.890	0.862	0.925	0.909	0.899	0.864	0.855
7	0.896	0.907	0.923	0.925	0.900	0.921	0.894	0.886	0.886	0.888
8	0.885	0.937	0.905	0.893	0.888	0.937	0.913	0.895	0.921	0.935
9	0.940	0.945	0.942	0.949	0.933	0.950	0.938	0.924	0.946	0.955
10	0.938	0.949	0.969	0.958	0.987	0.942	0.943	0.936	0.937	0.948
11	0.927	0.894	0.890	0.900	0.877	0.901	0.912	0.900	0.922	0.937
12	1.116	1.138	1.156	1.182	1.144	1.163	1.231	1.214	1.191	1.172
Primary factors										
Wages	1.024	1.024	1.022	1.023	1.023	1.023	1.030	1.030	1.029	1.028
Capital	1.000	1.001	1.001	1.004	1.000	1.000	1.013	1.013	1.008	1.008
Imports	0.700	0.682	0.711	0.719	0.726	0.726	0.709	0.696	0.676	0.728
Eigensurplus ratio	0.119	0.147	0.147	0.131	0.107	0.111	0.170	0.133	0.158	1.140

Production sectors

    1 - Agriculture and forestry
    2 - Food
    3 - Mining
    4 - Electricity
    5 - Chemicals
    6 - Metals
    7 - Machinery
    8 - Building materials
    9 - Building industry
    10 - Light industry and others
    11 - Trade, transports, communication and watersupplies
    12 - Public services (including health, economic and administrative services)

Primary factors

Wages   - Wages, salaries and contributions after wages paid for by the employers
Capital - Profits and amortization
Imports - Imports in rubles and in "non-ruble" currencies

Eigensurplus ratio: $\frac{1}{\phi} - 1$

AN ATTEMPT TO EVALUATE THE IMPACT OF CHANGES IN INTERINDUSTRY INTERACTIONS

Maurizio Ciaschini

Faculty of Economics and Commerce, University of Urbino, Urbino, Italy

1. INTRODUCTION

In recent times many of the important issues to government economic pol-icy involve problems of industrial development. Such problems that refer not only to economics but also to important instances in the social field, imply dealing with the technological change as having an impact on the production side and, more widely, on the general performance of the economic system to meet the households demands for consumption, to maintain a favourable balance on foreign trade, to allow a convenient growth of the capital stock and em-ployment.

The changes in the structure of economic systems experimented in recent decades reveal that such phenomenon is not temporary but appears to become stricktly connected with the growth patterns of the world's economies. They are linked, in fact, with the changes in the availability of primary re-sources and shifts in the composition of internal and external demands. In such environment the main problem seem to be the constant search of a struc-ture that can fit, to some extent, the present technical and behavioural situ-ation, starting from the given preexisting structure. Transferring resources form one economic activity to another that appears to warrant a better per-formance may imply relevant economic and social costs, so that economic pol-icy has to be supported by substantial information on the order of magnitude of the effects of modifications in the structure of the whole economic system and of the exogenous inputs, either instruments or exogenous data.

Modern Input Output (I-O) analysis provides a convenient framework for the identification of the economic structure. It allows, in fact, for the identification of the relevant variables implied in the representation of the economic process and, through the analysis of the structure of the nation-al economic acconts, for the "sectorization" of each variable, so that the complete set of causal relations among sectoral variables can be specified

---

[1] This paper is part of a research project on Input Output analysis at the Institute of Economics of University of Urbino supported by the Italian Ministry of Public Education. I wish to thank L. Stefanini for his collabor-ation in implementing the computing routines for singular value analysis.

and estimated.

Once determined the parametric set of a modern I-O model through a simulation procedure the forecasts for sectoral variables are easily obtained. Such forecasts describe the evolution of the inner composition of the major economic variables so thet changes in the structure of the economy can be detected and analyzed through the evolution of the structure of such variables.

Further information on   patterns of structural change can be obtained if we try to implement an analysis of the dynamics of the system based directly on its paramentric set, through the dynamical systems theory. Such method allows for the identification of the elementary structures and paths composing the systems complex dynamical behaviour and provides a tool for establishing which objectives combinations shall be priviledged by the inherent systems dynamics and which tend to remain blocked to a particular configuration.The effects of a change in a given subset of the paramentric structure can then be evaluated and quantified in terms of the changes in the elementary paths. In this context such "structural" analysis can be extended to the evaluation of the changing effects of exogenous shocks while time is going on, adapting for this purpose the concept of approximate controllability.

2 . MODERN I-O FRAMEWORK AND THE SIMULATION PROCEDURE

Modern I-O models have become a very powerful tool for analyzing the evolution and the modifications of the major economic variables. Starting from the classical problem of determining the sectoral output vector given a vector of final demands, we have assisted to an evolution that has incorporated in the classical problem many other aspects of the economic dynamics such as the final demand behaviour and the price formation process. See Almon (1982). We now dispose of a tool able to forecast in detail the evolution of the structure of economic variables that once were dealt with, prevalently, in aggregated schemes and we can model the behaviour of variables, such as disposable income, which cannot be referred to I-O sectors as such.

If we keep our attention on the real side of the economy,a modern I-O model can describe the internal dynamics of privatre consumption in terms of the items composing the family budgets, the behaviour of investment and inventory change in terms of the demands originating; from each industry, the evolution of the structure of foreign trade in terms of the major categories composing total imports and exports, the evolution of public and private social expenditure, the composition of employment and total output for each I-O sector. An abstract representation of the structure of a modern I-O model with a first order time lag on variables can be given by equation system (1).

In the left hand side- block vector each block represent a vector of the final demands, employment and output. In the case of INTIMO, a modern I-O model for Italy, see Ciaschini and Grassini (1981), such vector has 441 elements i.e. 40 for consumption vector,c, 23 for investment vector,i, 31 for inventory change vector ,s, 41 for export vector,e, 41 for import vector m, four vectors g for social expenditure with 45 elements, 41 for employment vector ,n, and 45 for total output vector x.

$$
\begin{bmatrix} c \\ i \\ s \\ e \\ m \\ g \\ n \\ x \end{bmatrix}_t
=
\begin{bmatrix} G_{11} \cdots G_{18} \\ \vdots \quad \vdots \\ B_1 \cdots B_7 \; M \end{bmatrix}
\begin{bmatrix} c \\ i \\ s \\ e \\ m \\ g \\ n \\ m \end{bmatrix}_t
+
\begin{bmatrix} \bar{G}_{11} \cdots \bar{G}_{18} \\ \vdots \quad \vdots \\ \bar{G}_{81} \cdots \bar{G}_{88} \end{bmatrix}
\begin{bmatrix} c \\ i \\ s \\ e \\ m \\ g \\ n \\ x \end{bmatrix}_{t-1}
+
\begin{bmatrix} F_{11} \cdots F_{15} \\ \vdots \quad \vdots \\ F_{18} \cdots F_{81} \end{bmatrix}
\begin{bmatrix} y \\ p \\ p^e \\ v \\ w \end{bmatrix}_t
+
\begin{bmatrix} \bar{F}_{11} \cdots \bar{F}_{15} \\ \vdots \quad \vdots \\ \bar{F}_{81} \quad \bar{F}_{85} \end{bmatrix}
\begin{bmatrix} y \\ p \\ p \\ v \\ w \end{bmatrix}_{t-1}
\quad (1)
$$

Matrices G_{ij}, when defferent from zero, show the degree of simultaneity among such subvectors, as in the case of impots when they are made dependent on internal demand. Blocks B_i are the bridge matrices that allow for the tranformation of each demand component into demands for I-O sectors, while M is the intermediate consumption matrix. Blocks $\bar{G}_{ij}$ show the dependence on the previous period's values and shall be different from zero for those vector variables that are explained by lagged values of endogenous variables. Blocks F_{ij} show the effect of exogenous on endogenous variables. Exogenous variables may be given by policy instruments, by data concerning economic phenomena outside the national economy, but also by variables outside the range of the model.

If we confine to the real side of the economy, we take exogenously given the disposable income,y, as the process that determines it starting from value added components is not modelled in the real side. Internal prices vector,p, is taken as exogenous for the same reason. Foreign prices, p^e, world demand, w, and the exchange rate,v, are exogenous data.

When a scheme of this type is used for simulation purposes some computing facilities are introduced in the routines that calculate the dynamic solution. They must,in fact, allow for an easy introduction in the computing procedure of the whole set of exogenous conditions usually referred to as scenario. The exogenous conditions may affect exogenous variables, a subset of the parametric structure of the model and also part of the endogenous variables.

As an example we can refer to the experiences made with INTIMO in the specification of a particular scenario representing a version of the national energy plan, for details see Ciaschini(1982) and Alessandroni(1982). Given a base scenario that drove the system under "normal" conditions modifications were introduced to take into account the "energy hypothesis". The input coefficients for electricity were, in fact, modified to take into consideration the expected mix-change in fuels that generate electricity and also the energy input coefficients in non energy sectors were changed according to the results of interviews to experts of manufacturing industries, transport and services.

Further modifications were adopted on the elements of bridge matrices: the column of fuel and electricity in consumption bridge matrix,B_1, had to give account of an increase in the shares of gas, electricity and coal and a decrease in the share of liquid fuels; the column of energy products in the investment bridge matrix,B_2, had to be adapted according to the composition of investment provided by the national energy plan.

Endogenous variables,too, may be affected by exogenous conditions.This is made not allowing the behavioural equatios of these variables work in the simulation and imposing to such variables the prefixed values. In the energy example investment in energy, i_2, and household expenditure for fuel and electricity,c_{17}, were made equal to the values indicated in the energy plan; for public expenditure,g, exogenous forecasts were also used.

The exogenous variables were supposed to follow the patterns established for the normal scenario.

The results obtained showed that at the aggregated level the energy scenario did not influence to a great extent the levels of the major variables; while at the sectoral level some interesting changes in the structure of such variables could be detected. Take as an example the dynamic pattern of employment as shown in fig.1.

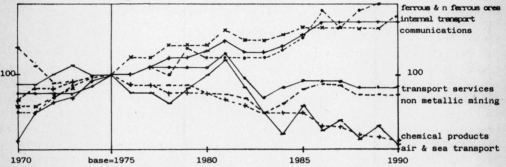

FIGURE 1   Employment path resulting from the simulation.

In this figure the evolution of employment is shown with reference to the base year 1975 in which it is made equal to 100 in each sector. As long as historical data are available such data are imposed to the model so that the simulated values for employment start from that period for which statistical data are no more available.Fig. 1 refers only to seven sectors out of the forty but they sufficiently represent various patterns of employment.

Similar type of results can be obtained for the balances of each I-0 sector. Fig. 2 shows the results obtained for I-0 sector 4: Petroleum, derivates and natural gas.

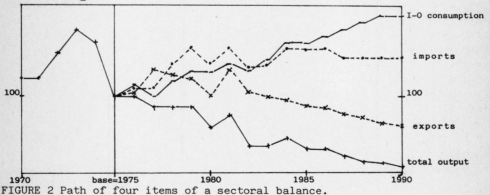

FIGURE 2 Path of four items of a sectoral balance.

As the figure shows, in the long run we assist to a shift from external to internal demand: sectoral I-0 consumption, that is composed according to the weights of consumption bridge matrix, by consumption sector 17:fuels and

electricity, and consumption sector 29: operating costs of private transportation, follows a slight expanding pattern that shall be alimented by a decrease
in exports. The slight falling trend in output is due to the increasing interest, specified in the energy plan, towards other type of energy sources.

The type of results shown demostrate the role played by the simulation
of a modern I-0 model in determining the evolution of the structure of economic variables. The changing relevance of the different items composing output, final demands, employment and I-0 sectoral balances can be evidenced and
quantified and on this basis the analysis of structural change can be implemented.
See Nyhus (1983). But structural change can be also analyzed with explicit
reference to the parametric set that characterizes the economic system so
that some further features of the system's dynamics can be put in evidence.

3. DYNAMICAL ANALYSIS OF AN I-0 STRUCTURE

The main features of the dynamical behaviour of an I-0 model are determined by the type of equations that describe the behaviour of final demands.
A time lag structure on the explanatory variables is often used in the specification of the final demand equations: investment may, in fact, be explained
by lagged values of sectoral output, consumption by lagged values of disposable
income and consumers' prices, imports by the previous year's value of internal
demand and foreign prices. For keeping exposition simple let us confine to
only one demand component endogenously explained and assume the remaining
demands as exogenous. Let investment in sector i at time t be explained by
the product of sectoral capital output ratio, k_i, and the difference beetween
sectoral output at time t-1, x_{t-1}^i, and sectoral output at time t-2, x_{t-2}^i, for
the m investing sectors. Investment demands to I-0 sectors shall then be
given by:

$$i_t = B K b (x_{t-1} - x_{t-2}) \tag{2}$$

where B is the investment bridge matrix with n rows corresponding to the n
I-0 sectors and m columns for the m investing sectors, K is a diagonal matrix with m diagonal elements corresponding to the m capital-output ratios,
and b is an (m x n) matrix that transforms I-0 sectors' to investing sectors'
outputs.

Equation (1) extended in the order of time lags and simplified with the
hypothesis assumed can be rewritten as:

$$x_t = M x_t + N x_{t-1} - N x_{t-2} + L u_t \tag{3}$$

where M represents the intermediate coefficient matrix, N is given by B K b,
matrix L is an (n x q) matrix representing the impact of the remaining demands.

A state space realization for eq. (3) can be given by:

$$\begin{bmatrix} v_1 \\ v_2 \end{bmatrix}_t = \begin{bmatrix} (I-M)^{-1}N & -(I-M)^{-1}N \\ 0 & I \end{bmatrix} \begin{bmatrix} v_1 \\ v_2 \end{bmatrix}_{t-1} + \begin{bmatrix} L \\ 0 \end{bmatrix} u_t \tag{4}$$

where $v_1 = x_t$, $v_2 = x_{t-1}$, I is an (n x n) unit matrix and 0 is a matrix
with elements equal to zero.

For the output transformation we shall write:

$$
\begin{bmatrix} c \\ i \\ s \\ e \\ m \\ g \\ n \\ x \end{bmatrix}
=
\begin{bmatrix} 0 & 0 \\ N & -N \\ 0 & 0 \\ \cdot & \cdot \\ \cdot & \cdot \\ \cdot & \cdot \\ & \\ 0 & 0 \end{bmatrix}
\begin{bmatrix} v_1 \\ v_2 \end{bmatrix}
+
\begin{bmatrix} F_1 \\ 0 \\ F_3 \\ \cdot \\ \cdot \\ \cdot \\ \cdot \\ F_8 \end{bmatrix}
u_t
\qquad (5)
$$

Eq. (4) and (5) are not the only possible realization of the dynamical system. Under our hypothesis it is easy to find a realization that implies a smaller dimension of the state space. Considering that matrix N has some rows whose elements are all equal to zero, correspondingto the I-O sectors that don't produce capital goods, we can partition the structural matrices according to the sectors that can produce also capital goods out of the n I-O sectors and obtain a state space realization that refers to these sectors following and adapting the results of Livesey(1978).

The problem of the state space realization for an I-O model can be satisfactorily solved when the complete parametric structure of a specific system is actually given. We can expect that the dimensions of the state space shall depend on the number of variables that are explained by lagged values of the engonenous and on the order of the time lags.See Ciaschini(1980).

In general we can write the implicit form of the system, analogous to (4) and (5) as:

$$
v_t = A\, v_{t-1} + B\, u_t \qquad (6)
$$
$$
w_t = C\, v_t + D\, u_t \qquad (7)
$$

Eq. (5) models the dynamic structure of the I-O model: the value of the state vactor at time t, v_t, depends through the state transition matrix A on its value in the previous period and throgh matrix B, on the value of exogenous inputs. Eq. (7) makes a simultaneous transformation of the state vector v_t and the input vector u_t into the systems' output vector w_t, through matrices C and D.

The paths described by the system during his evolution can now be expressed in terms of its structural matrices. From (6) and (7) we obtain the following trajectories:

$$
v_t = A^t v_o + \sum_{\delta=1}^{t} A^{t-\delta} B\, u_\delta \qquad (8)
$$
$$
w_t = C A^t v_o + \sum_{\delta=1}^{t} C A^{t-\delta} B\, u_\delta + D\, u_t \qquad (9)
$$

for $t \geqslant 1$.

Either the free evolution of the system, that is the evolution of the state and output starting from given initial conditions v_o with input sequence equal to zero, and its forced evolution, that is the evolution of the state and output when the system starts at rest with a non zero input sequence stricktly depend on the charateristics of A matrix, which can be rewritten in the form:

$$
A = \sum_i \lambda_i u_i v_i \qquad (10)
$$

where λ_i are the n distinct eigenvalues of A matrix, u_i is the right eigen-vector and v_i the ith left eigenvector so that

$$A^t = \sum_i \lambda_i^t u_i v_i \qquad (11)$$

eq. (11) shows that the dynamics of the system can be expressed in terms of a combination of elementary paths, each one having associated a specific structure of the state variable. Under particular assumptions on the composition of initial conditions or on the input sequence we can make the system follow a single elementary path. In this case for real eigenvalues the system shall exibit a steady state growth pattern whose rate of growth is given by $(1 - \lambda_i)$. in this particular case the structure of I-O sectoral outputs shall be confined to the proportions stated by the elementary structure u_i associated. When some eigenvalues are not real we have a couple of complex eigenvalues that determine a periodical behaviour. See Ruberti and Isidori (1975). The complete map of the elementary behaviours that can constitute the dynamics of the system is shown in fig. 3.

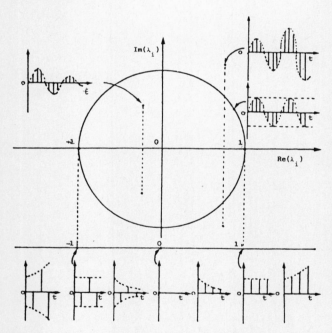

FIGURE 3 Elementary paths determining the system's motion.

On the complex plane the unit circle is the locus that separates the unstable paths from the stable ones. On the unit circle the paths are limited but not converging to zero.

The map of the eigenvalues characterizes a specific representation of the system and the whole class of stricktly equivalent representations i.e. the class of representations that can be obtained by a non singular linear transformation of the state space.

This central result of systems' theory allows for a qualitative and quantitative analysis of the impact of a change in a subset of the parametric

structure of the system. Such changes may introduce oscillatory behaviours
that were not present in the originary structure and can also introduce and
amplify unstable components. But even in the case where structural changes
are not so important to affect the nature of the elementary paths, we can get
a measure of the order of relevance of the change.

If we now refer to the impact of exogenous inputs, we can determine, without loss of generality, the value of the state vector at final time period
t=T, starting from initial conditions equal to zero $v_o = 0$. Such value shall
be given by

$$u_T = B u_T + A B u_{T-1} + \ldots + A^{T-2} B u_2 + A^{T-1} B u_1 \tag{12}$$

if the components of the input vector are not constrained to particular values
we can make the state vector assume predetermined values in a finite time
horizon if

$$\text{rank } G = \text{rank}(B \quad AB \quad A^2 B \quad \ldots \quad A^{n-1}B) = n \tag{13}$$

Eq. (13) pose a limit to the time period to be investigated. Since A
matrix satisfies its charateristic equation, powers of A higher than n-1 can
be expressed as linear combinations of powers of lower order. Since G matrix
describes the evolution of the state during n-1 periods the system is state
controllable either in n-1 periods or not at all.

Since the input vector u_t in general is composed by different types of
policy variables: policy instruments and exogenous data, condition (13) must
be specilized to be referred to a single input:

$$\text{rank } G_j = \text{rank } (B_j \quad AB_j \quad A^2 B_j \quad \ldots \quad A^{n-1}B_j) \tag{14}$$

where B_j is the result of the selection of column j of B matrix corresponding
to the jth input. If eq. (14) is fulfilled and the jth component of input vector u_t is a policy instrument we can make the state vector assume predetermined values in a finite time horizon using input u_j alone. If u_j is an exogenous data and eq. (14) is fulfilled then all the possible state structures
can be perturbed in a finite time horizon through shocks on the exogenous data variable u_j.

Conditions (13) and (14) refer to a concept of controllability that
doesn't appear adequate when applied to economic systems, see Hill and Sitzia
(1978), in particular to I-O models. Such conditions, in fact, are formally
fulfilled in the majority of economic models while it doesn't offer any articulated information on the evolution of the achievable states in that crucial
and relevant portion of time that is needed to attain the complete controllability. For a state space realization of a medium size I-O model the full
forecasting horizon T may well constitute only a small portion of the time
span required for complete controllability n.

If we consider G matrix for the T-1 periods

$$G = (B \quad AB \quad \ldots \quad A^{T-1}B) \tag{15}$$

we can write it in the following way

$$G = U S V' \tag{16}$$

where U and V are real orthogonal matrices of order (nxn) and (qxq) and s is a real (nxq) diagonal matrix whose diagonal elements can be arranged as:

$$s_1 \text{ ,} s_2 \text{ ,} s_3 \text{ , } \ldots \text{ ,} s_r \text{ , } 0 \tag{17}$$

and represent the singular values of matrix G. If we consider the particular structures of sectoral outputs indicated by matrix U and operate a state space transformation so that

$$v^*_t = U \, v_t \tag{18}$$

and consider those combinations of inputs indicated in matrix V so that

$$u^*_t = V' \, u_t \tag{19}$$

In the new coordinates we shall have:

$$v^*_t = s_i \, u^*_t \qquad i=1 \ldots . r \tag{20}$$

If we require the input vector describe a sphere in the input space , then v^*_t
describe an ellipsoid in the state space with semi axis of lenght s_1
$s_2 \ldots s_r$.
The properties of our multisectoral model as the planning period changes trom 1 to T-1 are then evidences by succesively applying the singular value decomposition to matrices G or G_j. We can then identify the fundamental state structures implicit in the I-O model and their different sensitivity to exogenous inputs. Fig.4 shows the structures identified by matrix U relative to a simplified example shown in the appendix.

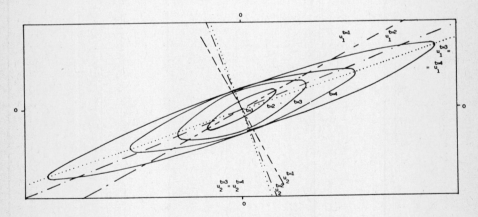

FIGURE 4 Implicit state structures and their unit input sensitivity.

Vectors u_1^t give the directions indicated by the culumn of matrix U associated with the highest singular value and represent the implicit trade offs among the levels of activity in the I-O sectors. Such structures,being associated with the highest singular value are the most "easy" to influence through exogenous inputs. Vector u_2^t describe the sectoral output structures along which growth is more difficult to stimulate. The relative "easiness" depends on the magnitude of singular values and whether or not they are relevantly different.

If the map in fig. 4 is calculated with respect to those columns of matrix G that are associated with the policy instruments fig. 4 shall show the "preferred" directions of the system i.e.the I-O structure that are easier to stimulate operating on the instruments and those that tend to remain blocked to a particular configuration. If it refers to the impact of exogenous data we can determine which structures are more exposed to shocks coming from the international environment and which tend to be more protected from external influence.

4 . CONCLUSIONS

The aims of the present work were to verify whether a structural analysis of the changes in interindustry interactions could be implemented and wheter it was possible to identify quantifiers of structural change.

These goals have been partially achieved in the sense that modern I-O models seem to constitute the convenient framework for the identification and specification of the economic structure and dynamical systems theory allows for the implementation of an analysis based on the parametric structure of the model that can become a valuable support to the simulation techniques.

Through systems theory we can in fact analyze separately the effects of the inherent dynamics of the system and the effect of changes in its parametric structure. The dynamics of the system tends to priviledge certain state state structures which are the easiest to control but also the most exposed to exogenous shocks. The identification of such growth patterns is of relevant interest in determining which combinations of objectives tend to remain blocked to a particular configuration and which tend to grow fastly creating the conditions for a structural change to take place.

When a structural change of whatever relevance has occurred, it can be detected through the analysis of the changes in the elementary paths and structures while through simulation it is not easy to separate the effect of inherent dynamics from that of changes in interindustry interactions, so that the order of magnitude of the structural change cannot be precisely determined.

From an applicative viewpoint the contribution has remained confined to a simplified example that has allowed to clarify the definitions but not to test the effectiveness of the concepts on an operating I-O model nor to iden-tify further synthetic indicators of structural change. Along this direction further research is being developed.

REFERENCES

Alessandroni, A. (1982) The effects of the Italian Energy Plan on sectoral
        outputs and private consumption. In M. Grassini and A. Smyshlaev(Ed.)
        Input Output Modeling.CP-83-S2. IIASA,Laxenburg,Austria.
Almon, C. (1982) Utilizzazione dei modelli Input Output per la politica eco-
        nomica. Banca Toscana, Studi e Informazioni. 1/1982
Ciaschini, M. (1980) L'approccio sistemistico ai modelli multisettoriali con
        capitale fisso. Quaderni di ricerca MONIF. Università di Roma,Facoltà
        di Scienze matematiche, Fisiche e Naturali. n.8.
Ciaschini, M. (1982) Modern Input Output Models as Simulation Tools for Pol-
        icy Making.CP-82-56. IIASA, Laxenburg,Austria.
Ciaschini, m. and Grassini, M. (1981) INTIMO:Il modello italiano nel sistema
        INFORUM. Aisre, Napoli.

Hill, R. and Sitzia B. (1981) A Definition of Approximate Controllability, in Castellani, G. and Mazzoleni, P. (Ed.) Mathematical Programming and its Economic Applications, F. Angeli, Milano.

Livesey, D. A. (1978) A Minimal Realization of the Leontief Dynamic Input Output Model. in K. Polensk and J. Sholka (Ed.) Advances in Input Output Analysis. North Holland. Amsterdam.

Nyhus, D. E.(1983) Observing Structural Change in the Japanese Economy: an Input Output Approach. Proc. of the IV Tasck Force Meeting on Input Out put Modeling CP-83-S2. IIASA, Laxenburg, Austria.

Ruberti, A. and Isidori, A. (1975) Teoria dei Sistemi. Edizioni Siderea, Roma.

5 . APPENDIX

Let $x_t = M x_t + N (x_t - x_{t-1}) + C f_t$ (1.A)

where x_t is the I-O sectoral output at time period t,

f_t is the vector of final demands excluded investment,

M is the intermediate consumption matrix,

C is the bridge matrix for final demands excluded investment,

and

$N = B K b$

where B is the investment bridge matrix,

K is the capital-output ratios matrix,

b is the bridge matrix for output;

The state transition equation for (1.A) shall be given by:

$$x_t = (N - (I - M))^{-1} N x_t + (- (N - (I - M))^{-1}) C f_t \quad (2.A)$$

if

$$M = \begin{bmatrix} .2 & .6 \\ .7 & .1 \end{bmatrix} ; B = \begin{bmatrix} .3 & .2 \\ .7 & .8 \end{bmatrix} ; b = \begin{bmatrix} .4 & .2 \\ .6 & .8 \end{bmatrix} ; K = \begin{bmatrix} .3 & .0 \\ .0 & .6 \end{bmatrix} ; C = \begin{bmatrix} .7 & .8 \\ .3 & .2 \end{bmatrix}$$

then

$$(N - (I - M))^{-1} N = \begin{bmatrix} 3.602 & 4.127 \\ 3.360 & 3.762 \end{bmatrix} = A$$

$$(-(N - (I - M))^{-1}) C = \begin{bmatrix} -3.7595 & -3.7070 \\ -8.1210 & -8.3570 \end{bmatrix} = B$$

from which

	preferred direction u_1		singular values	
			s1	s2
t=1	(.47	.87)	3.6	.06
t=2	(.36	.93)	6.9	.53
t=3	(.32	.94)	11.8	.57
t=4	(.32	.94)	20.6	.48

THE INTERNATIONAL INSTITUTE FOR APPLIED SYSTEMS ANALYSIS

is a nongovernmental research institution, bringing together scientists from around the world to work on problems of common concern. Situated in Laxenburg, Austria, IIASA was founded in October 1972 by the academies of science and equivalent organizations of twelve countries. Its founders gave IIASA a unique position outside national, disciplinary, and institutional boundaries so that it might take the broadest possible view in pursuing its objectives:

To promote international cooperation in solving problems arising from social, economic, technological, and environmental change

To create a network of institutions in the national member organization countries and elsewhere for joint scientific research

To develop and formalize systems analysis and the sciences contributing to it, and promote the use of analytical techniques needed to evaluate and address complex problems

To inform policy advisors and decision makers about the potential application of the Institute's work to such problems

The Institute now has national member organizations in the following countries:

Austria
The Austrian Academy of Sciences

Bulgaria
The National Committee for Applied Systems Analysis and Management

Canada
The Canadian Committee for IIASA

Czechoslovakia
The Committee for IIASA of the Czechoslovak Socialist Republic

Finland
The Finnish Committee for IIASA

France
The French Association for the Development of Systems Analysis

German Democratic Republic
The Academy of Sciences of the German Democratic Republic

Federal Republic of Germany
Association for the Advancement of IIASA

Hungary
The Hungarian Committee for Applied Systems Analysis

Italy
The National Research Council

Japan
The Japan Committee for IIASA

Netherlands
The Foundation IIASA—Netherlands

Poland
The Polish Academy of Sciences

Sweden
The Swedish Council for Planning and Coordination of Research

Union of Soviet Socialist Republics
The Academy of Sciences of the Union of Soviet Socialist Republics

United States of America
The American Academy of Arts and Sciences